EU Corporate Law and EU Company Tax Law

CORPORATIONS, GLOBALISATION AND THE LAW

Series Editor: Janet Dine, *Director, Centre for Commercial Law Studies, Queen Mary College, University of London, UK*

This new and uniquely positioned monograph series aims to draw together high quality research work from established and younger scholars on what is an intriguing and under-researched area of the law. The books will offer insights into a variety of legal issues that concern corporations operating on the global stage, including interaction with WTO, international financial institutions and nation states, in both developing and developed countries. Whilst the underlying foundation of the series will be that of company law, broadly-defined, authors are encouraged to take an approach that draws on the work of other social sciences, such as politics, economics and development studies and to offer an international or comparative perspective where appropriate. Specific topics to be considered will include corporate governance, corporate responsibility, taxation and criminal liability, amongst others. The series will undoubtedly offer an important contribution to legal thinking and to the wider globalisaton debate.

Titles in the series include:

Human Rights and Capitalism
A Multidisciplinary Perspective on Globalisation
Edited by Janet Dine and Andrew Fagan

Company Law in the New Europe
The EU *Acquis*, Comparative Methodology and Model Law
Janet Dine, Marios Koutsias and Michael Blecher

EU Corporate Law and EU Company Tax Law
Luca Cerioni

EU Corporate Law and EU Company Tax Law

Luca Cerioni

Academic Research Fellow at the University of Leeds, UK

CORPORATIONS, GLOBALISATION AND THE LAW

Edward Elgar

Cheltenham, UK • Northampton, MA, USA

Published by
Edward Elgar Publishing Limited
Glensanda House
Montpellier Parade
Cheltenham
Glos GL50 1UA
UK

Edward Elgar Publishing, Inc.
William Pratt House
9 Dewey Court
Northampton
Massachusetts 01060
USA

A catalogue record for this book
is available from the British Library

Library of Congress Cataloguing in Publication Data

Cerioni, Luca, 1969–
EU corporate law and EU company tax law / by Luca Cerioni.
p. cm. — (Corporations, globalisation and the law series)
Includes bibliographical references and index.
1. Corporation law—European Union countries. 2.
Corporations—Taxation—Law and legislation—European Union countries. I.
Title.
KJE2451.C47 2007
346.24'066—dc22

2006028682

ISBN 978 1 84542 774 0

Printed and bound in Great Britain by MPG Books Ltd, Bodmin, Cornwall

Contents

Abbreviations

ACT	Advance Corporation Tax
APCLCG	European Commission Action Plan on Company Law and Corporate Governance
CCBT	Common Consolidated Base Taxation
CCBTWG	Common Consolidated Base Taxation Working Group
CEN	capital export neutrality
CIN	capital import neutrality
Commission	the European Commission
Council	the Council of Ministers of the European Community
DTC	Double Tax Convention
EC	European Community
ECJ/the Court	European Court of Justice
ECR	European Court Report
ECS	European Company Statute
EEC	European Economic Community
EEIG	European Economic Interest Grouping
EPC	European Private Company
ESC	European Economic and Social Committee
EP	European Parliament
EUCIT	European Union Company Income Tax
EU	European Union
FFC	formally foreign companies
HST	Home State Taxation
HTB	Harmonised Tax Base
IBFD	International Bureau of Fiscal Documentation
OECD	Organisation for Economic Co-operation and Development
OECD Model	OECD Articles of the Model Convention with respect to taxes on income and capital
OJEC	Official Journal of the European Communities
PE	permanent establishment
SE	European Company
SCE	European Cooperative Society
SMEs	small and medium-sized enterprises
SNB	special negotiation body
Treaty	Treaty of Rome (as subsequently amended) establishing the EEC (and the EC)

Preface

WHY STUDY EC CORPORATE TAXATION AND EC COMPANY LAW TOGETHER IN THE CURRENT PHASE OF DEVELOPMENT OF EC LAW?

The European Community (EC), which since its foundation has been offering new and original issues to the international academic and extra-academic literature concerning both law and other disciplines, currently finds itself in a period of its history which presents unprecedented risks and opportunities. The risks have been well evidenced by the difficult times during 2005: the rejection of the 'European Constitution' in popular referenda in two founding states, and the difficulties in reaching agreement over the budget, indicate that the 'crisis of rejection' may paralyse any further progress of the European construction and even compromise its future when the ultimate objectives stated in the Treaty of Rome (such as harmonious and balanced development of economic activities, high level of employment, social cohesion, improvement in the standard of living) – objectives which would benefit all socio-economic actors in any Member State – are not reached, or when the advantages brought about by their achievement are not fully perceived. In these circumstances, the future of the European integration process risks being threatened to a greater extent than in any previous period in the history of the EC: as the current range of decisions taken at EC level affecting the everyday life of nationals (individuals and businesses) of Member States is wider than in any previous period, negative interdependencies are deemed to be amplified in the event of malfunctioning of the internal market. Together with (and because of) these risks, the current historical context also offers decision-makers and academic researchers unprecedented opportunities of identifying clear patterns that, on a lasting basis, could shape future developments in such a way as to minimize the risk of not achieving the goals stated in the Treaty and the EC's self-set objective of becoming the world's most competitive and knowledge-driven economy (the so-called 'Lisbon objective', the strategy towards which was revised in 2005). This challenge will need to find a response, among others, in those areas of EC law that create the essential framework enabling businesses (which are the main protagonists of market integration) to operate on a Community-wide scale: the areas of EC company law and EC company tax law.

The importance of future developments in these two areas was already understood, 50 years ago, by the founders of the (then) EEC, when they provided the institutions of the Community with the legal basis for creating, within the Community, a level playing field for all businesses from any Member State. For this purpose, they envisaged the removal of those obstacles that would hinder companies' free movement within the internal market, such as excessive differences in national company law provisions and risks of double taxation, and regarded the future Community's initiatives in these two areas of law as complementary. Moreover, in important Communications issued in recent years, the European Commission has highlighted the importance, in this historical phase, of developments in each of these areas for the proper functioning of the Community market and for the 'Lisbon objective'.

With these premises, the (developments in the areas of) EC company law and EC company taxation should be studied together, in the current phase, on the one hand from the perspective of academic research, of decision-making at EC level and of students of European law, of company law and of European and international tax law, and, on the other hand, from the perspective of businesses and practitioners. Important legislation in recent years, innovative rulings of the European Court of Justice (ECJ) on the freedom of establishment and new proposals from the Commission for legislative developments, which ultimately are all aimed at creating for cross-border activity within the Community the conditions of a domestic market, are deeply affecting both company law and company taxation systems of Member States. This is occurring at the same time when, in a global economy where capital and investments quickly move from one jurisdiction to another in search of the optimal location, company law and company taxation have been emerging as the two areas of law in which Member States are concentrating much of their efforts for improving their attractiveness as locations for businesses and investments. Company law and company taxation regimes of each of the Member States are thus being increasingly affected not only by Community initiatives, but also by this 'legal competition' with each other, which has been acquiring an increasing prominence in recent years and with which the Community initiatives are bound to interact. In such a context, the reason for studying the developments of EC company law and of EC corporate tax law together lies in the challenges it affords from the perspective of academic research, at the political decision-making level and for students, and in the unprecedented opportunities offered from the perspective of businesses and practitioners. Under the first perspective, the challenge is twofold: for academic researchers and decision-makers, it is the search for a comprehensive response to the questions whether and under which conditions the phenomenon of legal competition, in its interaction with developments of EC company law and of EC corporate tax law, can contribute to the proper functioning of the internal market (and thus minimize the risks of outcomes in conflict with the Treaty's objectives and with the Lisbon objective). For students, it is the turning of possible difficulties (in considering systematically the interdependencies between the developments in EC company law and in EC tax law and those of the national company law and company taxation systems in competition with each other) into major chances of increasing or consolidating an interdisciplinary and comparative approach of analysis and of building up an international legal curricula. From businesses' perspective, a unified approach towards EC company law and EC corporate tax law (which aims to consider together, in a systematic manner, the developments in these two areas of EC law and their impact on the competing national company law and corporate tax regimes) reveals opportunities for new strategies of expansion within the Community, which could take advantage from the legal competition in both areas while remaining within the ambit of exercise of the freedom of establishment granted by the Treaty. To the extent that these opportunities are being opened to businesses, the unified approach towards EC company law and EC tax law which makes it possible to identify the possible combinations of optimal choices becomes also a must from the viewpoint of tax and legal practitioners acting as their advisors.

In the overall situation where the two areas of EC law at stake have a crucial role to play in indicating clear patterns in order for future developments to contribute to the proper functioning of the internal market, and where studying EC company law and EC corporate tax law together becomes a suitable approach from the perspectives of academic research, of decision-makers, of students, of businesses and of practitioners, this book is intended to contribute to each of these perspectives. It seeks, in fact, to reconcile a contribution to new research themes suggested by the latest developments in EC company law and in EC corporate tax law, aimed at offering 'inputs' to the international academic debate and to decision-makers, with a description of the fundamental framework and of the key developments of interest to students, and with the illustration on new possibilities for companies' intra-EC expansion strategies that are of interest on the one hand from the academic viewpoint, and on the other hand to businesses and their consultants.

The book's structure has a main text and Appendices. The main text (a) in Part I illustrates the key EC legal framework in the two areas, the legislative developments and the most important ECJ rulings, and indicates how these developments, in the current context of the legal competition among the Member States, have contributed to this phenomenon; (b) in Part II formulates a hypothesis for future developments allowing the legal competition to meet some conditions under which it could aid the achievement of the ultimate EC law objectives. In pursuing these purposes, the book considers possible strategies for expansion by businesses on a Community scale, and pays particular attention to the latest 'supranational' developments and proposals, which have been attracting much international interest in recent years: the European company in the field of EC company law and the Commission's strategy for the introduction of a common consolidated base taxation in the field of EC corporate tax law.

The Appendices offer to businesses and practitioners an overview of the implementation of the key EC legislation in some Member States and of the resulting differences between national laws, with some examples of strategies for intra-Community expansion and restructuring that could be implemented as modalities of exercising the freedom of establishment from one state to another.

The author hopes that the book will become a useful instrument while, at the same time suggesting research ideas for the international debate on possible future developments in the two complex and fascinating areas of EC company law and EC company taxation.

Luca Cerioni
30 May 2006

Foreword and acknowledgments

At a time when – in singular coincidence with the 50th anniversary of the Treaty of Rome – the future of the European construction is the subject of frequent discussions where further 'supranational' developments often meet resistance, this book wishes to be academically provocative: it formulates a legal case for supranational developments as the only solution that under certain conditions, in the current historical phase, would deserve being regarded as a way forward in two 'sensitive' areas of EC law such as EC company tax law and EC corporate law, and ultimately suggests that this would also be in all Member States' interests.

Given the dynamic areas of EC law at issue, the construction of this case required a critical review of the relevant EC legislation and case law, in order to demonstrate that a clear pattern could be identified and would require the proposed way forward, as well as to draw the arguments, and a considerable period of time. This started with my PhD thesis, prepared at the University of Essex and submitted in 2004, and finished in late October 2006 at the University of Leeds, when it was realized that few further developments taking place after the start of the production process on the main text, which had been presented at the end of May 2006, made it appropriate to add a short updating that the reader will find in Appendix VI. During such a considerable period of time, several people gave their contribution to the finalization of this book, and I would like to express sincere thanks to all of them.

This work was developed with my PhD thesis as a starting point and with considerable revisions and updating that were made necessary by ongoing developments in EC corporate law and EC company tax law and by the need to address the comments that I was aware that work could attract. Therefore, I'm extremely grateful, first, to Prof. Janet Dine, who, at the University of Essex Law Department, supervised both my LLM dissertation in 1996 and my PhD thesis during a period – from 2001 to 2004 – when I was carrying out my doctoral research on a part-time basis while working abroad. She had great patience in re-reading the changes that new pieces of EC legislation and new ECJ case law made necessary from time to time to parts that had already been written and, after her transfer to the Centre for Commercial Law Studies at the Queen Mary College, University of London, in 2005 felt that the work would deserve inclusion in the 'Corporations, Globalisation and the Law' series. My gratitude to Prof. Dine is equally due for her encouragement, before and after the publication in the *Journal of Business Law* in 1999 of a part of my LLM dissertation, to pursue the doctoral research itself, and for her reading of the last version of this work in June 2006. I also would like to thank, for their appreciating the PhD thesis and for the useful comments, the two examiners, Prof. Steve Peers (University of Essex) and Prof. Charlotte Villiers (University of Bristol), and I'm also obliged to the anonymous academic referee for Edward Elgar, whose comments were useful to me in the latest refinement phase.

As regards the technical phase of finalization of the book, I'm also very grateful to Elisabetta Valdani, at Essex University, who in 2005 helped me to understand the difficulties that would have arisen had an alternative procedure for the technical preparation of the manuscript been followed and who therefore allowed me to save enough time that I could devote to the updatings and revisions, and to the entire Edward Elgar team for their advice and patience before and after I submitted the manuscript. In particular, I wish to thank Luke Adams and Nep Elverd for their flexibility in extending the deadline initially agreed for submission and their patience with my numerous queries relating to technical house style criteria, and I'm also particularly grateful to Kate Emmins, who, during the later phase of the production process, allowed me to add the short updating appendix (October 2006) and was willing to discuss by phone, point by point, a series of questions concerning the way of expressing the arguments put forward, which issue, due to my not being a native English language speaker, was also important in my final check of corrections made in the previous copyediting phase.

As for some of the material used, I'm obliged to the International Bureau of Fiscal Documentation (IBFD) in Amsterdam, for authorizing me to use, in Chapter 4 paragraph 2 of this work, part of the material concerning the compatibility of tax competition with EC law, which was published in my previous article: L. Cerioni, 'Harmful tax competition revisited: Why not a Purely Legal Perspective under EC law?' *European Taxation*, the IBFD – edited and published journal in EC, comparative and international taxation, Vol. 45, No. 7, July 2005. I'm also grateful to Prof. Adriano Di Pietro and his collaborators at the University of Bologna, Faculty of Law, for providing me, shortly after the start of my work on the PhD thesis, with comparative material, drawn from international Congresses held there, concerning the implementation of the first two EC tax directives in several EC Member States. Last but not least, I'm also very grateful to my family of origin for allowing me, in 1995–1996, to attend the LLM in European Community Law at Essex University, which was the preliminary step for the research that led to the PhD thesis and eventually, through the work I carried out over the last two years, to this book.

Luca Cerioni
School of Law
University of Leeds
30 October 2006

PART I

The developments of EC legislation and case law in corporate taxation and company law and their ultimate outcome: a contribution to the legal competition between Member States

Part I will indicate the key developments in EC corporate tax law and in EC company law and will demonstrate that, in both fields, the ultimate outcome is a contribution to the legal competition between Member States.

1. The ultimate result of EC legislation and case law in the field of companies' taxation: an increased scope for tax competition among Member States

In spite of the absence in the Treaty of Rome ('the Treaty') of provisions specifically dealing with companies' direct taxation, the general wording of Article 293 EC reveals one of the key aims of the Treaty's drafters. With a view to creating a level playing field for 'companies and firms' (defined by Article 48 EC) of all Member States (in connection with the establishment of a system of *undistorted market competition* under Article 3 EC) they regarded tax obstacles to cross-border economic activity within the Community (such as double taxation) as barriers to be eliminated. Such a goal, set out by Article 293 EC without distinctions ('the abolition of double taxation'), was bound to affect the developments in the important field of company (direct) taxation.

The achievement of this level playing field becomes even more important in view of the ambitious Lisbon objective, set out in 2000: that of making the European Union (EU) the world's most competitive and dynamic knowledge-based economy by 2010, capable of sustainable growth while attaining social and environmental standards. In fact, both before and after the 2005 revision of the 'Lisbon strategy' which attributed priority to economic growth, the Commission consistently stressed that the elimination of all company tax obstacles to cross-border business activity within the Community has a key role in providing the proper legal framework towards the Lisbon objective, and has committed itself to this end. Nevertheless, it can be demonstrated that the developments of EC legislation and case law in the field of corporate taxation over roughly the last two decades have been generating a particular result, which risks being strengthened by the Commission strategy for future developments: an increased scope for tax competition among Member States. This gives rise to a problematic issue, indicated at the end of this chapter.

1.1 THE TWO 1990 DIRECTIVES: FROM THE OBJECTIVE OF A 'COMMON SYSTEM OF TAXATION' TO THE RESULT OF A DISTORTED TAX COMPETITION

1.1.1 General Overview

EC corporate tax law finds its central legislation in Council Directive 90/434/EEC ('the Merger Directive')[1] and in Council Directive 90/435/EEC ('the Parent-Subsidiary Directive')[2] (both modified by amending Directives in 2004 and in 2005)[3] which have set out ambitious objectives. The Preambles to the two Directives clearly reflect the idea that the proper functioning of the EC internal market needs 'tax rules which are neutral from the viewpoint of competition', which makes necessary the introduction of a 'common system of taxation'. They recognize, in fact, that 'mergers, divisions, transfers of assets and exchanges of shares' (in the case of the Merger Directive) and 'the grouping together of companies' (in the case of the Parent-Subsidiary Directive) involving companies of different Member States 'may be necessary to create within the Community conditions analogous to those of an internal market' but underline that, for the time being, restrictions, disadvantages and distortions are caused by the different tax provisions of Member States.[4] Accordingly, the removal of such restrictions, disadvantages and distortions, and the creation of analogous conditions for these intra-EC operations in comparison with the corresponding operations concerning companies of the same Member State, emerge from the Preambles to both Directives as key objectives.

The goal of eliminating the tax disadvantages on intra-EC operations considered by the two Directives in comparison with the same operations at national level would certainly be achieved if competing companies falling within the scope of the second paragraph of Article 48 of the Treaty[5] found location in one Member State or another was immaterial for the purpose of carrying out these transactions at either intra-EC or domestic level. In such case, tax rules would be completely neutral from the viewpoint of competition. This would be the broadest concept of tax neutrality, and would be fully coherent with the objectives of the Treaty in terms of the proper functioning of the internal market and undistorted market competition. Nevertheless, it would be difficult to reconcile with that 'tax competition' between Member States which[6] lies at the root of those diversities between national provisions which make the conditions for intra-EC profits distributions and restructuring operations different from one Member State to another.

The tax literature, by analysing the two Directives' provisions, has already found such a number of omissions and interpretative uncertainties as to conclude that 'perhaps the most fundamental problem of the Directives is what they do not say'.[7] If examined in the light of the broadest concept of tax neutrality, they show even more limitations: their implementation was thus bound to generate a widely different result from tax rules which are truly neutral from the viewpoint of (market) competition.

1.1.2 The Parent-Subsidiary Directive

The 1990 version of the Parent-Subsidiary Directive, in order to eliminate the risk of double taxation of intra-Community dividends flows:

1. requires that where a 'parent company' resident in one Member State receives a dividend from a subsidiary company resident in another Member State, the Member State of the parent company should either exempt the dividend from tax in the parent company's hands (exemption method) or grant a full credit for the corporate tax paid by the subsidiary corresponding to the dividend (indirect tax credit method);[8]
2. abolishes withholding taxes on that dividend, specifying in this regard that a subsidiary is to be defined as such where the parent company holds at least 25 per cent of its capital and clarifying the term 'withholding tax';[9]
3. grants Member States the further options of replacing, by means of bilateral agreements, the criterion of a holding in the capital by that of a holding of voting rights, of not applying the Directive to those of their parent or subsidiary companies which do not comply with a two-year minimum holding period[10] and of providing that any charges relating to the holding in the capital of the subsidiary may not be deducted from the taxable profits of the parent company;[11]
4. contains an anti-abuse clause, whereby the Directive does not preclude the application of domestic or agreement-based provisions required to prevent fraud or abuse;[12]
5. does not affect the application of national or Double Tax Convention (DTC) provisions 'designed to eliminate or to lessen economic double taxation of dividends'.[13]

The 2004 amendments[14] have extended the scope of the Directive, by covering both new legal forms of companies and a wider range of profits distributions.[15] Whereas the types of companies covered by the original version are identified by general definitions and, mostly, by the typical limited liability companies forms which are corporate taxpayers in Member States,[16] the new range also includes new legal forms[17] which are equally subject in their Member States of residence to national corporate taxes,[18] as well as the two 'European' legal forms introduced to date: the European Company (SE)[19] and the European Cooperative Society (SCE).[20] All these types of companies fall within the scope of the Directive provided they have their fiscal residence in a Member State and are subject to one of the national typologies of corporation tax applied in Member States.[21]

As regards the range of distributions of profits covered, the amendments have introduced four innovations. First, they have included dividends received by a parent company through a permanent establishment located in a Member State other than that of its subsidiary (triangular cases),[22] where the definition of 'permanent establishment' (PE) mirrors that of the 2003 OECD Model Tax Convention[23] and of a third EC tax Directive issued in 2003 ('the Interest-Royalties Directive').[24] Secondly, the Member States of location of either the parent company or the PE, which choose to apply the indirect tax credit method, must grant the parent company or the PE a full credit from the amount of tax due, for that fraction of corporation tax paid by the subsidiary and by any lower tier subsidiary which relates to distributed profits.[25] Thirdly, because some of the newly included legal entities, treated by their Member States of residence as corporate taxpayers, are considered 'transparent' for tax purposes in other Member States on the basis of their applicable business law, the amended text requires the state of the parent company, if it considers a subsidiary to be fiscally transparent, to refrain from taxing the distributed profits of the subsidiary and, when taxing the parent company's share of the profits of its subsidiary as they arise, to grant the parent company a full credit against the tax due for the tax paid by the immediate subsidiary and by any lower-tier subsidiary.[26] Last, the minimum shareholding requirement is gradually reduced to 10 per cent.[27]

Globally considered, the amendments have therefore broadened the scope of the Directive, but have left unchanged the basic 1990 provisions.

1.1.3 Limits of the Directive

A vast literature has found in the 1990 text of the Parent-Subsidiary Directive important limitations.[28] The first is the lack of a definition of the key concepts of 'distributions of profits' and of 'fiscal residence',[29] which causes the effectiveness of the Directive to be undermined whenever national laws apply different definitions of these concepts,[30] with the ultimate results that the companies concerned risk escaping the application of the Directive and that the same profit, after having being taxed on the subsidiary, may constitute taxable income for the parent company too.[31] Another has been found in the importance of the options expressly granted and of the crucial choices left to Member States in answering the doubts raised by the text of the Directive: for example this latter excludes from the concept of 'distribution of profits' those profits which are received by the parent company at the winding up of the subsidiary,[32] thus raising the question as to what should be, in the country of origin, the tax treatment of these distributions when they are considered by the relevant provisions as equivalent to dividends.[33]

Further problems have consistently been raised: the anti-abuse clause,[34] which does not define exactly the limits up to which Member States can enact restrictive provisions for declared anti-abusive purposes without jeopardizing the application of the Directive,[35] the lack of tax relief on account of underlying tax paid by second and lower-tier subsidiaries where the tax credit method applies,[36] and the absence of any mention of distributions through PEs.[37] The 2004 amendments overcame the last two limitations but, by maintaining the basic 1990 provisions, left the others unaltered. Moreover, from the perspective of the broadest concept of tax neutrality, the Directive's crucial assumptions overlook the real situations which may derive from national laws and from companies' association strategies. Given the Directive's goal of eliminating the tax disadvantages faced by intra-EC profits distributions in comparison with profits distributions within one Member State,[38] the choice left to Member States between the exemption and the indirect tax credit methods could only be based on the assumption that the two methods are fully equivalent in their ultimate results. Yet, this assumption can only be valid – because of the working of the indirect tax credit method – if the level of taxation of the parent company is either *equal* or *higher* than that of the subsidiary, which may not be the case in the concrete situation. On the other hand, the choice offered between these two methods could accommodate the different methods used by national legislators, but this approach is consistent neither with the clear recognition (in the Preamble) that these differences create restrictions, disadvantages and distortions, nor with conditions analogous to those of an internal market. Such methods in fact reflect two different ideas of tax neutrality intended to prevent international double taxation at the parent company level, 'capital import neutrality' (CIN) and 'capital export neutrality' (CEN), which both make sense across distinct markets,[39] whereas a *unique* internal market implies the broadest concept of tax neutrality, which would cause the distinction between CIN and CEN to disappear. In turn, the possibility of replacing the criterion of a holding in the capital by that of a holding of voting rights, despite the implicit assumption that the two criteria lead to the same result, can obviously generate different tax effects (given a certain amount of profits received by a parent company) in the case of subsidiary companies having different categories of shares. For example, some preference shares typically entitle the holder to receive in preference to all other classes of share capital a dividend, but either exclude voting rights or bear limitations on such rights. It is evident that two companies, the first possessing 25 per cent of voting rights, the second 25 per cent of share capital (including a quota of preference shares without voting rights), and receiving by assumption the same amount of profits, would – if located in a Member State adopting the criterion of holding of voting rights – be treated differently: the first company would be considered as a 'parent company' under the terms of the Directive and would benefit from it, the second one would not qualify as a parent company and would still risk double taxation on the profits distributed by its subsidiary. This outcome, in turn, would also place the second company at a disadvantage in comparison with competing companies located in a Member State following the criterion of holding in the share capital.[40]

Moreover, although the amendments have greatly extended the number of legal forms, they do not appear to have included all profit-making 'companies and firms' entitled to the freedom of establishment under Article 48 of the Treaty.[41] For example, neither partnerships nor all possible types of limited partnerships, which are implicitly included within the scope of Article 48 EC, are expressly listed in the Annex.[42] On the one hand, this may generate a lack of tax neutrality affecting the choice of the legal form (between limited companies and other business forms with unlimited liability) to be made by limited liability companies envisaging the setting up of a subsidiary in another Member State.[43] On the other hand, unlimited liability entities may be discouraged from either setting up subsidiaries under the form of limited liability companies in other Member States or taking shareholdings in already existing corporate entities. The Directive text is therefore still far from capable of achieving complete tax neutrality.

1.1.4 The Merger Directive

The 1990 version of the Merger Directive included within its scope three types of 'mergers' (merger by creation of a new company, merger by acquisition, merger by acquisition of a wholly-owned subsidiary)[44] and one type each of 'division'[45] of 'transfer of assets'[46] and of 'exchanges of shares',[47] involving limited liability companies from two or more Member States, defined in the identical manner as in the Parent-Subsidiary Directive. The very nature of these operations generally gives rise to capital gains and to eliminate the tax disadvantages faced by these reorganizations when carried out at intra-EC level, the original version of the Directive grants a tax deferral regime of these capital gains. In a merger, division or transfer of assets, a company, without being dissolved, transfers its assets and liabilities to another in exchange for the issue to the shareholder of the transferring company (in a merger or division) or to the company itself (in a transfer of assets) of shares in the capital of the receiving company; in an exchange of shares, a company acquires the majority of the shares in another company from this second company's shareholders who, in exchange, receive shares in the acquiring company. According to the tax deferral regime, in a merger, division or transfer of assets receiving companies are not taxed on the capital gains at the time of the operation, but only when such capital gains are actually realized through a later disposal,[48] and on a merger, division or exchange of shares, a shareholder of the transferring or acquired company (who obtains shares of the receiving or acquiring company) is not taxed on the inherent 'income, profits or capital gains' until these are actually realized.[49] The tax deferral regime is subject to two conditions: the tax basis of the assets or of the shares transferred must remain the same as before the operation (thus, any capital gains must be rolled over to receiving companies or to shareholders of the transferring or acquired company), and these assets and liabilities must remain effectively connected with a PE of the receiving company in the Member State of the transferring company and contribute to generate the profits or losses for tax purposes. In providing for this regime, the Directive:

1. specifies that, if the receiving company has a holding in the capital of the transferring company, any gains accruing to the receiving company on the cancellation of its holding is not taxed,[50] with the option for Member States to derogate from this general rule when the shareholding does not exceed 25 per cent;
2. leaves Member States the freedom to maintain, in their national provisions concerning domestic operations, different and/or more favourable rules than the relief provided for by the Directive, while requiring them to extend such rules (if any) to operations involving non-resident companies;[51]
3. clarifies that, where the assets transferred in a merger, a division or a transfer of assets include a PE of the transferring company situated in a Member State other than that of the transferring company, the latter state must not tax that PE, and leaves to the state of the transferring company the tax treatment of the losses and gains of this PE;[52]
4. last, provides an anti-abuse clause whereby Member States *may* refuse to apply the benefits of 'all or any part' of the Directive when the principal objective, or one of the principal objectives of a restructuring operation, is tax evasion or avoidance.

This clause specifies that the lack of 'valid commercial reasons', such as restructuring or rationalization, 'may constitute a presumption that the operation has tax evasion or avoidance as its principal objective'.[53]

The 2005 amendments, which were proposed by the Commission on the ground that the 1990 version did not cover all the companies and situations it should have done,[54] extended the scope of the Directive to both additional types of companies and new operations. As regards the first aspect, the new version of the Merger Directive includes the additional types of legal entities falling within the scope of the amended Parent-Subsidiary Directive, the corresponding legal forms in the ten new Member States as well as the SE and the SCE.[55] The extension of its scope to new operations covers the partial division, where the transferring company transfers only parts of its assets and liabilities, constituting one or more branches of activity;[56] exchanges of shares consisting of acquisitions beyond the thresholds that are necessary to obtain a simple majority of voting rights;[57] the conversion of branches into subsidiaries;[58] and the transfer of the registered office of the SE and of the SCE from one Member State to another.[59]

All these operations benefit from the same tax relief as stipulated for the four types of operations already included in the 1990 version, under the two identical conditions regarding the transferred assets and liabilities.[60] Moreover, those Member States which consider some of the non-resident corporate entities falling in newly included typologies as fiscally transparent, are required to avoid economic double taxation of their resident taxpayers having an interest in these entities.[61] In its proposal for amendments, the Commission had also stressed that, in transfers of assets, the necessary roll-over of capital gains to receiving companies risks causing economic double taxation if the transferring company were requested by its state of residence to value the shares received in exchange at the book value of the assets and liabilities transferred, because the same gain would be considered the first time at the moment of disposal of assets by the receiving company, the second one at the time of any disposal of securities received by the transferring company. The Commission had evidenced this could occur in exchanges of shares too, due to the roll-over of capital gains to shareholders of the acquired company, if the acquiring company were requested, under its national law, to attribute to the shares it obtains the book value they had in the shareholders' hands, which would again cause taxation on the same gains, at the time of disposal, in two Member States. Nevertheless, the valuation rules proposed by the Commission[62] to prevent this economic double taxation were not included in the amendments.

Two last amendments to the 1990 version have, on the one hand, extended the possibilities of benefiting from the tax deferral and, on the other hand, widened the scope of the anti-abuse clause. In the first respect, the minimum holding in the capital of the transferring company required for the receiving company in order not to be taxed on the capital gains accruing to it on the cancellation of the shareholding, will gradually be reduced to 10 per cent.[63] In the second respect, the new anti-abuse clause includes the transfer of registered office of the SE or of the SCE amongst the operations to which Member States can refuse to apply the Directive on grounds of (presumption of) tax evasion or tax avoidance objectives.[64] Apart from the amendments, the 2005 Directive has left Member States all options granted by the 1990 version.

1.1.5 Limits of the Merger Directive

The limits on the achievement of a 'common system of taxation' and of conditions of tax neutrality 'analogous to those of an internal market' are evident in several aspects. The literature has already indicated two of the most significant ones. The first is the uncertainty on essential subjective features of the operations, such as the exact meaning of some restrictions imposed by the definitions of the qualifying transactions. Examples can be found in the definitions of the qualifying mergers, divisions and exchanges of shares, which state that any cash payment to shareholders may not exceed 10 per cent of the value of shares used as a consideration without specifying whether the limit applies to each shareholder individually or to the shareholders as a group;[65] in the provision which, by referring to the 'issue' of shares in relation to mergers, divisions and exchange of shares and to the 'transfer' of shares in transfer of assets, does not clarify whether the shares to be used as a consideration for the transfer of assets must be new or already existing shares[66] (this makes it uncertain whether or not the receiving company must necessarily increase its share capital). The second limitation is the uncertainty on the objective conditions of the 'involved' companies: for example, the Directive fails to clarify whether new companies coming into existence as a result of the operation may be considered involved exactly as those already established in more Member States which realize the operations with each other.[67] The widening of the scope of the Directive, by maintaining unchanged the formulations which originated such uncertainties in the 1990 version[68] and extending the requirements set by this version to the new operations envisaged, has not eliminated this type of limitation of the Directive. As a result, the 2005 amendments have caused these uncertainties to affect a greater number of companies and operations.[69] It can also be noted that, despite the amendments, the remaining risk of economic double taxation of the same capital gains, in transfers of assets and exchanges of shares, in two different Member States[70] can still make the overall treatment of these cross-border operations less favourable than the treatment of the corresponding type of domestic operations. Moreover, the Directive continues to assume,[71] and to require, that assets and liabilities transferred remain connected with a PE of the receiving company in the Member State of the transferring company, and that they play a part in generating taxable profits.[72] However, as a result of these operations, assets different from fixed assets (for example, assets such as intangible assets, specific equipment) but in some cases even more important in the business's overall economy and possibilities of growth, by their very nature might be transferred without requiring the 'connection' with a PE, so that this condition may not make sense in economic terms. In this hypothesis, the taxation of capital gains is excluded solely for some assets, which in the concrete situations may not be the most important ones, whilst others – in respect of which capital gains may be even greater – do not benefit from the relief. The possible tax charges arising on their transfer on intra-EC restructuring operations and not on domestic ones would fully contrast with the goals stated in the Preamble.[73] The amendments, by extending the requirement at stake to the transfer of the registered office of the SE or the SCE, have paradoxically created the risk of this obstacle for an operation, such as the transfer of seat, which ought to be the distinctive advantage of intended supranational instruments in comparison with companies governed by national laws. Moreover, the wording of the anti-abuse clause resulting from the 2005 amendments, according to which the transfer of registered office can be presumed to be aimed at tax evasion or avoidance if not carried out for valid commercial reasons such as restructuring or rationalization, would risk even placing the transfer of the registered office of the SE or the SCE at disadvantage in comparison with the seat transfer of domestic companies, as will be seen in Chapter 3.[74]

Another aspect can be highlighted. Although the definition of 'transferred assets and liabilities', when requiring the connection with the PE, does not distinguish between agencies, branches and subsidiaries, the very nature of the operations (in which transferring companies are 'dissolved without going into liquidation')[75] limits their choice to branches and agencies, which are included in the international tax law concept of PE derived from the OECD Model.[76] Accordingly, in those cases in which the receiving companies preferred the creation of a subsidiary in the Member State of the transferring company, the requirement set out by the Directive may distort the exercise of the freedom of establishment. A more far-reaching effect would thus have been secured, in terms of removal of tax obstacles and achievement of tax neutrality, if the 'transferred assets and liabilities' had been defined as 'all rights and obligations which, as a consequence of the operation, are transferred to the receiving company and, as a whole, make possible the carrying out of a business activity'.

Moreover, in addition to Member States' freedom to maintain, in their national provisions concerning domestic operations, different and/or more favourable rules than the relief provided for,[77] in essential provisions of the Directive it is possible to find not only an explicit choice (such as the option not to grant the tax relief when the receiving company's holding in the capital of the transferring company does not exceed the threshold indicated)[78] but also an implicit option for Member States. For example, national legislators can decide when the assets and liabilities connected with a PE play a part in generating taxable profits, and can thus be regarded as 'transferred';[79] which are the necessary measures that, as required by the Directive, must be taken to ensure that tax-exempt provisions or reserves may be carried over by the PEs of the receiving company which are situated in the Member State of the transferring company.[80] Consequently, the individual states are left even more space than in the case of the Parent-Subsidiary Directive, for national legislators are given the task both of implementing this greater number of options and of exactly defining some underlying technical concepts (such as 'provisions', 'reserves', 'losses'), for which (like the Parent-Subsidiary Directive) the Merger Directives does not provide uniform definitions.

A thorough review of the Directive suggests, in conclusion, that it was bound to be unable to achieve all the objectives set out in the Preamble to an even greater extent than in the case of the Parent-Subsidiary Directive, owing to the broader range of the operations involved which, in itself, calls for the solutions of a far greater number of technical issues. Apart from the difficulty of reconciling the omissions and the technically ambiguous formulations with tax neutrality, those legal requirements potentially contrasting with the economically preferable solutions to certain issues contradict the further intentions, stated in the Preamble, to increase companies' productivity and to improve their competitive strength at international level.[81] Last, the options left to Member States over some crucial issues would seem, on their own, consistent with a 'minimalist approach', but the introduction of rules which are truly 'neutral' on competition would require a high degree of uniformity of application of the tax relief.

1.1.6 Common Outcome of the Directives' Implementation: a Distorted Tax Competition rather than a Common Tax System

The protection of national revenue interests, traditionally regarded by Member States as one of the main expressions of national sovereignty, can be pursued through two alternative kinds of fiscal policies: (a) the restriction of the conditions under which taxpayers can benefit from certain tax reliefs or the complete refusal to grant these reliefs, policies which enable a state to increase its revenue from the taxpayers, both individuals and companies, having their residence for tax purposes within its jurisdiction in a given tax year, but which risk discouraging foreign investments and producing companies' migration to other states; (b) the granting of more favourable tax reliefs than those provided for by other states, which on the one hand generates a lower revenue from the already resident taxpayers but, on the other hand, frequently attracts new companies from other states and increases the overall number of taxpayers.

The implementation of the two Directives, because of the indicated features, has offered Member States the occasion to combine these two choices in the tax treatment of both intra-EC dividends flows and restructuring operations, with the ultimate result of generating, throughout the Community, a distorted tax competition which increases the number and the complexity of the relevant elements under national tax laws which groups of companies are forced to consider, in order to avoid the risk of double taxation on the same income or capital gain, when deciding to structure themselves within the EC. Such an outcome clearly emerges from the effects of the choices made by Member States in implementing each of the two Directives.

Comparative surveys on the implementation of both Directives by each Member State[82] have, in fact, unequivocally shown this result: considerable differences have survived between national laws in essential aspects, mainly relating to the conditions to be fulfilled by involved companies for enjoying the tax benefits granted by the two Directives. Member States have not only used the expressly-left options in considerably different ways, but also introduced further requirements in addition to the conditions set by the Directives which make the conditions for the tax relief more restrictive than envisaged by the Directives, and often different from one state to another. In fact, these additional requirements, frequently justified on the basis of the anti-abuse clauses, are in general of the same type: similarity of the level of taxation in the case of the Parent-Subsidiary Directive, forms of prior authorization or qualification on the persons of shareholders in the case of the Merger Directive, but stricter in some Member States than in others.[83] Consequently, national legislators have been ‘competing’ with each other in a distorted manner to the extent that the additional conditions imposed by a given state or group of states, although not envisaged by the Directives and therefore, as argued by commentators,[84] in breach of these latter, are less restrictive than those imposed by other national legislations and, for this reason, are capable of making this state or states more ‘attractive’ than others as locations for groups of companies wishing to structure themselves within the EC.

Moreover, the effects of a distorted tax competition can continue to be generated by the different national definitions of the underlying technical concepts (thus, by the ‘implicit options’ left by the two Directives). As regards the Parent-Subsidiary Directive, its transposition into national tax laws still characterized by wide differences as between the regimes of determination of taxable profits (and the rates of taxation), of which distributed profits are just a part, leaves scope for tax competition as between Member States, competition which in turn is bound to be distorted, just because it openly concentrates on the tax treatment of dividends while leaving the different national definitions of ‘taxable profits’ (and the possibility of modifying them over time) completely unchanged. As regards the Merger Directive, the identical effect derives from the importance of the underlying concepts (‘tax-exempted provisions’, ‘reserves’) left to national laws in determining the actual amount of the tax relief. Accordingly, in addition to being distorted, this tax competition lacks transparency to the extent that, after the implementation of the Directives, it may tend to concentrate on elements not expressly defined by the Directives themselves, but which are decisive in affecting the overall tax treatment. Furthermore, as regards the Merger Directive, three Member States[85] have long avoided implementing the provisions relating to cross-border mergers and divisions on the ground of the lack of EC company law provisions.

Owing to the limitations of the text of the two Directives, their implementation by Member States does not thus seem to have resulted in an effective approximation of the tax treatment for intra-EC profits distributions and restructuring operations at a global level within the EC. This leaves to the ECJ case law (examined below)[86] the decisive role.

1.1.7 Concluding Observation

The history of both Directives may certainly give force to the argument that they are 'very good examples of the limits of the EC legislative process'[87] (a legislative process ultimately dominated by the interests of all Member States), that they also reflect the trade-off between the needs for efficiency at EC level and for autonomy at Member State level and that they would appear to be consistent with the 1990 Commission Communication on 'guidelines on company taxation'.[88] This Communication had, on the one hand, stressed the importance of tax neutrality as a guiding principle regarding company taxation, and on the other hand, accepted as guidelines on the Commission's policy on company taxation the principle of subsidiarity and the inherent concept of 'minimum harmonization', the need for action when necessary to complete the single market and the taking of any action in concert with all the Member States and with companies. Apparently, the drafters of the Directives thus intended tax neutrality as absence of tax obstacles to intra-EC profits distributions and restructuring operations subject to certain conditions, rather than in its broadest concept of irrelevance of location within the EC for the purpose of carrying out these operations at either Community or domestic level. With this narrower concept of tax neutrality, they regarded the concepts of 'common tax system' and of 'national tax systems with common features' as equivalent, and used the words 'common system of taxation' to indicate the approximation of national tax laws to such an extent that, after the implementation of the two Directives, they ought to have, as a common feature, the absence of taxation of intra-EC dividends flows and of all the restructuring operations dealt with. This approach appears to be confirmed by an important Commission Report on *Company Taxation in the Internal Market*, released in 2001,[89] which indicated the amendments of the two Directives as important 'short term' measures to tackle the most urgent company tax obstacles still existing within the EC.[90] The Report expressed doubts concerning the implementation by Member States, in particular with regard to the anti-abuse clauses, and regarded a closer view of this implementation as necessary, but it did not carry out an overall assessment of the contribution of the two Directives to the achievement of 'conditions analogous to those of an internal market'[91] from the tax law perspective, which would have required a scrutiny of the outcome of the Directives' implementation under the broadest concept of tax neutrality.

Nevertheless, the adoption of this concept would effectively have ensured neutrality from the viewpoint of (market) competition, thus between competing companies located in different Member States. This would have enabled the objectives stated in the Preambles to the two Directives to be fully achieved and would also have been coherent with their legal basis: Article 94 EC, that is the provisions of the Treaty requiring Community institutions to approximate national laws which directly affect the functioning of the internal market. The choice of this legal basis supposes in fact a recognition that differences in national provisions on companies' direct taxation directly affect (as stated by Article 94 EC) the functioning of the internal market and that Member States are more reluctant to have their autonomy restricted in this sector than in others (as implicit in the Treaty's rule requiring unanimity in the Council of Ministers for EC intervention in the tax field). With this premise, the approximation of national laws to such an extent as to limit differences between national provisions to secondary aspects for the carrying out of the operations considered – which, in companies' overall evaluations, would have probably not affected the location decisions within the EC – would have been consistent with the maintaining for Member States of margins of autonomy which would no longer directly affect the functioning of the market. Ultimately, due to the drafting of the two tax Directives according to a concept of tax neutrality stricter than that required to fully achieve the goals stated in their Preambles, it can thus be reaffirmed that their ultimate outcome has not been a system of taxation truly common to Member States. This system would have reduced the margins for tax competition between Member States: instead, the outcome has been that of approximating one aspect of national tax regimes for intra-EC profits distributions and restructuring operations (the absence of taxation) while allowing some other essential aspects (the conditions for companies based in different Member States to enjoy this tax benefit) to remain widely divergent from one Member State to another. As the surveys referred to above demonstrate, a distorted tax competition has been the ultimate outcome in regulating just these aspects.

The approved amendments to the Parent-Subsidiary Directive[92] and to the Merger Directive[93] maintain unaltered the options expressly granted to Member States as well as their margins of autonomy in defining the underlying technical concepts, which indicates the continuation (on the part of the Commission when proposing these amendments in 2003, and of the Council in adopting them) of the approach already adopted by the 1990 drafters. Consequently, the results of the implementation, despite the amendments, are unlikely to show significant changes. By contrast, the extension of the tax benefits of the two Directives to a greater number of cases may induce national legislators to use the options and the margins of autonomy to compete with each other in attracting companies into their jurisdictions to an even greater extent than they may have done to date.[94] Member States may, in fact, consider this strategy as necessary in order to 'compensate' for the reduction in tax revenues caused by the extension of the scope of the tax benefits. In turn, the higher the number of elements (including those outside the options granted, as well as the possibility of minor and/or less evident infringements of the Directive than in other states) on which competition between Member States may concentrate and is actually concentrating after the entry of the ten East European states into the EC,[95] the higher the incentive for companies to devise complicated tax-planning strategies to take their location decisions. Such an effect would not be welcomed by the Commission, which would consider it detrimental to the achievement of the strategic 'Lisbon objective'.[96]

1.2 THE 2003 INTEREST-ROYALTIES DIRECTIVE: OVERVIEW

In June 2003, the EC Council issued an 'Interest-Royalties Directive', which exempts interest and royalties payments between associated companies of different Member States from 'any tax' in the country where they arise.[97] This Directive[98] covers the same typologies of companies as the original version of the 1990 Directives, with the same participation threshold,[99] which makes the definition of 'associated companies' similar to those of parent company and subsidiary,[100] and it leaves identical options for Member States as regards the replacement of the criteria of holding in the capital with that of holding in the voting rights;[101] the setting of a two-year minimum holding period requirement;[102] the anti-abuse clause[103] and the safeguard of national or DTCs provisions,[104] both formulated with the identical wording of the corresponding provisions of the Parent-Subsidiary Directive and, in the case of the anti-abuse clause, with similar wording to the corresponding provision of the Merger Directive too.[105] Moreover, this Directive also covers (like the amended version of the Parent-Subsidiary Directive) the payments made and received by a company through a PE, defined in accordance with the OECD Model, situated in a Member State different from that of its associated company.[106] The goal of this Directive is the elimination of the disadvantage faced by intra-EC interest and royalties payments in comparison with domestic payments,[107] where 'interest and royalties', the main technical concept, are defined in the same way as the OECD Model.[108]

Member States are granted implicit options: the limitation of the scope of the Directive to the amount of such payments agreed by the associated companies in the absence of a 'special relationship',[109] where the features which this relationship should have in order to be regarded as 'special' are not indicated; complete discretion as to whether to apply it to some cases of payments in which they are not obliged to do so;[110] the possibility for Member States to set a number of substantive and procedural conditions not contemplated by the two 1990 Directives directly affecting the scope of the tax exemption granted.[111]

Moreover, after the extension of the scope of the Parent-Subsidiary Directive to new types of companies, amongst which are the SE and the SCE,[112] the Commission has proposed similar amendments to this new Directive: they would extend its scope to new legal entities, including the SE and the SCE, without lowering the participation threshold.[113] Member States are, in any case, completely free to introduce implementing measures reflecting all these amendments.

Ultimately, the 2003 Interest-Royalties Directive was able to introduce a common method of taxation of interest and royalties payments between associated companies of different Member States, rather than a truly common system.[114] The gradual implementation by Member States shows, in fact, a wide choice of instruments[115] to compete with each other in the tax treatment of intra-EC interest and royalties payments. The latest ECJ case law on the Parent-Subsidiary Directive would seem, however,[116] applicable to this Directive too, giving clear indications regarding the most effective national tax policies.

1.3 UNINTENTIONAL CONTRIBUTION OF THE LATEST ECJ CASE LAW ON THE 1990 DIRECTIVES TO TAX COMPETITION

The absence in the Treaty of provisions specifically governing direct taxation has led the overall case law of the ECJ in this field, concerning both companies and natural persons, to express the fundamental principle that, although direct taxation falls within the competence of Member States, they must exercise that competence consistently with EC law.[117] The application of this principle to the two 1990 Directives offers Member States clear guidelines.

1.3.1 Three Phases of the ECJ Case Law on the Parent-Subsidiary Directive

The case law on the Parent-Subsidiary Directive, developed from 1996 onwards, has dealt with six crucial interpretative issues: the content of the anti-abuse clause contained in Article 1, second paragraph, in the 1996 *Denkavit* case[118] (the first ruling); the direct effect of the Directive provisions, in *Denkavit* and in the 2001 *Zythopiia* case;[119] the right of compensation for damages incurred by involved companies as a result of improper implementation by Member States, in *Denkavit* and *Zythopiia*; the concept of 'withholding tax' prohibited under Article 5, first paragraph, in the 1998 *Epson* case,[120] in *Zythopiia* and in the 2003 *Van der Grinten* case;[121] the scope of the clause which safeguards the application of domestic provisions or DTCs designed to eliminate or to lessen economic double taxation of dividends, laid down by Article 7, second paragraph, in *Zythopiia* and in *Van der Grinten*; the relationship between the options allowed by the Directive and the freedom of establishment in the 2003 *Bosal Holding*[122] ruling (whose finding was reiterated in the 2006 *Keller Holding* ruling[123]) and, indirectly, in *Van der Grinten*. Three phases can be recognized in the development of this case law.

a. Search for compromise in *Denkavit*

The *Denkavit* ruling related to an application of the holding period requirement, by the state of the subsidiary, which caused damages to the non-resident parent company, and which was justified by that state on the basis of the anti-abuse clause. A Dutch parent company holding a qualifying participation in a German subsidiary had to await the elapsing date of the minimum holding period under German law in order to receive dividends with the benefit of the exemption from withholding tax under the Directive, even though the dividends distribution had originally been planned to take place before that date. If dividends had been distributed before the elapsing of the minimum holding period, withholding tax would in fact have been charged. The ECJ ruled that: (a) the granting of this tax advantage could not be subject to the condition that the minimum holding period had elapsed at the time of profits distribution, but Member States were free to devise rules ensuring compliance with this period; (b) a parent company could rely on the provision granting exemption from withholding tax before the courts of another Member State, when the relevant state interpreted the minimum holding period contrary to the Directive; (c) the plaintiffs were not entitled to damages suffered as a result of the erroneous interpretation of the Directive.[124] Whereas the first finding was based on recognition of the anti-abuse clause as a provision of principle, explained in detail by the provision allowing Member States to set the minimum holding period in order to avoid abuses whereby temporary holdings are taken in the capital of companies for the sole purpose of benefiting from the tax advantage available, the second conclusion indicates the ECJ's willingness to recognize the 'direct effect' of the provision granting exemption from withholding tax. This however in *Denkavit* was limited to the event of wrongful interpretation of the minimum holding period. The last finding – the absence of a right of compensation for damages – would deprive of any practical effect the right to resort to national courts if it were intended as the statement of a general principle, but the ECJ in reaching this decision relied on the absence, up to that moment, of case law offering guidance on the interpretation of the provision relating to the holding period, as well as on the circumstance that many other Member States had interpreted this provision in the same way as Germany.

Globally considered, the *Denkavit* ruling could thus be seen as a search for compromise between the interests of companies and of Member States. It raised two important issues: whether the possible resort to national courts could be extended to all cases of national provisions apparently contrasting with the wording and the objective of the Directive; and whether the ECJ would have reached the same conclusion about the right to compensation for damages if other Member States had not shared the arguments of the state involved.

b. Recognition of the Directive's 'direct effect' in *Zythopiia*

The answers to these questions can be deduced from the 2001 '*Zythopiia*' ruling, which also reaffirmed the interpretation of the concept of 'withholding tax', from which profits distribution must be exempted under Article 5, first paragraph, followed in the previous *Epson* ruling.[125]

A Greek company, controlled by a Netherlands parent company, claimed from the competent national tax authority the refund of a part of the corporation tax which it had paid at the time of the distribution of profits to its parent company in accordance with national tax provisions, on the ground that these provisions infringed Article 5, first paragraph. According to the national provisions at issue, the distribution of profits to its parent company made the subsidiary subject to tax on two categories of income which would not have been made taxable had the subsidiary not distributed them to the parent company.[126]

Although the Greek Government basically contended that since the profits were subjected to taxation as the subsidiary's profits, the tax paid was merely an advance payment of the corporation tax by the subsidiary made in connection with a profits distribution to its parent company,[127] the ECJ followed a different reasoning. After underlining the importance of the exemption from the withholding tax for eliminating double taxation, it on the one hand stated that Article 5 does not limit the notion of withholding tax to specific types of national taxes, and on the other hand stressed, in accordance with its previous case law in the taxation field, that any national tax or duty must be examined, under Community law, on the basis of its objective features, irrespective of the way in which it is classified by national legislation.[128] In the case at issue, the analysis of these objective features evidenced that the tax was generated by the distribution of dividends rather than by the production of income:[129] this led the ECJ to exclude the nature of an advance payment of the corporation tax made in connection with profits distribution.

The Greek Government also argued that the taxation of dividends by the state of residence of the distributing subsidiary, in addition to the taxation by the state of residence of the shareholder, was allowed, up to a rate of 35 per cent, by the DTC concluded with the Netherlands, which, in its opinion, was authorized by Article 7, second paragraph of the Parent-Subsidiary Directive. Nevertheless, the ECJ, on the basis of the provisions of that DTC, found no difficulty in holding that this latter had created the double taxation of dividends, instead of either eliminating or reducing it, since the DTC ultimately did authorize both states to tax the distributed dividends, despite the ceiling on the rate set to the taxation of dividends distributed by a subsidiary located in Greece to a shareholder resident in the Netherlands. Consequently, the ECJ stated that the DTC could not fall within the scope of Article 7, second paragraph of the Directive and, by recognizing, outside the hypothesis of application of this provision, the absolute and unconditional nature of the rights conferred to economic operators by Article 5, first paragraph,[130] it definitively concluded that the form of taxation at issue did represent a 'withholding tax', in breach of the Directive.

This first part of *Zythopiia* establishes two key principles, both capable of strengthening the effectiveness of the Directive. Firstly, the nature of withholding tax, if deriving from the objective features of a particular tax, is completely independent from either the classification or the name attributed by the national legislation involved. As a result, and as a disincentive for Member States from devising complicated provisions or combinations of provisions, no combination of provisions relating to a single tax, which might be present in national laws, can serve to disguise the nature of withholding tax: the necessity to examine the objective features logically implies the need to analyse all parts of national tax law referring to the tax, in order to consider all the objective features of this latter. These are the only elements which may lead to making a distinction with advance payments of corporation tax made in connection with distributions of profits by subsidiaries to parent companies. Secondly, but equally important, *Zythopiia* indicates that, even though formally, by their very nature, all DTCs are 'designed to eliminate or lessen economic double taxation'[131] the ECJ reserves the right to analyse in each case whether the relevant Convention, in the light of all its relevant provisions, actually produces the result of either eliminating or lessening economic double taxation. This obviously affects Member States' margins of freedom when signing DTCs between themselves if they wish to be certain that the Convention will be safeguarded by Article 7, second paragraph, of the Parent-Subsidiary Directive.

The second part of the ruling dealt with the Greek Government's request for a limitation in time of the effects of the ECJ's finding, to allow the national administration to lessen the considerable financial liability otherwise deriving from the refund of the unduly collected withholding tax. The Court rejected this request on the grounds that: (a) according to the settled case law, the interpretation of an EC law provision given by the ECJ in the exercise of a power conferred on it by Article 234 of the Treaty, clarifies the ambit and the meaning of the provision as it was intended and should have been applied from the time of its entry into force and, therefore, even before the interpretative ruling; (b) the effects of an interpretative ruling may be limited only in exceptional cases, which cases had been identified by previous ECJ case law in the risk of negative economic effects involving a great number of legally binding obligations entered into in good faith on the basis of a specific provision and in a relevant and objective uncertainty about the scope of the provision in question.[132] These exceptional circumstances were considered to be absent in *Zythopiia,* because Greece had not demonstrated that, at the time of introduction of the national provisions establishing the contested tax, it was reasonably possible to suppose that EC law allowed such a tax.[133] Accordingly, the ECJ could have reached a different conclusion, had the Greek Government proved, by assumption, a relevant and objective uncertainty in the application of Article 5, first paragraph of the Directive. With these premises, the argument based on the amount of the financial liability deriving from the refund of the withholding tax collected from the time of entry into force of the national provisions establishing it was easily rejected. It was sufficient for the ECJ to stress that, if the financial damages arising for Member States from the unlawful nature of a tax justified the limitation of the effects of an interpretative ruling (from the date of the ruling), the final outcome would (paradoxically) be a better treatment for the most significant violations and that, in addition, a limitation of the effects of the ruling based solely on financial reasons would substantially reduce the enforcement of the rights conferred to taxpayers by EC tax law.[134] Given the ECJ's reasoning, this second part of the ruling greatly strengthens the outcome (already generated by the first part) of discouraging Member States from introducing taxes whose lawfulness may appear doubtful in the light of EC law, to the extent to which it leaves them with the burden of proof of demonstrating the objective uncertainty of the relevant EC tax law provisions, including those of the

Parent-Subsidiary Directive. Moreover, the ECJ's final statement above, referring in general terms to the rights conferred to taxpayers by Community tax law, implicitly suggests (if read with reference to the Directive, as is necessary, it being contained in an interpretative ruling on the Directive's provision) that this Directive, conferring enforceable rights on taxpayers, is considered as having 'direct effect' and classified amongst the Directives formulated in clear and specific terms.[135]

The ECJ's conclusions in the last part of the *Zythopiia* ruling, and their implications, read together with the Court's above-mentioned findings in *Denkavit,* can provide the answers to the two issues left unresolved by that ruling. Whereas the implicit recognition in the ECJ's statement in *Zythopiia* of the Directive's direct effect is fully consistent with the finding in *Denkavit* of the parent company's right to rely directly on the fundamental tax relief provisions of the Directive before the national courts of another Member State, and it appears to be the extension of such right (initially recognized in the event of a wrong interpretation of the minimum holding period requirement) to all the Directive's main provisions, the issue concerning damages compensation seems to deserve to be distinguished. In fact, it can be noted that, in *Zythopiia*, by affirming outside particular and exceptional cases the financial liability of Member States for the refund of the withholding tax collected from the time of entry into force of the national provisions establishing it, the ECJ also recognized, as a general rule, the right of companies to the full refund of a tax which they ought not to have paid under a Directive's fundamental provision. Consequently, the two rulings may be reconciled as follows: as a general principle, after *Zythopiia* companies are entitled to compensation for direct damages which consist of the payment of clearly undue taxes under Articles 4 and 5 of the Directive, whereas in cases of indirect damages (such as, in *Denkavit,* the postponing of the receipt of income until the expiry of the minimum holding period), the result may be the opposite. Companies will thus in practice be interested, in any doubtful case, in trying to argue and to prove that, ultimately, any damages suffered may be regarded as equivalent to direct damages deriving from the infringement by the Member State involved of the Directive's fundamental provisions.[136]

c. Interpretation based on the freedom of establishment: *Bosal Holding*, *Keller Holding* and *Van der Grinten*

In *Bosal Holding,* a company resident in the Netherlands and carrying on holding, financing and licensing/royalty-related activities, declared, for a given financial year, costs in relation to the financing of its holdings in companies established in nine other Member States and claimed that those costs should be deducted from its own taxable profits in the Netherlands. The tax authority denied the deduction on the ground that the national Law on

Corporation Tax applicable at the time made the deduction conditional upon such costs being indirectly instrumental in making profits taxable in the Netherlands: the ECJ had to establish whether the Treaty's provisions on the freedom of establishment (Articles 43 and 48), the Parent-Subsidiary Directive or any other rule of EC law precluded a Member State from granting a parent company subject to tax in that Member State a deduction of costs relating to a holding owned by it subject to the condition that the relevant subsidiary makes taxable profits in its jurisdiction. The ECJ considered, amongst the relevant rules of EC law other than the provisions on the freedom of establishment, Articles 1 and 4 of the Parent-Subsidiary Directive, together with the key recital in its Preamble, and interpreted the Directive in the light of Article 43 EC on the freedom of establishment. Amongst the provisions of the Directive,[137] Article 4, second paragraph, in allowing Member States to apply either the exemption or the tax credit methods, leaves Member States the option of making any charges relating to the holding not deductible from the taxable profits of the parent company. Against the Dutch argument that the refusal to allow the deductibility of the costs at issue was legitimate as it was allowed by this option, the Court admitted that, in so far as the national law merely implemented the possibility offered by Article 4, it was compatible with the Directive, but went on to state that the option could be exercised only in compliance with the Treaty's rules on the right of establishment. From this viewpoint, it found that the limitation to the deductibility of costs contained in the national provision might dissuade a parent company from carrying on its activities through the intermediary of a subsidiary established in another Member State (since, normally, such subsidiaries did not generate profits that are taxable in the Netherlands) and that such a limitation conflicted with the objective, spelt out in recital (3) of the Directive's Preamble, to eliminate the disadvantages in the tax treatment of relations between parent companies and subsidiaries of different Member States in comparison with the relations between parent companies and subsidiaries of the same Member State.[138] It thus concluded that the Directive, which admits no exception concerning the territory where the profits of the subsidiaries might be taxed, interpreted in the light of Article 43 EC, precluded the national provision examined.

The *Keller Holding* ruling extended the interpretation based on the freedom of establishment to second tier subsidiaries in another Member State. The German tax authority had excluded the deduction of financing costs, related to the participation in a German subsidiary, incurred by a resident parent company which had received, through the intermediary of such subsidiary, dividends from a second tier subsidiary established in Austria, because these dividends were tax exempt in Germany. The deduction was allowed for dividends distributed by a German (second tier) subsidiary, in which case the dividends were taxable but the German parent was entitled to credit the distributing company's corporation tax against its own tax liability under the imputation system applied by Germany at the time. The ECJ first rejected an argument, submitted by the German and the UK Governments, according to which the deduction of costs related to the participation of a German holding in the German subsidiary was a purely internal matter: in fact, it found a direct economic link between the refusal to allow the deduction and the dividends paid by the indirect Austrian subsidiary and, consequently, it regarded the situation as falling within the scope of EC law. Subsequently, it observed that domestic dividends flows, although formally taxed, were effectively tax exempted under the imputation system, so that the situation was ultimately the same as that of tax-exempt dividends distributed by the indirect Austrian subsidiary, except for the deduction allowed in one case and disallowed in another. Accordingly, the ECJ found that the tax position of a company with an indirect subsidiary in Austria was less favourable than it would have been had the indirect subsidiary been established in Germany, and that this difference in treatment could dissuade a company from carrying out its activity through direct or indirect subsidiaries in other Member States. Last, it stated that Germany could not rely, to justify the refusal to allow the deduction, on the same option left by the Parent-Subsidiary Directive at issue in *Bosal*, by concluding again that this option must be exercised in compliance with the freedom of establishment.[139]

The *Bosal* and *Keller* rulings set a limit of general character to Member States' margin of discretion in implementing the options left by the Directive. Although these options on their own may allow the Member States to introduce or maintain some restrictive provisions (like the one at issue), their *implementation* must be tested against the objective, consistent with the freedom of establishment, of eliminating the disadvantage which the relations between parent companies and direct or indirect subsidiaries of different Member States have been facing in comparison with those between parent companies and direct or indirect subsidiaries of the same Member State. This implies that the scrutiny in the light of Articles 43 and 48 of the Treaty, which can be directly relied upon also by an indirect parent company (*Keller*), extends to this implementation too, with potentially far-reaching consequences for the tax systems not only of the Member States of destination, but also of the Member States of origin (as the Netherlands and Germany were in *Bosal* and *Keller*). Accordingly, the Commission's observation that the *Bosal* ruling opens up new legal possibilities for tax planning and could create further difficulties for Member States,[140] can certainly apply to both rulings.

The question whether the application of the freedom of establishment to the implementation of the Directive meets any exception (and, if so, which), left open by *Bosal* and *Keller*, may perhaps find an indirect response in the interesting *Van der Grinten* ruling. In the situation at issue, a Dutch parent company received dividends from a wholly owned British subsidiary, which, under the UK tax legislation of the time, had to pay advance corporation tax (ACT) calculated at a certain rate on a sum equal to the distribution made. Whereas any distribution of dividends subject to ACT by a UK subsidiary to a UK parent company entitled this latter to a tax credit equal to the amount of the ACT, under the United Kingdom-Netherlands DTC the Dutch parent company receiving the dividends was only entitled to a 50 per cent tax credit and was subject to a 5 per cent charge, in the United Kingdom, on the aggregate amount of the dividend and of that tax credit. The half tax credit, redeemable in cash, was included in the taxable profits of the Dutch company in the Netherlands; the Convention required the Netherlands to allow this parent company to deduct, from any national tax payable on the dividend, the amount of the 5 per cent United Kingdom charge. Having to assess, first, whether this 5 per cent charge was a withholding tax under Article 5 of the Parent-Subsidiary Directive, the ECJ stated, after recalling its previous case law[141] and consistently with it, that the part of the 5 per cent charge applying to dividends was a withholding tax, in principle prohibited by Article 5, but found that the part of the charge applying to the half tax credit was not such, for three reasons. Its first argument was that the tax credit is a fiscal instrument designed to avoid double taxation, in economic terms, of the profits distributed as dividends, and not an income from shares. Secondly, it found that the effects of the charge on the tax credit were not contrary to the prohibition of withholding tax, on the ground that the partial reduction of the tax credit, caused by the 5 per cent charge to which it was subject, did not apply to the distribution of dividends and did not diminish their value in the hands of the recipient parent company. Thirdly, it stressed that, under the United Kingdom-Netherlands DTC, the 5 per cent charge in the United Kingdom had as its counterpart the obligation on the Netherlands to allow it to be set against the tax of the parent company.[142]

This first conclusion of *Van der Grinten* evidences two key points: (a) in contrast with the argument it had adopted as regards the nature of withholding tax of the part of the charge applying to dividends, where it had concentrated on the characteristics of it irrespective of the formal classification (in line with *Zythopiia*), the ECJ seems to have paid attention to the formal classification of the half tax credit, as a fiscal instrument designed to *avoid* double taxation in economic terms, irrespective of its actual capacity to do so in the concrete case and of its inclusion in the taxable base in the Netherlands; (b) consequently, and even more important, the notion of fiscal neutrality of the cross-border distribution of dividends emerging from the above statement is not that of a complete equality of treatment between domestic shareholders (entitled to a full tax credit, without the 5 per cent charge, which completely compensates the ACT) and shareholders from other Member States (entitled to half tax credit, with the 5 per cent charge, insufficient to fully compensate the ACT): it is solely that of absence of reduction of the part of the distributions which is regarded as dividends. Whereas the first point will need to be clarified by future case law, the second one gives rise to an important question: in what way that notion of neutrality could be reconciled with the same recital (3) of the Directive's Preamble, stating the goal of eliminating disadvantages on cross-border operations in comparison with domestic ones, which had been regarded as decisive in *Bosal*?[143]

An answer can be drawn from the further finding of the ECJ, which held that the part of the 5 per cent charge applying to dividends, amounting to a withholding tax, was allowed by Article 7, second paragraph on the grounds that (a) account was taken when drawing up Article 7, second paragraph of the UK system, under which the distribution of dividends was accompanied by a right to payment of a partial tax credit where a DTC concluded between the Member State of the parent company and the United Kingdom so provides; (b) the 5 per cent charge, viewed as an inseparable whole with the provisions relating to the payment of the half tax credit which was introduced to mitigate the economic double taxation of dividends paid by a UK subsidiary to its Dutch parent company, was not set at a rate such as to cancel out the effects of that lessening of the economic double taxation of dividends; (c) in any event, any UK tax in respect of dividends, such as the 5 per cent charge, was deductible from the tax due in the Netherlands.[144]

Consequently, *Van der Grinten* indicates that Article 7, second paragraph allows, by way of exception from Article 5, first paragraph, the maintaining of withholding taxes, provided they are part of a DTC which does not generate an (even partial) juridical double taxation of dividends on the same recipient. In that case, due to the right of deduction of the 5 per cent charge from the Netherlands tax, juridical double taxation was in fact avoided, as would have happened if the withholding tax represented by that charge had not been applied at all by the United Kingdom (in accordance with Article 5, first paragraph). Member States can thus allocate between themselves the power of taxation of dividends distributed to a given recipient but, once one of the states involved taxes them, the other state must compensate. There can be, therefore, no restriction to the achievement of the goal of Article 5, first paragraph. As a result, the emphasis placed by the ECJ's holding in *Van der Grinten* on the lessening in itself of economic double taxation would seem to generate an exception not to Article 5, first paragraph, but to Article 4, first paragraph, which, by providing either the exemption or the tax credit method, aims to avoid economic double taxation on intra-EC distributions.

Although issues corresponding to those raised in *Bosal* were not dealt with in *Van der Grinten*, where they were raised neither by the parent company nor by the national court asking the preliminary ruling, two questions may indirectly find a response. These questions are: (a) whether a difference in treatment such as that at issue (between a UK resident parent company, which could benefit from the avoidance of economic double taxation, and the Netherlands parent company, which could only benefit from a lessening of economic double taxation) can constitute a restriction to the Netherlands company's right of establishment in the United Kingdom; (b) if so, whether it can be justified, in which case the application of the freedom of establishment to the implementation of the Directive's provisions, as stated in *Bosal* and *Keller*, would find an exception. As regards the first issue, an indication can be drawn from the ECJ's findings, which rejected a submission that Article 7, second paragraph of the Parent-Subsidiary Directive was invalid for want of reasoning, or for procedural defects lying in the fact that its inclusion in the final version of the Directive was a substantial change to a previous version without the necessary consultation of the European Parliament (EP) and of the European Economic and Social Committee (ESC). The ECJ found that a specific statement of reasons for Article 7, second paragraph was not necessary on the ground that the existing statement of reasons, which indicated the objective of fiscal neutrality of cross-border distributions of dividends, was sufficient to cover this clause preserving domestic or agreement-based provisions pursuing the same objective. This led it to conclude that the insertion of Article 7, second paragraph must be regarded as a technical adjustment, rather than as a substantial change, which 'merely enables specific sets of domestic or agreement-based rules to continue to apply, where consistent with the aim of the Directive' as set out in the same recital of the Preamble considered in *Bosal*.[145]

It can thus be argued that, provided there is no reduction of what are regarded as dividends and juridical double taxation is avoided, cross-border operations are not considered to be disadvantaged in comparison with domestic ones even if, as a result of a DTC, they benefit from a lessening of economic double taxation instead of an elimination of this as may be the case for domestic distributions.

The ultimate response to the issue left open by *Bosal* and *Keller*, to be drawn from *Van der Grinten*, would thus be that the application of the freedom of establishment to the implementation of the Directive's provisions meets no exception, because a difference of treatment in the host Member State (as the United Kingdom was from the viewpoint of the Netherlands parent company) deriving from the mere allocation of taxing powers between Member States would not fall within the concept of restriction of that freedom in the present position of ECJ case law. However, this is only due to the notion of dividends, and consequently of fiscal neutrality, adopted in *Van der Grinten*, which does not include in the concept of profits every amount redeemable in cash (as the half tax credit was in *Van der Grinten*).

1.3.2 ECJ Case Law on the Merger Directive

The case law on the Merger Directive has dealt with three basic issues: (a) the ECJ competence to rule on situations not directly governed by EC law where the national legislation, in implementing the provisions of the Directive, has chosen to apply the same treatment to purely internal situations and to those governed by the Directive; (b) the interpretation of the anti-abuse clause; (c) the failure of Member States to implement part of the Directive.

The first two issues were first dealt with in the *Leur-Bloem*[146] ruling, whose first finding was reaffirmed in the subsequent *Andersen og. Jensen* rulings.[147] In *Leur-Bloem,* the sole shareholder and director of two private Dutch companies was planning to use its shares in both companies as the means of payment for acquiring the shares of a holding company, thereby realizing a transaction after which he was to become, no longer directly but only indirectly, the sole shareholder in the first two companies. The shareholder, subject to the Netherlands Income Tax Law which, in the situation defined by its provisions as 'merger by exchange of shares', excludes from taxation gains arising on major shareholdings, had asked national authorities to treat the proposed transaction as 'merger by exchange of shares' within the meaning of the Netherlands legislation. This required the fulfilment of certain general conditions which were considered to be absent in the specific case, and the relevant national court took the view that a national provision introduced at the time of transposition of the Merger Directive into domestic law required interpretation.[148] Although the Directive was not directly applicable to the specific circumstances of the case, the relevant provision stated that the circumstances at issue had to be treated in the same manner as a situation to which the Directive does apply. The situation was similar in *Andersen og. Jensen,* where a Danish limited liability company claimed the benefit of the tax exemption granted for 'transfers of assets' by a national provision, implementing the Merger Directive, which, in regulating purely national situations, had adopted the same definitions as those adopted in EC law. In that case, the tax exemption was claimed for the planned transfer of all the business of the claimant to a new company, set up by its own shareholders, under a particular arrangement which created a dissociation between an asset (the proceeds of a large loan, which was to remain with the transferring company) and the related liability (the obligation arising from such loan) which was to be transferred to the new (receiving) company, and which did foresee a security for the benefit of the receiving company:[149] the Danish tax authority made the granting of the requested authorization to carry out the planned transfer with the tax exemption subject to the condition that the operation be made without this particular arrangement.[150] In both cases, the ECJ had to assess whether it had competence under Article 234 of the Treaty[151] and, in the affirmative case, to clarify technical questions concerning the concepts of 'exchange of shares' (in *Leur-Bloem*) and of 'transfer of assets' and 'branch of activity' (in *Andersen og. Jensen*) under the Merger Directive.

On the one hand, the importance of these rulings lies therefore in the circumstance that they provided the occasion to clarify the limits of the jurisdiction of the ECJ and, with them, the potential of EC (tax) law to attract within its definitions cases to which it does not directly apply, but for the solution of which it is *necessary* and *sufficient* that its provisions be referred to by national law. On the other hand, and as a consequence, such importance lies in their potential to identify the extent to which Member States may be free to adopt restrictive definitions of the relevant concepts. Had the ECJ answered the question concerning its competence in the negative, national tax administrations could have had the discretion to interpret both their internal provisions concerning such operations, and the Merger Directive provisions, as restrictively as they wish. This would have added to the above indicated limits of the formulation of the Directive an element capable, on its own, of greatly defeating its objectives.

On the contrary, the ECJ started these rulings by stating that its jurisdiction to interpret Community law, under Article 234 of the Treaty, extends to situations which are not directly governed by EC law but for which the national legislature, in transposing the provision of a Directive into domestic law, has chosen to apply the same treatment to purely internal situations and to those regulated by EC law.[152] This statement has, in itself, a decisive importance. Although in the situations at issue in these rulings national legislators had expressly made such choice, the general EC law principle of non-discrimination on grounds of nationality, as well as the already consolidated ECJ case law on covert discriminations,[153] reveals that, even in the absence of a specific directive regulating the operations at issue, Member States have the obligation to apply the same treatment to purely domestic situations and to the cases involving companies from other Member States. Consequently, the ECJ's statement has, in itself, the potential of extending its jurisdiction (and the ambit of EC tax law) to virtually every situation not directly regulated by EC law. This may deprive Member States of any incentive to introduce types of operations similar to those envisaged by the Directive and aimed at the same practical results (such as, in *Leur-Bloem*, the 'merger by exchange of shares' rather than directly the 'exchange of shares'), and to interpret restrictively the conditions for tax neutrality when examining these operations. Equally important is the second part of these rulings. In *Leur-Bloem,* the ECJ basically dealt with two issues:[154] (a) whether there can still be an exchange of shares within the meaning of the Directive in particular circumstances concerning either the acquiring company or the identity of its shareholder or the ultimate effect of the operation, that is, whether the concept of exchange of shares ought to be interpreted in a restrictive or in a wider sense;[155] (b) whether the clear purpose of the companies involved to obtain tax advantages can be sufficient to resort to the anti-abuse clause of Article 11.[156] The answer to the first point was inevitably bound to affect the second: a restrictive interpretation of the concept at issue could in fact broaden the discretion of Member States in establishing both the *criteria* and the *extent* through which to decide whether the tax benefit ought to be denied under the anti-abuse clause. In *Andersen og. Jensen,* the ECJ had to ascertain again, as it did when examining the above indicated first point in *Leur-Bloem*, whether the operation at issue, with its particular arrangement, could fall within the definition of 'transfer of assets' provided for by the Directive.

The ECJ's findings in the two rulings, considered together, offer both Member States and companies clear indications. In *Leur-Bloem,* the ECJ, by adopting a liberal interpretation of the concept of 'exchange of shares', stated that this notion requires general conditions to be fulfilled neither by the participating companies nor by the shareholders.[157] In *Andersen og. Jensen,* it relied on the literal wording of the definitions of 'transfer of assets' and 'branch of activity' and found that a transfer of assets must include *all* the assets and liabilities relating to a branch of activity, that 'the assets and liabilities relating to a branch … should be transferred in their entirety' and that if the transferring company retains the proceeds of a large loan contracted by it and transfers the obligations deriving from that loan to the receiving company, 'those two elements are dissociated'.[158]

Accordingly, the two rulings clarify aspects which are complementary to each other. *Leur-Bloem* suggests that, as *general* conditions are not envisaged by the Directive, there is also no other *particular* condition which could be legally imposed in addition to the literal wording of the Directive, and that this applies not only as regards the concept of 'exchange of shares' but also to the concepts of all three other operations governed by the Directive. This is because its text does not suggest in any part that with regard to one of the envisaged operations, Member States might adopt restrictive interpretations of the relevant concepts which are not admitted for the other operations, so that national legislators remain within a correct transposition of the Directive so long as they do not introduce requirements which are not contemplated by the options expressly left. The ECJ's ruling in *Leur-Bloem* may well serve as a potential base for a case law which would force Member States to amend their provisions, with regard to all operations involved, in order to abolish the number of additional restrictions introduced in the implementation, evidenced by all surveys. However, whereas Member States cannot impose conditions other than those literally set out by the technical definitions contained in the Directive, companies, given the *Andersen og. Jensen* findings, cannot rely on the benefit granted by the Directive and by national legislations adopting the same concepts if the conditions emerging from the literal definitions of the Directive are not exactly met. In turn, the concrete assessment whether they are exactly fulfilled does not seem to be based on a purely formal criteria: the ECJ reasoning in *Andersen og. Jensen* suggests that, perhaps, if the transferring company had retained the proceeds of a small (rather than of a large) loan while transferring the related obligations to the receiving company, the formal dissociation would not have been considered as important as the transfer of substantially all assets and liabilities to the receiving company. This might be seen as confirmed by a further finding by the ECJ in the same ruling, which regarded the retention by the transferring company of a small number of shares in a third company as immaterial on the ground that such retention 'cannot exclude the transfer of a branch of activity unrelated to those shares'.[159] The lack in the ruling of any indications on how small a formal dissociation between assets and liabilities elements should be in order for an operation to remain within the definition of transfer of assets paves the way for a case-by-case solution (with an assessment left to national courts), expressly indicated with regard to the last question concerning the arrangement of the operation. This question was, in essence, whether the business transferred is an independent one, as required by Article 2 of the Merger Directive for a transfer of assets, if, as occurred in that case, it could not be regarded as such from a financial viewpoint.[160] The ECJ, after deducing from Article 2 that the independent operation of the business must be assessed primarily from a functional and only secondarily from a financial point of view, admitted that the position may be different where the financial situation of the receiving company as a whole makes evident that it will very probably be unable to survive by its own means, and, after offering national courts these general guidelines, it concluded by leaving them an assessment based on the particular circumstances of each case.[161]

The ECJ approach allows companies to draw an important conclusion. To meet the requirements for enjoying the tax exemption, they only need to avoid designing operations with such a structure as to make it evident that literal definitions are not complied with, from both a formal and a substantive viewpoint (as occurred in the situation at issue in this ruling, due to the dissociation between the proceeds of a large loan and the related obligations). Such a strategy may allow them to limit the risk of falling within the doubtful cases, where the ruling leaves national tax authorities and courts the possibility of a case-by-case solution in the assessment whether or not the literal conditions contained in the relevant definitions are met.

The ECJ's conclusion on the anti-abuse clause in *Leur-Bloem* can equally generate far-reaching effects. The ECJ found that the anti-abuse clause was to be interpreted as requiring a general examination, open to judicial review, of each particular case, and that the laying down of a general rule automatically excluding certain categories of operations from the tax advantage, on the basis of general criteria, whether or not there is actually tax evasion or tax avoidance, would go beyond the purpose of this clause and would undermine the aim pursued by the Directive.[162]

Accordingly, Member States are allowed neither to set a general presumption that certain operations have tax evasion or tax avoidance amongst their principal objectives nor to provide that in particular cases such operations have, due to the specific nature of the situation at issue, tax evasion or tax avoidance objectives. With this premise, the logical question as to whether there may be some situations (and, if so, which ones) where the lack of valid commercial reasons (referred to in Article 11(a) as a possible (but not necessary) ground for establishing a presumption) may instead just be considered as a particular case of which a general examination is necessary, would have deserved an answer. It has, in fact, great practical importance: the setting of a presumption leaves companies with the burden of proof of demonstrating the lack of objectives of tax avoidance or evasion, whereas the need to carry out, by the competent national authorities, a general examination leads to the opposite result. Had the ECJ addressed this issue – which it did not – the outcome would have been an important contribution towards the achievement of a tax system common to all Member States.

In the third part of *Leur-Bloem*, the ECJ found that a restructuring operation carried out for the unique purpose of benefiting from a tax advantage (of which horizontal off-setting of losses is just an example) cannot be considered as having valid commercial reasons.[163] This indicates to Member States circumstances where they may establish a (not absolute) presumption of tax avoidance or tax evasion objectives. It could be argued to the contrary that it is also a particular case of which a general examination is not necessary: however, the ECJ's finding may give rise to the question as to whether it refers solely to operations of which the tax advantage is the unique and immediate purpose or if it also includes operations implying economic transactions which have, as a unique and ultimate goal, the achievement of a tax advantage. At practical level, the distinction is certainly not immaterial.

On balance, *Leur-Bloem* (and, indirectly, *Andersen og. Jensen*) thus limit the Member States' possible tendency to restrictively interpret the concept of the restructuring operations falling within the scope of the tax relief provided for by the Directive; moreover, it definitively confirms the unlawfulness of the *a priori* restrictions, which, as indicated by the comparative overviews, some Member States have introduced (in the form of requirements of discretionary prior approval or of absolute presumptions of fraud) by justifying them on the basis of the anti-abuse clause.

Last, the failure of a Member State to implement part of the Directive was at issue in the ruling in *Commission of the European Communities v. Hellenic*

Republic,[164] issued after an action brought by the Commission against the Greek Government for failure to adopt the laws, regulations and administrative provisions necessary to comply with the Merger Directive. The ECJ considered well-founded the action brought by the Commission and extended to the Merger Directive its findings in other areas of EC law,[165] whereby a Member State cannot rely on provisions, practices or situations arising in its own internal legal order to justify its failure to respect the obligations and time limits laid down by a Directive. In rejecting the justifications of the Greek Government, based on internal difficulties in national legal order as well as on the lack of adoption at Community level, at that time, of the proposals for a Tenth Company Law Directive on intra-EC mergers and for the SE, the ECJ did not deal with the same crucial aspects touched on *Denkavit* and *Zythopiia*:[166] the direct effect of the Directive and the right to damages reparation. Nevertheless, these issues, which would most probably have been dealt with had the action been brought by a company, can reasonably find the same response they were given in *Zythopiia*, in particular after the *Bosal Holding* ruling which, as subsequently indicated,[167] can offer the ECJ the base for scrutinizing the effects on the freedom of establishment of the lack of implementation of the Merger Directive also.

1.3.3 ECJ Case Law 'Lessons' for Member States and their Effect on Tax Competition

The analysis of the case law concerning the (first two) Tax Directives which had been developed before *Bosal, Keller* and *Van der Grinten* could already evidence, as a common feature, the ECJ's tendency to interpret broadly the relevant concepts (such as 'exchange of shares' in *Leur-Bloem* and 'withholding tax' in *Zythopiia*) and to limit Member States' discretion, which, as can be inferred from *Andersen og. Jensen*, can to some extent be exercised through a liberal assessment of the fulfilment of the conditions laid down by the literal definitions of these technical concepts (which must be met by companies).

Accordingly, from the viewpoint of Member States wishing to retain as much as possible of their national autonomy in the tax field and to safeguard their financial interests, two key 'lessons' could already be deduced from the case law up to 2003:

a. the safeguard of national financial interests can no longer be effectively pursued by attempting to limit the application of the tax benefits provided for by the Directives, through either restrictive interpretations of their technical concepts or additional requirements to be met imposed on companies; in fact, the national provisions deriving from such 'strategies' risk falling under scrutiny of the ECJ at the initiative of interested parties and being recognized as infringements of EC law, with the additional risk of financial liabilities for damages incurred by the plaintiff, particularly when no objective uncertainty in the Directives' provisions at issue can be invoked;

b. any attempt to protect national budget interests by introducing provisions or combinations of provisions which, even without mentioning the concepts referred to in the Directives, aim at either denying or restricting access to the tax benefits, is also likely to fail.

However, the question could arise as to whether *any* national provisions potentially concerning the situations covered by each of the Directives might fall under the ECJ's scrutiny, on the basis of the statements made in *Leur-Bloem* and *Zythopiia*,[168] or whether the Court's scrutiny could find a limit, to be expressed in a general principle, in the recognition of a degree of Member States' autonomy consistent with the notion of 'minimum harmonization' (thus, with the principle of subsidiarity) in the fields covered by the Directives.[169] *Bosal* (strengthened by *Keller*) can be seen as providing a response which, even if issued in respect of the Parent-Subsidiary Directive, appears to be applicable by analogy to the Merger Directive and to the new Interest-Royalties Directive too: the objective of eliminating disadvantages on intra-EC operations in comparison with the corresponding domestic ones, the decisive element of the ECJ's reasoning in these rulings (coordinated with *Van der Grinten*), is in fact stated in the Preambles to all the three tax Directives.[170] This response is negative: the ECJ's scrutiny finds no limit as long as any restrictive choice (even if deriving from an expressly granted option) creates a possible disincentive to the exercise of the freedom of establishment from the state of origin (*Bosal*, *Keller*) or to the state of destination (as it can be deduced from *Van der Grinten*). Moreover, this objective refers to all three kinds of intra-EC operations considered (inbound and outbound dividend distributions; restructuring operations; interest and royalties payments), including those carried out through PEs in a state other than those of residence of the companies involved:[171] thus, the response indicated should apply to the state of location of the PE too, with reference to the 'triangular cases' included in the amendments to the Parent-Subsidiary Directive or to interest/royalties payments to and by PEs.[172]

Similar 'lessons' cannot but suggest to Member States the alternative route to meet the need to safeguard their budget revenues: if attempts at reducing the tax benefits available to their corporate taxpayers under the EC Tax Directives turn out to be ineffective, the financial interests can certainly be safeguarded by increasing the number of corporate taxpayers having either a source of taxable income or their fiscal residence within their jurisdictions, that is by attempting to attract companies from other Member States (as well as from third countries). This outcome – the creation of agencies, branches and subsidiaries by companies incorporated in other countries – can easily be achieved by competing with EC partners in introducing national provisions granting even more favourable benefits than those envisaged by the Tax Directives. Such a strategy does not risk finding obstacles to the extent that the right of establishment of companies in other Member States is guaranteed under Articles 43 and 48 of the Treaty, whose effectiveness is strengthened by the case law of the ECJ on the right of establishment itself.[173] Moreover, the success of a similar tax policy also derives from the current standard content of DTCs, which, by leaving to the state of location of the PE the right to tax the income deriving from it, can induce companies incorporated in a given state to create secondary establishments in another country offering a more favourable tax regime and/or to concentrate most or the whole of the business activity in this country, particularly in the light of the latest ECJ company law rulings.[174]

It may thus be argued that by (implicitly) suggesting the attempt to attract corporate taxpayers from other states as the alternative and effective route to safeguard national revenue interests, the case law of the ECJ on the first two Tax Directives offers an unintentional contribution to tax competition among the Member States.[175]

1.4 CRUCIAL DEVELOPMENTS OF THE ECJ TAX CASE LAW ON COMPANIES' FREEDOM OF ESTABLISHMENT AND THEIR POTENTIAL EFFECTS ON TAX COMPETITION

1.4.1 Developments of the ECJ Case Law on the Freedom of Establishment: Overall Evolution

In addition to the rulings on the application of the two 1990 Tax Directives, an ever growing number of corporate tax cases brought before the ECJ since the 1980s has been dealing with the tax obstacles to the exercise of the freedom of establishment within the Community which is granted by Articles 43 and 48 of the Treaty. The resulting case law, which the ECJ has been developing contemporaneously with a case law on the application to direct taxation of other fundamental freedoms (that is the free movement of persons, services and capital), is deemed to affect an increasing number of aspects of national company taxation systems, and to offer Member States (exactly like the case law on the 1990 Tax Directives) crucial indications on how to develop their tax policies. As noted[176] the striking features of the evolution of the ECJ's jurisprudence lie in the approach adopted, in the attitude towards the justifications submitted by Member States for their national provisions under scrutiny and in the issues dealt with.

With regard to the approach, the overall developments, including the rulings concerning natural persons (from which the literature[177] is drawing principles applicable by analogy to a company's freedom of establishment) indicate that the ECJ, after having initially relied on the prohibition against (overt and covert) discriminations,[178] in recent years has made an increasing use of terms such as 'restriction', 'difference of treatment' or 'barriers',[179] rather than simply 'discrimination'. This widening of the concepts used has enabled the ECJ to examine the compliance of national provisions with the freedom of establishment (and with other fundamental freedoms) in a broader range of cases, including those where the comparative approach, inherent in the non-discrimination rule, proves to be inappropriate. Whereas the concept of discrimination requires the scrutiny of a question of equality between residents and non-residents (companies as well as individuals) to discover different treatments applied in comparable situations, the concept of restriction (or of 'barriers') merely involves a question of obstacles, which can exist even without a legally different treatment of residents and of non-residents. Since the ECJ has ruled that freedom of establishment applies both to the state of destination and to the state of origin,[180] there are at least two types of restrictions: the application in the state of destination of the same conditions to residents and non-residents alike, but with more burdensome fulfilments on non-residents, and any barriers raised by the laws of the state of origin hindering the freedom of establishment of domestic companies (or natural persons) in other Member States. These cases have both come under the scrutiny of the ECJ.[181] The indicated approach has been leading the ECJ to define the obligation to exercise the national fiscal competence consistently with EC law as the prohibition of any discrimination, either direct or indirect, on grounds of nationality, and of any restriction to the exercise of a fundamental freedom guaranteed by the Treaty,[182] unless they are justified.

As regards the attitude towards justifications submitted by Member States, it was observed that, although 'barriers' or 'restrictions' might theoretically be justified more easily than discriminations, as they could be acceptable in the presence of 'reasons of overriding general interest', whereas discriminations can be justified only by the reasons expressly provided for by the Treaty,[183] the ECJ has developed a method of analysis which, in practice, makes the usefulness of the distinction doubtful from the viewpoint of Member States:[184] after realizing that a 'difference of treatment' exists, the ECJ directly examines one by one all justifications put forward and, when all of them are rejected, it no longer has to establish whether the difference of treatment is a discrimination or a restriction. The concept of 'restrictions' thus allows the Court to examine a broader range of situations than would be possible only with resort to the notion of discrimination, without helping the Member States to support their arguments better. In turn, the ECJ, which since 1986 has issued more than 40 rulings[185] declaring national provisions in breach of the Treaty, has rejected all justifications in 95 per cent of cases.[186] A frequently submitted justification, which consists in the necessity to prevent reduction of the tax yield, has always been rejected by the ECJ,[187] which has simply stated that loss of tax revenue is not one of the grounds listed in Article 46 of the Treaty and cannot be regarded as a matter of overriding general interest which may be relied upon to justify unequal treatments.[188] Moreover, the ECJ has increasingly rejected the other justifications invoked by national governments which, all together, seem to cover all possible reasons for differences of treatment between residents and non-residents, as well as for barriers on resident taxpayers wishing to migrate to other Member States: the non-comparability of situations, the cohesion of the tax system, the principle of territoriality of the tax system, the need to counteract tax avoidance or tax evasion, and the effectiveness of fiscal supervision.

The reasons underlying the increasing rejection of these justifications have been affirmed by the ECJ in dealing with three key issues, which, in this overall evolution, have marked the crucial developments of the tax case law on companies' freedom of establishment: (a) the equal treatment of subsidiaries and branches of non-resident companies; (b) the possibility of creating anti-abuse provisions; (c) the treatment of costs and losses within intra-EC groups of companies.

1.4.2 Landmark Findings on the Key Issues

a. Branches/subsidiaries comparative treatment after the *St-Gobain* (1999) and *CLT-UFA* (2006) rulings

The 1999 *St-Gobain* judgment,[189] interpreted together with the first corporate tax ruling, the 1986 *Avoir fiscal* case,[190] and with the 1995 *Schumacker* case[191] (concerning the free movement of workers, whose reasoning has generally been recognized as applicable by analogy to companies' freedom of establishment)[192] definitively clarifies the criteria of the branch/subsidiary comparison and goes beyond the previous rulings by extending this comparison to the application of treaty-based tax rules. In *Avoir fiscal*, the ECJ had to decide whether branches of companies resident in other Member States could qualify for tax credits on dividends which national rules reserved to resident companies. The *Schumacker* finding has been considered to be applicable by analogy as it dealt with an issue of principle, namely the status under EC law of the residents/non-residents distinction operated by all Member States in the direct taxation area: the ECJ had to examine German tax rules which denied a Belgian resident, who had worked for a while in Germany and obtained there the major part of his taxable income in the relevant period, tax advantages connected with personal and family circumstances which were granted to German residents. Moreover, after having considered residents and non-residents to be in a comparable situation for the application of rules of fiscal procedure and of progressive scales of taxation in cases concerning natural persons,[193] in the 2006 *CLT-UFA* judgment[194] the ECJ had to decide on the comparability between a branch of a non-resident company and a subsidiary of that company with regard to the application of the corporation tax rates, and thus completed the scrutiny of different aspects of national corporate tax systems which it had started in *Avoir fiscal*.

In both *Avoir fiscal* and *Schumacker,* the ECJ had considered the national provisions to be incompatible with the Treaty, but it had also formulated two important statements. In *Avoir fiscal*, it had admitted that there could be certain circumstances[195] (regarded as absent in the specific case) under which a distinction based on a (subjective) criteria, such as the location of the registered office (which was also the fiscal residence of the companies concerned) could be justified in tax law. In *Schumacker,* it had accepted, in principle, different treatments based on fiscal residence when the major part of taxable income of non-residents (individuals as well as companies) was concentrated in the state of reference[196] (which was not the case in the situation examined).

The ECJ's reasoning in both *St-Gobain* and *CLT-UFA*, where it also concluded that the provisions at issue were incompatible with the freedom of establishment, can be seen as complementary to both these statements. In *St-Gobain,* the German tax authorities had refused to grant to a non-resident company, which operated a branch in Germany through which it held shares in companies established in non-member states and through which it received dividends on such shares, certain tax concessions (provided for by the DTC between Germany and the extra-EC countries concerned and by German legislation) available to resident companies. In *CLT-UFA*, Germany had applied, on the taxable profits of the German branch of a Luxembourg-resident company, a corporation tax rate higher than that which would have been applied had the profit been generated by a German-resident subsidiary of such company and distributed in full to the parent company. In both cases, the ECJ rejected the key German justification, based on the non-comparability of situations: the reasoning of the ECJ in each of the two rulings generates far-reaching implications.

In *St-Gobain*, the German justification was that, as regards direct taxation, the situations of resident companies and of non-resident companies are, as a general rule, not comparable because non-resident companies are subject to limited tax liability, whilst resident companies are subject to unlimited tax liability. The ECJ simply adopted a different criteria for establishing the comparability at issue: it regarded as a decisive element not the fact that non-resident companies are *only* taxed on the income received through their branches in Germany and the assets held in them, but the circumstance that, on such income and assets, both categories of companies were liable to taxation. On this basis, it thus considered the situations of resident companies and of non-resident companies as *objectively* comparable.[197] Whereas in *St-Gobain* the ECJ adopted an *objective* criteria, based on the tax treatment of the source of income at issue, in *Avoir fiscal* and in *Schumacker* it had refused, in the specific cases, the validity of a *subjective* criteria, based on the status of resident or non-resident, as a justification for a difference of treatment. In *Avoir fiscal,* it had excluded the relevance of this status due to an identical treatment of resident and non-resident companies with regard to the method of determining the taxable income and the rate of taxation. In *Schumacker,* it had refused it because the non-resident received no significant income in the state of residence, which implied the absence of the condition in order for a difference of treatment based on the residents/non-residents distinction to be justified (and thus an unlawful discrimination, in comparison with German residents, because his personal and family circumstances were considered neither in the state of residence (which, owing to his employment abroad, was in no position to grant tax advantages corresponding to these circumstances) nor in the state of employment).

Consequently, *Avoir fiscal*, *Schumacker* and *St-Gobain*, if taken together, indicate that, unless a Member State shows that the major part of the taxable income of companies from other Member States is concentrated in their state of residence (which circumstance may be defined as the '*Schumacker* condition'), no difference of treatment on grounds of formal and subjective criteria (such as the status of resident or of non-resident, or of company with unlimited or with limited tax liability) can be accepted between resident companies and branches (or agencies) of companies resident in other Member States. This applies to the extent that the situations of resident and of non-resident companies are made objectively comparable by the application of the same method of determining the taxable income defined in the widest technical sense (including the taxation of a specific source of income). If the *Schumacker* condition is met, the state of location of the branch may apply a different treatment based on specific rules and methods for determining that minor part of the taxable income attributable to the PE located in its territory, which may be justified on the ground that the subjective status (of companies with limited tax liability) of non-resident companies corresponds to a situation objectively non-comparable with resident companies. Otherwise, after adopting the same rules and methods without regard to the importance of the part of the taxable income deriving from the branch, a Member State can never refuse non-resident companies the same tax treatment available to domestic companies.

The ECJ reasoning in *CLT-UFA* adds a further detail to this conclusion. In this case, the rejected German justification on the non-comparability of situations was based on the allegation that profits distributed by a subsidiary to its parent company are no longer assets of the subsidiary, whereas remittance of profits by a branch to the head office constitutes transfer of profits within the same company. The ECJ reasoned that, in both cases, the profits are made available to the company which controls the subsidiary and the branch respectively, and that the only real difference between the two situations lies in the fact that distribution of profits by a subsidiary to the parent company, unlike remittance by a branch, presupposes a formal decision to that effect. This formal element was regarded as irrelevant by the ECJ, which, furthermore, considered it apparent that, even if the profits distributed to the parent company were no longer part of the subsidiary's assets, these profits could still be made available to the subsidiary by its parent company in the form of share capital or shareholder loan.[198] In addition the ECJ rejected a further German argument, according to which the lower tax rate on profits-distributing subsidiaries was justified by the 'imputation credit system' in force at the relevant time, through which double taxation of resident taxpayers was avoided. In this regard, the ECJ observed that the lower tax rate also applied to the distribution of profits by German subsidiaries to parent companies resident in other Member States, and expressly stated that, in the light of the information provided by the German tax authority, the national legislation on the determination of the taxable amount drew no distinction between companies with their seat in another Member State according to whether they had a branch or a subsidiary, which distinction, in the ECJ wording, is capable of justifying a difference in treatment between the two categories of companies.[199] The ECJ thus concluded that German subsidiaries and branches of companies based in Luxembourg are in a situation in which they can be compared objectively, which makes it necessary to apply, to profits made by a branch, a tax rate which is equivalent to the overall tax rate which would have been applicable in the same circumstances to the distribution of profits by a subsidiary.

Consequently, CLT-UFA not only confirms that the adoption of the same methods for determining the taxable amount determines an objective comparability between branches and subsidiaries, but also indicates that a formal and subjective difference, if it derives from an act of one of the companies involved (formal decision to distribute profits by a subsidiary) rather than from a status (residents/non-residents), is always irrelevant whenever the situations considered can lead to the same final outcome and the objective comparability between branches and subsidiaries exists due to their being placed on the same footing for determining the taxable profits.

As indicated in *St-Gobain*, another important ECJ finding concerns the relationship between DTCs and EC law. The Court, after accepting that, in the absence of unifying or harmonizing measures adopted by the EC, Member States are free, in the framework of DTCs, to allocate powers of taxation between themselves, distinguished the *allocation* of the power of taxation from its *exercise*. In this regard, it stated that, once allocated the power of taxation, Member States must exercise it consistently with EC law. Accordingly it found, in the case of DTCs concluded by a Member State with a non-member country, that this Member State must, under the EC law principle of non-discrimination, grant PEs of companies from other Member States the advantages contemplated by the Treaty for its resident companies, on the same conditions. It also evidenced that the balance and the reciprocity of the DTCs concluded by Germany with the extra-EC countries would not be called into question by a unilateral extension of the range of recipients in Germany of the tax advantages provided for by those DTCs, because such extension would not in any way affect the rights of non-member states which are parties to the DTCs and would not impose any new obligation on them.[200] Consequently this ECJ finding, together with the previous statement in *Avoir fiscal* that the rights of establishment conferred by the Treaty are unconditional and cannot be made subject to DTCs entered into between Member States,[201] is important from a dual viewpoint. On the one hand, it clarifies that as Member States are under the obligation to comply with EC law general rules when concluding DTCs both between themselves and with non-member states, as well as when exercising the powers of taxation so allocated, their liberty is restricted to the attribution of the powers of taxation through such treaties. On the other hand, it underlines that the obligations imposed by EC law on the contracting Member States are completely independent from, and co-exist with, the rights and obligations deriving from DTCs, in so far as they stand at a different level: the obligation to comply with EC law concerns the (natural and) legal persons interested by the ambit of application of the DTC; the rights and obligations deriving from the treaties themselves reflect the objective balance of conditions between the Member States involved.

After *St-Gobain* and *CLT-UFA* it can, thus, be concluded that the obligation on Member States to ensure equivalence of treatment between resident companies and branches of non-resident companies has been, in principle, extended by the ECJ to whatever type of rules concerned, because any difference in treatment, in the ECJ's wording, would make it less attractive for non-resident companies to create branches and would thus restrict their freedom to choose the most appropriate legal form to exercise their right of establishment.[202]

b. *Langhorst-Hohorst* (2002) and the anti-abuse rules

The possibility for Member States to put in place anti-abuse rules came under the scrutiny of the ECJ, with specific regard to thin capitalization rules, in the 2002 *Langhorst-Hohorst* ruling.[203] German thin capitalization rules that reclassified interests as dividends in the case of non-resident shareholders, and thus prohibited the deduction of interests paid to them by their resident subsidiaries, were regarded by the ECJ as creating a difference in treatment between resident subsidiaries according to the seat of their parent companies, which made it less attractive for companies established in other Member States to exercise their freedom of establishment in Germany and could discourage such companies from creating, acquiring or maintaining a subsidiary in the state concerned. The ECJ found this situation incompatible with the Treaty: consequently, general anti-abuse rules – of which thin capitalization rules are one of the most widely used types – are incompatible with the freedom of establishment when they do not place shareholders resident in the Member State of the subsidiary and shareholders resident in another Member State on an equal footing. *Langhorst-Hohorst* owes its importance, on the one hand, to the rejection, even in respect of anti-abuse rules, of the typically invoked justifications and, on the other hand, to the innovative emphasis placed by the ECJ on the effect of making the exercise of the freedom of establishment less attractive for companies from other Member States.

In the first respect, the rejection of the justifications based on the coherence of the tax system, on the risk of tax avoidance and on the effectiveness of the fiscal supervision marks the extension of findings which the ECJ had already reached in previous rulings concerning natural persons and companies. In fact, the argument based on the coherence of the tax system, almost always submitted by Member States after its initial acceptance by the ECJ in the 1992 *Bachmann* ruling[204], had already been systematically refused afterwards. The conditions which had led the ECJ to accept it in *Bachmann* were always found to be absent in subsequent rulings concerning both individuals and companies. These conditions are: (a) a direct link between the element causing the difference of treatment (typically, a tax advantage) and the taxation element; (b) the application of one type of tax only; (c) its application to a single taxpayer. In previous judgments concerning companies, the 1998 *ICI* and the 2001 *Metallgesellsschaft* rulings[205] (which both involved the issue of cross-border losses compensation),[206] the ECJ had in fact rejected a defence based on the cohesion argument on the ground that the single taxpayer condition is not fulfilled in the case of groups of companies, where parent companies and subsidiaries are involved, whereas, in cases involving individuals,[207] the one taxation requirement was found to be lacking in the event of compensation between different taxes.[208] Moreover, the ECJ had already begun restricting the scope of the coherence argument by stating, in another case involving individuals,[209] that it cannot be invoked at individual level when, under a DTC, the coherence of the tax system is realized at the level of the global relationship between the two countries concerned. After these findings, in *Langhorst-Hohorst* the ECJ considered the direct link requirement to be absent, because the subsidiary of a non-resident parent company suffered less favourable treatment due to the thin capitalization rules and the German Government did not indicate any tax advantage to off-set such treatment: exceptions are thus admitted to none of the strict requirements for coherence and if the German Government had granted those tax advantages, it is evident that the effectiveness itself of the anti-abuse rules would have been at least partly reduced. With regard to the need to combat tax evasion and tax avoidance as a possible justification, the national provision concerned, according to the ECJ, should specifically aim to prevent wholly artificial arrangements designed to circumvent national tax legislation:[210] nevertheless, these arrangements can be presumed to exist neither for the establishment of a subsidiary abroad (as stated in the *ICI* ruling)[211] nor (as stated for this purpose in *Langhorst-Hohorst*) for any situation where a parent company, for whatever reason, has its seat abroad.[212] Last, the argument based on the effectiveness of fiscal supervision, already submitted as a justification for different treatments in cases dealing with natural persons[213] and generally refused on the ground that Directive 77/799/EEC concerning mutual assistance in the field of direct taxation provides adequate means[214] to ensure this supervision, was also refused in *Langhorst-Hohorst* on the ground that the German Government had not shown how the anti-abuse rule would enable national tax authorities to supervise the amount of the taxable income. Consequently, *Langhorst-Hohorst* charges Member States with the burden to prove and to explain in the concrete cases, with no exception, the existence of wholly artificial arrangements and the suitability of anti-abuse clauses to do no more than prevent them (and no more than ensure fiscal supervision), which may certainly be difficult.

On the other hand, the new ECJ statement on the effect of making the exercise of the freedom of establishment less attractive[215] generalizes a finding which, *in St-Gobain*, had been reached as regards a form of exercise of this freedom in comparison to another,[216] and can thus potentially apply to any situation, as shown by the *Bosal Holding* and *Keller Holding* rulings.[217]

c. Cross-border loss compensation for 'Community groups' of companies after the *Marks & Spencer* (2005) ruling

The Commission has consistently indicated the impossibility of cross-border off-setting of losses and costs for groups of companies operating in different Member States as a major and persisting tax obstacle to business operations within the Community and, in a 2005 Communication, as the main tax obstacle in particular for small and medium-sized enterprises (SMEs).[218] Nonetheless the ECJ, in two cases relating to branches, the 1997 *Futura*[219] and the 1999 *AMID*[220] rulings, had considered the refusal to allow the off-setting or carrying over of losses from foreign sources by the country in which the branch is situated as compatible with the Treaty on the basis of the principle of territoriality. In particular in *Futura*, the ECJ, in accordance with this principle, had accepted that the state of establishment could make the carrying forward of previous losses requested by the non-resident taxpayer which has a branch in its territory subject to the condition that the losses must be economically related to the income earned by the taxpayer in that state, provided that resident taxpayers do not receive a better treatment. Nevertheless, the ECJ subsequently starting restricting the margins for justifications based on both the territoriality principle and the principle of cohesion of the tax system. In the 1998 *ICI* ruling,[221] it found that neither the risk of tax avoidance in one Member State nor the principle of cohesion of the tax system can justify a refusal to grant resident companies forming a consortium, through which they hold shares in subsidiaries located in other Member States, a relief for the trading losses of these subsidiaries if this relief is available to holding companies wholly or mainly holding shares in resident subsidiaries. The ECJ argued, in fact, that the residence of the subsidiary outside the Member State concerned (the United Kingdom in that case) does not of itself necessarily entail tax avoidance, since foreign subsidiaries are subject to tax in the state of establishment, and that the cohesion of the tax system does not apply when more legal persons are involved. This latter reason for rejecting the cohesion argument was repeated in *Bosal Holding*.[222] Subsequently, the ECJ ignored the principle of territoriality in the 2001 *Metallgesellschaft* ruling[223] and went further in *Bosal Holding*, where it expressly refused it. In *Metallgesellschaft,* concerning the tax treatment in the United Kingdom of a subsidiary which varied in relation to the seat of the parent company, the ECJ regarded as incompatible with Article 43 of the Treaty the refusal to grant a tax relief to subsidiaries, resident in the United Kingdom, of parent companies having their seat in another Member State, where that advantage is available to subsidiaries, resident in the United Kingdom, of parent companies also resident in the United Kingdom, and ruled that the parent company and subsidiary concerned were entitled to reparation, without attaching importance to an argument based on the territoriality principle. According to this argument, under the territoriality principle the state involved – the United Kingdom – would not tax the subsidiary but it would be able to charge the tax to another level within the same group of companies, whereas, if the relief were granted to subsidiaries of parent companies not resident in the United Kingdom, no tax would be charged in the United Kingdom on transactions within the group since the other group companies would be in another Member State and not subject to corporation tax in the United Kingdom. Against the UK Government's argument that this would be tantamount to tax avoidance, the ECJ repeated its statement, already formulated in *ICI*, according to which the establishment of a company outside the United Kingdom does not, of itself, necessarily entail this risk, because that company will in any event be taxed in the state of establishment.[224]

Considered together with these previous rulings, *Bosal Holding* marked one more step in overcoming the territoriality principle. One of the justifications submitted by the Member State concerned, the Netherlands, was in fact that, according to the territoriality principle, the costs incurred in activities abroad, including financing costs and costs in relation to holdings in foreign subsidiaries, should be set off against the profits generated by those subsidiaries rather than against those of parent companies in the Netherlands. The ECJ rejected this argument by stressing that the difference in tax treatment ultimately concerned not the subsidiaries but the parent companies, according to whether or not they have subsidiaries making profits taxable in the Netherlands, even though those parent companies are all established in the Netherlands. In *Bosal Holding*, the ECJ seems thus to have paid attention to the *difference in treatment* caused by the application of the territoriality principle rather than to the *merit* of this principle (which, in *Futura,* it had accepted at the level of the single taxpayer) and, in essence, it followed this approach again in *Keller Holding* where, having regard basically to the disadvantage created to companies with indirect subsidiaries in other Member States as opposed to companies with indirect subsidiaries in the state concerned, it rejected justifications based on both the coherence of the tax system and the principle of territoriality.[225]

The ruling where the ECJ most directly dealt with the issue of cross-border loss compensation within the Community is the 2005 *Marks & Spencer*[226] ruling. One of the largest UK retailers was denied by the British tax administration the deduction from its own tax base of losses incurred by its subsidiaries in other Member States, which subsidiaries had been sold or had ceased trading at the time the parent company claimed the tax deduction. The refusal to allow cross-border loss relief created a difference of treatment in comparison with losses of subsidiaries resident in the United Kingdom, which latter, under a 'group relief' regime allowing resident companies in a group to off-set profits and losses against each other, can be deducted from the taxable profits of a parent company. The ECJ, after highlighting that the exclusion of group relief in respect of losses incurred by a non-resident subsidiary constitutes a restriction on freedom of establishment (in the form of an 'exit restriction' applied by the state of origin) within the meaning of Articles 43 and 48 EC, found that the application of the territoriality principle, resulting in the fact that the United Kingdom does not tax the profits of non-resident subsidiaries of resident companies, does not in itself justify this restriction, but accepted three arguments submitted by the United Kingdom and by other Member States. These arguments were that: (a) profits and losses need to be treated symmetrically in the same tax system to preserve a balanced allocation of the power to impose taxes between the different Member States concerned, which might make it necessary to apply to companies established in one of those states only the tax rules of that state in respect of both profits and losses; (b) if the losses of the non-resident subsidiary were deducted in the parent company's Member State, they might be used twice, and Member States must be able to prevent a double deduction of losses; (c) if the losses were not deducted in the Member State in which the subsidiary is located, there would be the risk of tax avoidance, because the possible transfer of losses of a non-resident subsidiary to a resident company would imply that, within a group of companies, losses could be transferred to companies resident in the Member States which apply the highest rates of taxation and in which, thus, they generate the highest tax savings. In the light of these three arguments, taken together, the ECJ found that the exclusion from 'group relief' of losses incurred by non-resident subsidiaries pursued legitimate objectives which were compatible with the Treaty and constituted overriding reasons in the public interest justifying the restriction. Nonetheless, it concluded that the restrictive measure at issue went beyond what was necessary to attain the essential part of the objectives pursued, and breached Articles 43 and 48 of the Treaty, where the parent company could demonstrate that the non-resident subsidiary, in its state of residence, had exhausted all possibilities of having the losses taken into account, for the accounting period concerned by the claim for relief, for previous accounting periods or for future periods, either by the subsidiary itself or by a third party.[227]

This condition, under which cross-border loss compensation must be allowed, if considered against the underlying arguments, is certainly such as to avoid the risk of a double deduction of losses and to prevent multinational groups from choosing in which Member State to deduct the losses. Nevertheless, it does not necessarily preserve the power of a Member State to treat profits and losses symmetrically because, if met, it allows a parent company to deduct the losses incurred by the non-resident subsidiary from its taxable profits even though its Member State of residence does not tax the profits of this subsidiary. In addition, it does not necessarily prevent the losses from being deducted from the taxable profit of a parent company located in the jurisdiction where these losses can generate the highest tax savings if the only state in which they can still be deducted applies a higher corporate tax rate (resulting in a higher tax value of the loss deduction) than the Member State of residence of the subsidiary. The essential part of the reasons of overriding public interest justifying restricting cross-border loss compensation between parent companies and subsidiaries of different Member States lies, therefore, in the risk of a legal or economic doubling in the deduction of the same losses in two Member States, and in the risk of tax planning for deduction purposes once a loss has been incurred. A legal doubling of the deduction of the same losses would occur if these losses were deductible by two companies under a legal relationship of control of one over another (parent company and subsidiary); an economic doubling of the deduction would be possible if the same losses were deducted by a parent company of a group and by an unrelated (third) party who has acquired one of the former subsidiaries of this company. Moreover, tax planning for loss deduction purposes would be possible if a group were free to opt for the deduction of a loss incurred by a subsidiary in a Member State or in another one. The ECJ's conclusions thus imply that, in the situation where the interested parent company manages to prove that neither the risk of the same losses being deducted twice nor the choice of the jurisdiction where to deduct the losses exist (which situation could correspond to the conditions of loss relief within a domestic group: deduction only once, no possibilities of choosing the jurisdiction), Member States cannot invoke the principle of territoriality to prevent the cross-border loss relief within the Community. In fact, in these cases, the prohibition of intra-EC losses off-setting between parent companies and subsidiaries by a Member State where a parent company is resident would fail the 'proportionality' test under EC law. Except for the need to maintain conditions that could be the same as within a single jurisdiction, the *Marks & Spencer* ruling thus results in the disappearance of any other legitimate reasons for Member States to apply the territoriality principle.

Moreover, if the ECJ's reasoning and conclusions in *Marks & Spencer* are considered together with *ICI* and *Bosal Holding*, it may be argued that *Marks & Spencer* complements the findings of the ECJ in those rulings. In *ICI* and *Bosal Holding*, the ECJ's reasoning appeared to focus on the specific treatment of the parent company in its Member State of residence, irrespective of the possibilities available to non-resident subsidiaries in their states of residence; in *Marks & Spencer,* this focus appeared to have been shifted on to the overall treatment, within the Community territory, of an international group of companies on the whole (in terms of possibilities available to parent companies and subsidiaries) as compared to the overall treatment of a group only operating within one Member State. Accordingly, after *ICI* and *Bosal Holding*, the question could be raised whether a multinational group could, under EC law, be allowed to deduct losses and costs in two jurisdictions or to choose the one where to deduct losses and costs: if this had been possible, it would have resulted in a more favourable treatment to multinational groups than to domestic groups. *Marks & Spencer* answers this question in the negative and indicates that double deduction of losses, as well as tax planning practices encouraged by the significant differences in corporate tax rates between Member States and aimed at transferring losses to the jurisdiction where they can generate the highest tax savings, are to be regarded as distortions in the functioning of the internal market, to be prevented to the same extent as wholly artificial arrangements designed to circumvent national laws. The ECJ findings in *Marks & Spencer* may also be regarded as symmetrical with *ICI*: from the viewpoint of a group of companies as a whole and of its treatment within the EC, the establishment of a subsidiary outside the Member State of residence of the parent company does not necessarily entail the risk of tax avoidance, because this subsidiary will be subject to tax in its state of establishment (*ICI*), to the same extent that it does not necessarily entail the risk of preventing losses deduction, since the subsidiary will be able to deduct the losses in its state of establishment (*Marks & Spencer*). In any case, the impossibility of taking the non-resident subsidiary's losses into account in any way in its state of residence, required by the ECJ, appears to refer to year-to-year losses rather than to losses deriving from the liquidation of the subsidiary, on which no argument was raised in *Marks & Spencer.* As liquidation losses cannot, by definition, be carried backward or forward or transferred to third parties, the ECJ's conclusions in *Marks & Spencer* can be seen as implying that liquidation losses relating to a subsidiary in another Member State could be deducted from the taxable profits of the parent company to the same extent as liquidation losses relating to a subsidiary in its own Member State. From the viewpoint of intra-EC groups having parent companies located in different Member States, *Marks & Spencer* can also be considered against the different treatment of losses in domestic group taxation schemes of the twenty-five Member States. Seven countries (the United Kingdom, Ireland, Finland, Sweden, Latvia, Cyprus and Malta) offer intra-group loss relief, whereby every group member is taxed separately but losses may be transferred on a definitive basis from one group member to another. In ten other jurisdictions (Germany, France, Spain, Denmark, Italy, Austria, Luxembourg, Poland, Portugal and Slovenia) which adopt a system of pooling the results of a group, each group member determines its taxable base, which is then pooled at the parent company's level. The Netherlands adopts a full tax consolidation, which considers a group as a single unit and thus treats the results of the subsidiaries as if realized by the parent company. Amongst the remaining Member States, loss compensation is not necessary in Estonia, where a parent company cannot receive profits distributions, and is not taxed accordingly, until after the subsidiary's losses have been set off against the subsidiary's profits, whereas no group relief is allowed in Belgium, in the Czech Republic, in Greece, in Lithuania, in Hungary and in Slovenia, as a group of companies is disregarded for tax purposes in these states. Against this variety of different treatments,[228] the fact that the *Marks & Spencer* ruling was delivered in the context of a particular kind of loss compensation (intra-group loss relief), but specified the general condition under which the refusal by Member States to allow intra-EC loss off-set breaches Articles 43 and 48 EC, has a twofold implication. On the one hand, when they can prove this condition, parent companies resident in any states permitting any form of loss off-set for domestic groups can claim the extension of the same form (intra-group loss relief, pooling of the group's results, full tax consolidation) to losses incurred by EC subsidiaries, in order not to have their freedom of establishment disproportionately restricted. On the other hand, parent companies resident in any Member States where no loss relief is available for domestic groups, when proving the condition set by *Marks & Spencer*, are not prevented from off-setting losses incurred by their EC subsidiaries. This is because, otherwise, subsidiaries in other Member States (whose losses, in these circumstances, could be taken into account by no party) would become 'less attractive' than domestic subsidiaries (whose losses could be taken into account by the subsidiary) and the freedom of establishment would be (disproportionately) discouraged.

These implications of *Marks & Spencer* make it convenient, from Member States' perspective, both to allow domestic loss compensation (or consolidation) schemes for groups and to compete with each other in designing the most attractive ones, in order to enable parent companies meeting the condition laid down in *Marks & Spencer* to use these schemes for losses incurred by their EC subsidiaries and thus, ultimately, to become more competitive as jurisdictions of location of parent companies of intra-EC groups. *Marks & Spencer* therefore risks further encouraging the corporate groups' strategies aimed at maximizing the tax benefits deriving from choices of location in some Member States rather than in others, which choices are the result of tax competition.

1.5 CURRENT COMPANY TAXATION ENVIRONMENT WITHIN THE COMMUNITY, COMMISSION ORIENTATIONS AND UNDERLYING ATTITUDE TOWARDS TAX COMPETITION

1.5.1 Acceptable Playing Field or Level Playing Field?

The corporate tax law environment within the EC would have the features of a level playing field if the overall approximation of national company taxation regimes were such as to make the location in whatever Member State: (a) possible without company tax obstacles; and (b) immaterial from the viewpoint of the influence of tax provisions on companies' competitive position. This would require the elimination of both of the two types of possible distortions: (1) tax obstacles preventing companies from freely moving throughout the EC; (2) investments decisions merely based on wholly artificial circumventions of national tax laws, that is on abusive forum shopping strategies (including those aimed at artificially doubling tax benefits)[229] encouraged by different national provisions. Whereas any company tax obstacles represent distortions by their very nature as they are deemed to hinder the exercise of a fundamental freedom guaranteed by the Treaty and thus to prevent companies from fully exploiting the benefits of the internal market, the fact that all kinds of forum shopping practices motivated only by artificial circumvention of tax laws of a Member State and/or only by artificial doublings of tax benefits are to be regarded as distortions can be clearly deduced from the series of ECJ findings that the freedom of establishment could be restricted to prevent such practices (such as in *Marks & Spencer*, where the ECJ clearly stated that tax planning practices aimed at doubling a tax advantage such as loss deduction need to be prevented).

In a situation where both the two types of distortion were eliminated, companies could only choose to locate in one state or in another for market-related reasons and the goal of a market competition not distorted by different legal provisions, fully consistent with the Treaty and with the strategic 'Lisbon objective', would be achieved. Consequently, a situation where only the first one of the two types of distortions were eliminated could be described as an acceptable playing field: companies would be able to operate throughout the EC without company tax obstacles, but the choices of location in one state or in another could be based on abusive tax planning strategies rather than on market grounds.

In the light of this distinction, at the current time the Commission's objective can be identified in the achievement of an acceptable playing field. The Commission highlighted in its Report[230] the existence of company tax obstacles to cross-border business activity within the EC, despite the two 1990 Directives and despite an Arbitration Convention also issued in 1990[231] to reduce the risk of double taxation that may arise for intra-EC companies in case of adjustment by national tax authorities of the taxable profits related to the pricing policy applied by these companies when trading with associated enterprises in other Member States (transfer pricing cases). The Commission identified these obstacles, caused by the co-existence of many different national tax systems, in the remaining risk of (economic) double taxation of dividends and of cross-border restructuring operations, in the absence of cross-border loss relief, in the risk of transfer pricing disputes with national tax administrations, and in the incapacity of existing DTCs (which create situations of uncertainty) to meet all internal market requirements regarding elimination of double taxation.[232] The Commission recognized the potential of the ECJ case law to remove such obstacles, but also presented a 'two track strategy': it regarded as necessary both short-term targeted measures, trying to find a solution for each specific problem, and longer term solutions which, through comprehensive approaches to company taxation within the EC, could eventually remove altogether the obstacles in a more unified manner.

The short-term targeted measures that, to date, have been enacted are basically aimed at eliminating or reducing the risk of double taxation regarding the intra-EC dividends flows and the restructuring operations, on the one hand, and the cases of transfer pricing adjustments by the tax authorities of Member States on the other hand. In relation to intra-EC dividends flows and to the restructuring operations, these measures consist of the amendments that have already been introduced to the two 1990 Directives, and of the proposed amendments to the 2003 Interest-Royalties directive.[233] In relation to transfer pricing, the measures consist of 'soft law' pieces aimed at minimizing the risk of double taxation that can arise in transfer pricing adjustments by the tax authorities of the different Member States of location of associated enterprises. These soft law pieces are two 'Codes of Conduct', which derive from the work of a consultative experts group established by the Commission in 2002, composed of representatives of Member States and of businesses and called the 'EU Joint Transfer Pricing Forum', which was entrusted with the task of identifying improvements to the existing situation and of formulating practical recommendations. A first Code of Conduct, issued in 2004, aims at ensuring an effective and uniform application by Member States of the 1990 Arbitration Convention and a second one, proposed in 2005, standardizes the documentation that multi-national companies must provide to national tax authorities on their pricing on cross-border intra-group transactions, and aims at reducing the costs of compliance with different national documentation obligations.[234] As soft law pieces, these Codes are not legally binding measures but political commitments by Member States, which are more likely to be easily accepted than legislative harmonization measures as they do not affect Member States' rights and obligations and can, thus, complement legislative harmonization in areas where this could find more opposition. The short-term measures introduced to date, amongst them the amendments to the 1990 Directives, have eliminated, at least in part, the tax obstacles identified in the Report, together with the overall progress of the ECJ's tax rulings in this direction.

1.5.2 Overall Progress Achieved by the ECJ Tax Case Law on the Removal of Tax Obstacles to the Freedom of Establishment, Lessons for National Legislators and Effects on Tax Competition

If the ECJ's tax rulings concerning both the application of the 1990 Directives and the freedom of establishment are considered together, it may be noted that companies wishing to set up branches and/or subsidiaries in other Member States and/or to carry on cross-border restructuring operations, can rely on the certainty that:

1. when receiving dividends from either direct (*Zythopiia, Bosal Holding*) or indirect (*Keller Holding*) EC subsidiaries and when wishing to implement cross-border restructuring operations (*Leur-Bloem*, *Andersen og. Jensen*), no juridical double taxation can exist and no difference of treatment can be applied in comparison with domestic operations, except for those differences deriving from mere allocations of taxing powers between Member States (*Van der Grinten*) as a result of DTCs;
2. when creating branches in other Member States (*Avoir fiscal*, *St-Gobain*), they cannot be refused in principle tax benefits available to companies resident in those states (and thus their freedom of choice between branches and subsidiaries is not affected);
3. when creating subsidiaries or branches, anti-abuse clauses (*Langhorst-Hohorst*) applied by the host Member States do not discourage their freedom of establishment to those states by applying stricter conditions than to domestic operations;
4. when creating branches and subsidiaries in other Member States, their state of origin cannot apply provisions that, within the Community territory (*Marks & Spencer*), prevent their rights of deduction of costs and losses relating to these secondary establishments.

From the viewpoint of national legislators this means that, with the ECJ's increasing tendency to reject justifications for different treatments of all situations involving companies from other Member States, any choice, other than the objective establishment of rules and methods for determining the taxable income and the allocation of the powers of taxation, both between themselves and with non-member countries, risks breaching EC law, if placing cross-border situations at a disadvantage in comparison with domestic situations.

The 'lesson' for Member States seems to be evident: the most effective strategy to safeguard national revenue interests may be that of using the margin of discretion left to compete with other Member States in the setting of objectively more favourable methods and rules for determining taxable income (to be equally applied to every kind of both intra-EC and domestic situation), in order to increase the number of resident taxpayers. More specifically, from the viewpoint of Member States, with regard in particular to the treatment of resident companies and PEs, the application of such (more favourable) methods to PEs of non-resident companies may turn out to be convenient even when such PEs generate just a marginal part of the overall taxable income of the non-resident company (in which case different methods might be justifiable: *Schumacker* and *St-Gobain*), since such strategy can induce the non-resident companies to organize their overall business activity in such a manner as to produce a more relevant part of their taxable income through the PEs concerned. A legislative policy aimed at attracting companies, to the extent that it leads to neither discrimination nor restrictions towards companies coming from other Member States, is the only one which at present would not risk being regarded as inconsistent with EC law by the ECJ.

Ultimately, it appears thus unquestionable that the tax case law of the ECJ, on the application of the 1990 Directives as well as on the freedom of establishment, has made considerable progress in reaching an acceptable playing field and, in so doing, it has unintentionally been providing an incentive for (further) tax competition between Member States.

1.5.3 The Commission's Long-term Orientation

The Commission's preferred long-term choice about the comprehensive company taxation approach to be adopted within the EC is a Common Consolidated Base Taxation (CCBT) solution, which would allow companies to use a single company tax base for all their EC-wide activities and would require the adoption of a new, supranational code as regards the definition of a common tax base. First expressed in 2001, this choice which, in the Commission's view, should contribute to the Lisbon objective by removing all remaining company tax obstacles, has been consistently reaffirmed and, in April 2006, the Commission clarified its intention to present a comprehensive EC legislative measure by 2008 for introducing CCBT.[235] Companies which operate through subsidiaries or branches throughout the EC, including those choosing the SE form, would thus be allowed to opt for an EC-wide consolidation of all profits and losses under a new European CCBT Code, which would be applied irrespective of the residence of the parent company: the tax base would then be apportioned amongst the Member States involved and each Member State would apply its own national tax rate to its share of this tax base.

The option for this 'partly supranational' solution, which finds the support of the EP and leaves completely open tax competition between Member States in establishing tax rates, reflects a specific attitude towards tax competition: tax rates are considered the instruments of a sound tax competition, that is of a 'fair tax competition' which can contribute to the attainment of the objectives of growth and competitiveness in the EU and encourage a positive approach by the Member States, helping to prevent tax pressure reaching excessive levels.[236] Two reasons basically lie behind this position. First, it is emphasized that tax rates must remain within the exclusive competence of Member States, as the level of taxation, under the principle of subsidiarity, 'is a matter for Member States to decide'.[237] Secondly, shortly before the release of the Report, the EC Commissioner for internal market and taxation expressly recognized that the differences in corporate tax rates may generate 'welfare losses due to locational inefficiencies', which, in turn, may derive from (abusive) forum shopping practices, but argued that Community action on tax rates was not to be undertaken on the ground that 'at this stage' the locational inefficiencies 'are not quantifiable' and that 'taxation is only one of the factors in any location decision'.[238] Assuming that the CCBT solution will finally be adopted, if multinational enterprises throughout the EC opt for the CCBT rather than for national tax bases, Member States will only be able to induce companies to concentrate the greatest part of their activities into their jurisdictions by competing on tax rates. Consequently, the desired long-term development would go in the same direction as the developments which have characterized EC tax law to date: that of providing scope for further tax competition among the Member States. Although this competition, after the adoption of the CCBT, might produce in the medium to long term the effect of approximating tax rates, until such 'spontaneous' approximation takes place companies would find plenty of scope for tax planning strategies when deciding the location of their investments. In fact, the comparison of the tax burden in different countries would become even easier than it may currently be, due to the application of the different rates to the same tax base, and tax-driven strategies aimed at choosing the location so as to reduce the tax burden would be simplified.

The start of the current attitude towards tax competition concentrating on structural elements, such as tax rates and tax bases, may be dated back to 1997, when the Commission released an important Communication against harmful tax competition[239] which led to the adoption by ECOFIN of a Code of Good Conduct on business taxation.[240] As they resulted from a campaign by some Member States, which suffered revenue losses, against the resort by other Member States to special tax facilities designed to attract foreign investments, these 'soft law' measures identified harmful tax competition in that kind of tax competition which works through special tax regimes. This Code of Good Conduct (just like the more recent Code of Conduct on transfer pricing) is a political compromise of the Member States not to introduce tax facilities which could harm other Member States, as well as to review and, eventually, to eliminate existing measures which are causing problems to other Member States. This instrument has produced results: Member States have in fact revised a good part of the existing special tax facilities.[241] The delimitation of the notion of harmful tax competition to these measures has generated the identical effect as the implementation of the tax Directives and the overall developments of the ECJ tax case law: once again, Member States have been induced to compete with each other in the structural aspects of their corporate tax regimes, typically by reducing their corporate tax rates.[242] The implementation of the Code of Good Conduct has thus been strengthening this 'lesson' to the national tax legislators, and its contribution in this direction may become even greater than it has been up to date. This is because, if 'soft law' extends to the object of the rules of conduct the 'principle of Community loyalty' implying for Member States a duty to make 'any effort to comply with soft law and not to act against it unless good reasons for doing so are set out',[243] then even on those aspects of corporate taxation to date covered by soft law (such as the special tax regimes), the ECJ may convert such duty into a legally binding obligation (as it did, for example, in the state aids field)[244] with far-reaching effects on the legislative options which remain open to Member States.

1.6 A PROBLEMATIC, UNRESOLVED ISSUE

To the extent that both the developments of EC corporate tax law to date and the key objective that the Commission wishes to pursue (that is the introduction of the CCBT) go in the same direction of encouraging tax competition based on tax rates and, in general, on structural aspects of corporate taxation regimes, the question could be asked whether the conception of this kind of tax competition as a 'fair' one can be regarded as a legal conclusion or as the expression of a political strategy. The two reasons on which the Commission and the EP have been basing this conception – the principle of subsidiarity (and of national sovereignty) in direct taxation on the one hand, the realization that distortions created by this competition are not quantifiable at this stage, on the other hand – suggest that this conception can be considered as expressing just a *political* strategy.[245] Considered together, these two arguments in fact offer a negative answer to the question whether, for the time being, the Community ought to undertake action in structural aspects of corporate taxation regimes such as tax rates, but cannot be regarded as a clear acceptance, from a legal viewpoint, of this kind of tax competition: if the competence of Member States under the principle of subsidiarity and national tax sovereignty had been regarded as sufficient to definitively consider the tax competition at issue compatible with the Treaty, the argument that those distortions of the functioning of the market which consist of locational inefficiencies are not quantifiable at this stage would have made no sense. In this case, action would in fact need to be undertaken neither currently nor in the future, irrespective of the effects of this tax competition, that is irrespective of whether those distortions are quantifiable or not and of their size: in other words, even the greatest and more evident distortions would need to be accepted. Nevertheless, this conclusion not only would renounce any attempt at reconciling the principle of subsidiarity with other principles emerging from the Treaty, but would also ignore the ECJ's reasoning in *Marks & Spencer*. Here, the ECJ expressly recognized that a specific kind of tax practices may be inspired by the significant differences between the national rates of taxation, which differences are to be seen as a result of the tax competition based on tax rates, but admitted that restrictive provisions preventing these tax practices pursue legitimate objectives compatible with the Treaty.[246] Implicitly, the ECJ thus regarded tax practices generated, in ultimate analysis, by the competition based on tax rates as distortions to be eliminated. Moreover, a position that considered tax competition based on general tax measures as compatible with the Treaty irrespective of its effects would be in sharp contrast with the Lisbon objective.

This leads to a problematic issue: whether, from the perspective of the legal analysis, there are some conditions under which the competition among the Member States in the structural aspects of corporate taxation is to be regarded as compatible with EC law and helpful in achieving the EC's general objectives. It might perhaps be objected that, if the ultimate result of EC legislation and case law in the field of company taxation has to date been an increased scope for tax competition among the Member States in structural aspects of companiy taxation, this automatically means that such competition is compatible with EC law: if this were true, this issue presented as unresolved would only be a tautology. Nonetheless, the objection is unfounded: it confuses a de facto result, of which, as shown above, the current positions considering tax competition compatible with the completion of the internal market seem to neglect the potential scale of a specific kind of distortion, with the goal to avoid or minimize all types of distortions in the functioning of this market, in order to ensure the best achievement of the Treaty's objectives and of the Lisbon objective. The solution of the issue thus implies an attempt, which will be made in Chapter 4, to interpret all the Treaty's provisions which might be relevant and the secondary legislation issued to date to draw a conclusion in the light of this goal.[247]

NOTES

1. Of 23 July 1990, originally entitled 'Common system of taxation applicable to mergers, divisions, transfers of assets and exchanges of shares concerning companies of different Member States', in OJEC L225/1 [1990].
2. Of 23 July 1990, on 'Common system of taxation applicable in the case of parent companies and subsidiaries of different Member States', in OJEC L225/6 [1990].
3. Directive 2003/123/EC of 22 December 2003 amending Directive 90/435/EEC, in OJEC L7/41 [2004]; Directive 2005/19/EC of 17 February 2005 amending Directive 90/434/EEC, in OJEC L58/19 [2005].

4. The quoted text is contained in recital (1) of the Preamble to both the Merger Directive and the Parent-Subsidiary Directive. The Preambles to the two Directives have most recitals in common, which reflect the view that differences between the corporate tax provisions of Member States in such fields tend to produce distortions within the EC market. Apart from the process of harmonizing indirect taxation (particularly in the field of VAT), prior to 1990 only the EC Directive on mutual assistance between national fiscal administrations in direct tax matters (Directive 77/799/EEC) had been adopted in the field of direct taxation.
5. Which includes all profit-making entities.
6. Together with their tendency to safeguard as much as possible of their sovereignty in the tax field.
7. IBFD (1995), *Survey of the Implementation of the EC Corporate Tax Directives*, IBFD Publications, Amsterdam, p. 5; this conclusion is still regarded as topical by the later IBFD (2003), *Survey on the Societas Europaea*, International Bureau of Fiscal Documentation, Amsterdam, p. 7.
8. Parent-Subsidiary Directive, Article 4, first paragraph.
9. See ibid. Article 5, first paragraph, Article 6 and the wording of Article 7, first paragraph, whereby the term 'withholding tax' does not cover an advance payment or prepayment of corporation tax to the Member State of the subsidiary which is made in connection with a distribution of profits to its parent company.
10. Ibid. Article 3, second paragraph.
11. Ibid. Article 4, second paragraph.
12. Ibid. Article 1, second paragraph.
13. Ibid. Article 7, second paragraph.
14. Which had to be transposed into national legislations by 1 January 2005: Article 5 of Directive 2003/123/EC, in OJEC L7/43 [2004].
15. See Article 1, n. (1), n. (3), n. (4) and n. (5) of Directive 2003/123/EC, in OJEC L7/42–43 [2004]. These amendments have been described in Cerioni, L. (2004), 'The amendments to the 1990 EC Tax Directives', *The European Legal Forum*, 02 (04), 139–148. Before the amendments, Maisto, G. (2002), 'Shaping EU company tax policy: amending the Tax Directives', *European Taxation*, 8 (42), 287–308.
16. See Parent-Subsidiary Directive, Article 2, let. (b) and (c), and the Annex to the 1990 version. These forms coincide for most countries with public and private limited companies and include some types of limited partnerships: see OJEC L225/6–9 [1990], Annex 'List of companies referred to in Article 2(a)'. See below 4.1.2.
17. Such as cooperatives, savings banks, mutual funds, some non capital-based companies and legal forms created after 1990: see OJEC L7/44 [2004], Annex 'List of companies referred to in Article 2, paragraph 1, letter (a)'.
18. This requirement – set by Parent-Subsidiary Directive Article 2 – is extended to the newly included legal forms by Directive 2003/123/EC.
19. Introduced by Regulation 2157/2001 and Directive 2001/86/EC: see below 3.2.1.
20. Introduced by Regulation 1435/2003 and Directive 2003/72/EC: see below 3.3.
21. With the possibility neither of opting for a different tax regime nor of being exempted: Parent-Subsidiary Directive Article 2.
22. See Article 1, n. (1) and n. (4) of Directive 2003/123/EC, OJEC L7/42 [2004].
23. Article 1, n. (2) of Directive 2003/123/EC (OJEC L7/42 [2004]) defines the PE as a 'fixed place of business' situated in a Member State through which the business of a company of another Member State 'is wholly or partly carried on', provided the profits of that establishment are subject to tax in the Member State where this is situated under the applicable DTC or under national law. In turn, Article 5 of the 2003 OECD Model Convention defines the PE as a fixed place of business situated in a state through which the business of a company of another state of the OECD is wholly or partly carried on.
24. Article 3, let. (c) of Directive 2003/49/EC of 3 June 2003, in OJEC L157/49 [2003]: see below 1.2.
25. See Article 1, n. (4) of Directive 2003/123/EC.
26. See Article 1, n. (4), let. (b) of Directive 2003/123/EC.
27. Which reduction (to 20 per cent from the entry into force of the amending Directive, to

15 per cent from 2007 and to 10 per cent from 2009) also applies, consistently with the inclusion of the distributions through permanent establishments, to the holding in the capital of a subsidiary through a PE. See Article 1, n. (3), let. (a) of Directive 2003/123/EC (see note 23).

28. Inter alia IBFD, *Survey on the Implementation of the EC Corporate Tax Directives*, note 7; Williams, David William (1998), *EC Tax Law*, Longman, London, New York, pp. 143–144; International Congress 'Gruppi di societa' ed imposizione sui redditi: l'attuazione della Direttiva CEE 90/435' ['Groups of companies and corporate taxation: the implementation of Directive EEC 90/435'], Faculty of Law, University of Bologna, 2000.
29. So that such gaps are to be filled by national tax laws and, in the case of 'distribution of profits', interpreted as synonymous with 'dividends' by the provisions contained in the DTCs entered into by Member States with third countries.
30. As frequently occurs since Member States still follow different interpretations about these basic notions. This aspect was evidenced in the International Congress, in note 28.
31. This could either discourage subsidiaries from distributing profits to their parent companies (and defeat, for these latter, one of the reasons for exercising their freedom of establishment through the creation of subsidiaries) or force the creation of subsidiaries in those countries which appear to adopt the same interpretations of the concept at issue, even when purely economic and market reasons would suggest the choice of other Member States.
32. See Parent-Subsidiary Directive, Article 4, first paragraph.
33. Thus to profits distributions during the life of the subsidiary company. The answer, left to Member States, creates further space for differences concerning important aspects between national legislations.
34. Parent-Subsidiary Directive, Article 1, second paragraph quoted below 1.1.2.
35. As regards this problem raised by the wording of the anti-abuse clause, see IBFD, *Survey on the Implementation of the EC Corporate Tax Directives*, note 7, pp. 12 and 368. However, on the scope of the anti-abuse clause, see the subsequent case law of the ECJ: below 1.3.1.a.
36. IBFD, *Survey on the Implementation of the EC Corporate Tax Directive*, note 7, p. 367.
37. Ibid. p. 12.
38. See above 1.1.1 and Preamble, recital (3).
39. The exemption method is regarded as representing the CIN idea of equal treatment of local investors and foreign investors in the same national market (local and foreign investors should thus obtain the same after-tax rate of return on similar investments in that market). The indirect tax credit method is considered the expression of CEN, whereby in a given state there should be equal treatment of resident taxpayers investing at home and of resident taxpayers investing abroad. Terra, Ben and Paul Wattel (1997), *European Tax Law*, Kluwer Law International, London, p. 242.
40. This situation may well occur in practice, as large companies often issue preference shares.
41. See above note 5.
42. In many countries, national company law rules allow the membership of limited liability companies in partnerships and in all limited liability partnerships, but the Annex to the Directive only lists some types of limited partnerships which are generally considered as belonging to the same category as limited companies (such as the Belgian or French *sociétés en commandite par actions* or the Italian *società in accomandita per azioni*) and not other types of limited partnerships (such as the Belgian or French *société en commandite simple* or the Italian *società in accomandita semplice*) and partnerships.
43. Which can lead to the incorporation of subsidiaries under forms of limited liability companies even when economic reasons would suggest the choice of unlimited liability forms (or partly unlimited liability, such as limited partnerships).
44. See definition of the merger in Merger Directive, Article 2, lit. (a).
45. See definition of the division in ibid. Article 2, lit. (b).
46. See definition of transfer of assets: ibid. Article 2, lit. (c).
47. See definition of exchange of shares: ibid. Article 2, lit. (d).
48. See ibid. Article 4, first and second paragraphs.
49. Ibid. Article 8.
50. Ibid. Article 7.

51. Examples can be found in ibid. Article 4, third paragraph, Article 5, Article 6 and Article 8.
52. Ibid. Article 10.
53. Ibid. Article 11, first paragraph, let. (a).
54. Commission's proposal (COM (2003) 613 final) of 17 October 2003, 'Impact Assessment Form' at pp. 28–29.
55. See Directive 2005/19/EC of 17 February 2005, in OJEC L58/19 [2005], Annex ('List of companies referred to in Article 3(a)') and see note 17.
56. See ibid. Article 1, third paragraph, let. (a).
57. See ibid. Article 1, third paragraph, let. (b).
58. See ibid. recital (14).
59. See ibid. Title IV b Rules applicable to the transfer of the registered office of an SE or an SCE, 10a to 10d.
60. See ibid. Title II and Title VI b and the two conditions referred to above for the tax deferral regime.
61. See ibid. Articles 6 and 9 which inserted in the Merger Directive new Article 4, second paragraph and Article 8, third paragraph.
62. Commission proposal, note 54, sentences 26 and 27 of the Explanatory Memorandum, pp. 7–8.
63. See Directive 2005/19/EC, Title II, paragraph 8.
64. See ibid. Title IV b, paragraph 13. This amendment was not proposed by the Commission.
65. IBFD, *Survey on the Implementation of the EC Corporate Tax Directives*, note 7, p. 23. On this aspect, also, Cerioni, L. (2004), 'The amendments to the 1990 EC Tax Directives', note 15.
66. IBFD, *Survey on the Implementation of the EC Corporate Tax Directives*, note 7, p. 40.
67. Ibid. p. 23.
68. See above 1.1.4.
69. See above 1.1.4.
70. See above 1.1.4.
71. See Merger Directive, Preamble, fifth recital (5).
72. Ibid. Article 4, first paragraph.
73. See above 1.1.1.
74. See below 3.2.4.d.
75. Merger Directive, Article 2, let. (a) and (b).
76. Article 5 of the OECD Model.
77. See above 1.1.4 and note 51.
78. Merger Directive, Article 7, second paragraph. Other examples are the options left to the state of the transferring company as regards the tax treatment of the losses and gains of a PE of this transferring company situated in another Member State (ibid. Article 10).
79. See ibid. Article 4, first paragraph, the definition of 'transferred assets and liabilities'.
80. See ibid. Article 5.
81. Ibid. Preamble, recital (1).
82. IBFD, *Survey on the Implementation of the EC Corporate Tax Directives*, note 7; International Congresses 'Le imposte sui redditi e le riorganizzazioni societarie nell'esperienza Europea: l'attuazione della Direttiva 434/90' ['Corporate taxation and companies' reorganisation in Europe: the implementation of Directive 434/90 EEC'], Faculty of Law, University of Bologna, 1999; and 'Gruppi di societa' ed imposizione sui redditi: l'attuazione della Direttiva CEE 90/435' ['Groups of companies and corporate taxation: the implementation of Directive 90/435 EEC'], Faculty of Law, University of Bologna, 2000; last, on the Merger Directive, also IBFD, *Survey on the Societas Europaea*, note 7, which, on the assumption that the Merger Directive would apply to the SE, made a comparative overview of the differences which would characterize its tax treatment on the basis of the implementation of the Merger Directive in each Member State.
83. See Appendix III on the implementation of both Directives.
84. See above note 82.
85. The United Kingdom, Germany and Belgium: see Appendix III on the implementation of the Merger Directive.

86. See below 1.3.
87. Martin Jiménez, Alfonso J. (1999), *Towards Corporate Tax Harmonisation in the European Community: an Institutional and Procedural Analysis*, Kluwer Law International, London, p. 129.
88. SEC (90) 601 final of 20 April 1990.
89. Commission Staff Working Paper, *Company Taxation in the Internal Market* (SEC (2001) 1681) of 23 October 2001.
90. See ibid. pp. 225–232 and pp. 327–329 as regards the Parent-Subsidiary Directive; ibid. pp. 232–242 and pp. 331–333 as regards the Merger Directive.
91. See above 1.1.1, the objective stated in the Preambles to the two Directives.
92. See above 1.1.2.
93. See above 1.1.5.
94. See above 1.1.6.
95. Since the ten new Member States, which entered the EC on 1 May 2004, have been trying to be competitive in attracting businesses: see Appendix III on the implementation of the tax Directives.
96. See Commission Communication, 'An internal market without tax obstacles: achievements, ongoing initiatives and remaining challenges' (COM (2003) 726 final), p. 6.
97. Directive 2003/49/EC of 3 June 2003 'on a common system of taxation applicable to interest and royalties payments made between associated companies of different Member States', in OJEC L157/49 [2003]. This Directive, which set 1 January 2004 as a deadline for implementation, has not yet been implemented by all Member States: see Appendix III.
98. Examined in more depth in Cerioni, L. (2004), 'Intra-EC interest and royalties tax treatment', *European Taxation*, 1 (44), 47–53.
99. Article 3, let. (a) and (b) of the Interest-Royalties Directive, in OJEC L157/51 [2003].
100. The only difference is that the notion of 'associated company' also includes (together with a company in which another holds a direct minimum quota of 25 per cent) each of two companies where a third company holds at least 25 per cent in the capital of both: Article 3 of the Interest-Royalties Directive.
101. Ibid. Article 3, let. (b).
102. Ibid. Article 1, tenth paragraph.
103. Ibid. Article 5, first paragraph, as compared with Article 1, second paragraph of the Parent-Subsidiary Directive.
104. Article 9 of the Interest-Royalties Directive as compared with Article 7, second paragraph of the Parent-Subsidiary Directive.
105. Article 5, second paragraph of the Interest-Royalties Directive as compared with Article 11, second paragraph of the Merger Directive.
106. Article 1, second and fifth paragraph, Article 3 let. (c) of the Interest-Royalties Directive; Article 5 of the OECD Model.
107. Interest-Royalties Directive, Preamble, recitals (1) and (2).
108. Ibid. Article 2 as compared with Articles 11 (interest) and 12 (royalties) of the OECD Model.
109. Interest-Royalties Directive, Article 4, second paragraph. This aspect was analysed in Cerioni, note 98, pp. 51–52.
110. Interest-Royalties Directive, Article 4, first paragraph.
111. Ibid. Article 1, eighth to tenth paragraphs.
112. See above 1.1.2.
113. Commission proposal (COM (2003) 841 final) of 30 December 2003 (2003/0331(CSN)). This proposal reflects the Commission's approach of extending the current body of EC tax legislation to the SE and the SCE (see below 5.1.2), so that the 2003 Directive should also be amended to add the SE and the SCE to the types of companies covered.
114. Which would have required, just as in the case of the two 1990 Directives, greater uniformity in the conditions for access to the tax benefit.
115. See Appendix III on the current results of the implementation.
116. See below 1.3.3.

117. This has been repeatedly stated by the ECJ in its tax rulings: see below 1.4. A list of cases of relevance for direct taxation is included at Appendix IV.
118. Joined Cases C-283/94, C-291/94 and C-292/94, *Denkavit, Vitic Voormer* [1996] ECR I-5063. On the *Denkavit* ruling, see inter alia, Bouzoraa, D. (1997), 'The Parent-Subsidiary Directive: Denkavit's lessons', *European Taxation*, 1 (37), 14–18.
119. Case C-294/99, *Athinaiki Zythopiia* [2001] ECR I- 6797.
120. Case C-375/98, *Epson Europe* [2000] ECR I-4243.
121. Case C-58/01, *Océ Van der Grinten* [2003] ECR I-9809.
122. Case C-168/01, *Bosal Holding* [2003] ECR I-9401.
123. Case C-471/04, *Keller Holding* OJEC C19/14 [2005], ruling delivered on 23 February 2006 (not yet reported).
124. *Denkavit*, note 118, paras 31, 51 and 52 of the ruling.
125. Which is not separately analysed, since its conclusions have been repeated and given greater emphasis in *Zythopiia*.
126. See, for a description of these Greek provisions, *Zythopiia*, note 119, paras 13, 14 and 15 of the ruling.
127. As such, it would be expressly excluded by Article 7 from the concept of withholding tax, and would be legitimate as the Directive does not provide for an exemption from the corporation tax on the subsidiary.
128. *Zythopiia*, note 119, para. 27 of the ruling, and Joined Cases C-197/94 and C-252/94, *Bautiaa et Société francaise maritime* [1996] ECR I-505; *Epson Europe*, note 120.
129. See *Zythopiia*, note 119, paras 28 and 29 of the ruling.
130. The unconditional nature of the rights conferred by the Treaty had been affirmed in the '*avoir fiscal*' case (Case 270/83, *Commission v. France* [1986] ECR 273); *Zythopiia*, by recognizing an unconditional right deriving from the Parent-Subsidiary Directive, marks an important step in the overall case law on the two Directives (see the final observations below 1.3.3).
131. See the wording of Article 7, second paragraph.
132. *Zythopiia*, note 119, paras 35 and 36 of the ruling, where the ECJ again cited, to indicate its settled case law, *Bautiaa et Société francaise maritime,* note 128, para. 47. Article 234 EC is, after the Treaty of Amsterdam, the former Article 177.
133. *Zythopiia*, para. 38 of the ruling.
134. Ibid. para. 39 of the ruling.
135. Which formulation is required for a Directive to have direct effect: Joined Cases C-6/90 and C-9/90, *Francovich and others* [1991] ECR I-5357, para. 11 ('unconditional and sufficiently precise terms').
136. In other words, *Zythopiia* makes it convenient for the companies involved to consider as interconnected two issues that are traditionally seen as separate: Member States' liability for damages for breach of EC law, on the one hand, and Member States' liability to pay back taxes that were wrongly levied, on the other hand. According to the settled case law, which was referred to by the ECJ in *Denkavit,* damage liability for breach of EC law is a general principle. In particular, it is inherent in the Treaty, and it gives rise to a right to reparation when three conditions exist: a right granted to individuals by the rule infringed, a sufficiently serious breach and a causal link between this breach and the damage suffered by the injured parties (Joined Cases C-46/93 and 48/93, *Brasserie du Pecheur and Factortame* [1996] ECR I-01029, para. 51; Joined Cases C-178/94, C-179/94, C-188/94, C-189/94 and C-190/94, *Dillenkofer and others* [1996] ECR I-04845, paras 21 to 23; *Denkavit, Vitic Voormer*, note 118, paras 47 and 48; *Francovich and others*, note 135, paras 38 to 42). Though these conditions apply when a Member State incorrectly transposes an EC Directive into national law (*Denkavit*, note 118, para. 48), a Member State might still try (as Germany did in *Denkavit*) to avoid reparation by calling into discussion the clarity and precision of the rule of the Directive involved, which would prevent the sufficiently serious breach (*Brasserie du Pecheur and Factortame*, above, paras 55 and 56; *Denkavit, Vitic Voormer*, note 118, para. 49). By contrast, the liability for repayment of taxes unduly collected by a state in breach of fundamental provisions of the Parent-Subsidiary Directive cannot in principle be limited (*Zythopiia*). Accordingly, in doubtful cases companies have

a practical interest to try to prove that any damage resulting from improper transposition of this Directive, to the extent that it deprives them of financial resources, originates from a violation by a state of clear and precise rules (the fundamental provisions of the Directive) and is equivalent to the direct damage consisting of the payment of clearly undue taxes, which latter per se also satisfies all three conditions for damages liability (right not to pay taxes, and thus to have more financial resources available; sufficiently serious breach, given the clear and precise terms of the Directive's fundamental provisions; casual link, by definition).

137. Article 1 includes both inbound and outbound profits distributions in its scope of application and contains the anti-abuse clause: see above 1.1.2 and 1.1.3.
138. *Bosal Holding*, note 122, paras 21 and 28 of the ruling and Recital (3) of the Preamble to the Directive. On the ECJ's approach to emphasize the possible effect of making the exercise of the freedom of establishment less attractive, see below 1.4.2.b and c.
139. *Keller Holding*, note 123, paras 21 to 24, 31 to 35 and 45 of the ruling.
140. Commission Communication, 'An internal market without tax obstacles: achievements, ongoing initiatives and remaining challenges' (COM (2003) 726 final), p. 8.
141. See *Zythopiia*, note 119.
142. See *Van der Grinten*, note 121, paras 56, 57 and 58 of the ruling.
143. See the analysis of *Bosal Holding*, note 122.
144. See *Van der Grinten*, note 121, paras 85 to 89 of the ruling.
145. See *Bosal Holding*, note 122, paras 97 to 103 of the ruling.
146. Case C-28/95, *Leur-Bloem* [1997] ECR I-4161.
147. Case C-43/00, *Andersen og. Jensen* [2002] ECR I-379.
148. *Leur-Bloem*, note 146, para. 5, let. (b) and paras 7 to 11 of the ruling.
149. See, for the description of this arrangement, *Andersen og. Jensen*, note 147, para. 8 of the ruling.
150. See ibid. para. 10.
151. The former Article 177 EC at the time when the *Leur-Bloem* case was brought, which empowers the ECJ to interpret Community law through preliminary rulings. See *Leur-Bloem*, note 146, para. 16 of the ruling and *Andersen og. Jensen*, note 147, paras 14 to 16 of the ruling.
152. See *Leur-Bloem*, note 146, para 34 of the ruling and *Andersen og. Jensen*, note 147, para. 19 of the ruling.
153. The ECJ case law on covert discriminations is the same case law which, from the 1980s, has started removing fiscal barriers to the right of establishment: see below 1.4.
154. In response to five specific questions: see *Leur-Bloem*, note 146, para. 15 of the ruling, questions (a) to (e).
155. See ibid. para. 15 of the ruling, questions (a) to (d).
156. See ibid. para. 15 of the ruling, question (e).
157. See ibid. paras 37 and 48, let. (a) of the ruling.
158. So that the requirements set by the definitions contained in the Directive are not met: see *Andersen og. Jensen*, note 147, paras 24, 25 and 27 of the ruling.
159. See *Andersen og. Jensen*, note 147, para. 28 of the ruling.
160. See ibid. para. 30 and Article 2, let. (c) and (i) of the Merger Directive.
161. See *Andersen og. Jensen*, note 147, paras 34 to 37 of the ruling.
162. See *Leur-Bloem*, note 146, para. 48, let. (a) and (b) of the ruling.
163. See ibid. para. 48, let. (c) of the ruling.
164. Case C- 8/97, *Commission v. Hellenic Republic* [1998] ECR I-00823.
165. Case C-208/96, *Commission v. Belgium* [1997] ECR I-5375.
166. Concerning the Parent-Subsidiary Directive: see above 1.3.1.a and b.
167. See below 1.3.3.
168. See above 1.3.1.b on the *Zythopoiia* ruling and 1.3.2 on the *Leur-Bloem* ruling.
169. Evident in their history: see above 1.1.8.
170. See above 1.1.1 for the Merger Directive and 1.2 for the Interest-Royalties Directive.
171. See above 1.1.2 for the amended version of the Parent-Subsidiary Directive, 1.1.4 for the Merger Directive and 1.2 for the Interest-Royalties Directive.

172. See above 1.1.2 for the amended version of the Parent-Subsidiary Directive and 1.2 for the Interest-Royalties Directive.
173. See below 1.4 as to the latest and key developments of the tax case law and Chapter 2 on the company law rulings of the ECJ.
174. See Article 7 (business profits), first paragraph of the OECD Model, on which DTCs are generally based, which provides for the taxation of profits attributable to the PE in the Contracting State where this PE is situated, and Chapter 2 regarding the latest company law rulings.
175. Which seems to be tolerated without a comprehensive legal analysis by the current Commission attitude, after having been regarded as 'harmful' by an early proposal at the start of the 1990s: see below 1.5 and 1.6 and 4.2.
176. 'Direct taxation falls within the competence of the Member States but the Member States must exercise that competence consistently with Community law', presentation by M. Wathelet, a former ECJ judge, at the European Conference on Company Taxation: EU Corporate Tax Reform: Progress and New Challenges, 5–6 December 2003. On the importance of the case law of the ECJ in the direct taxation field, see also Van Thiel, S. (2003), 'Removal of income tax barriers to market integration in the European Community: litigation by Community citizen instead of harmonization by the Community Legislature?', *EC Tax Review*, 4–19.
177. Tridimas, T. (1993), 'The case-law of the European Court of Justice on corporate entities', *Yearbook of European Law*, (13), 335–347; Wouters, J. (1994), 'Fiscal barriers to companies' cross-border establishment in the case-law of the EC Court of Justice', *Yearbook of European Law*, (14), 73–107, 79–108; Wathelet, M. (2001), 'The influence of free movement of persons, services and capital on national direct taxation: trends in the case-law of the Court of Justice', *Yearbook of European Law*, (20), 1–33.
178. With regard to the tax law cases on companies' freedom of establishment, see Case C-270/83, *Avoir fiscal* [1986] ECR 273; Case C-330/91, *Commerzbank* [1993] ECR I-4017; Case C-1/93, *Halliburton Services* [1994] ECR I-1137; Case C-311/97, *Royal Bank of Scotland* [1999] ECR I-2651. The ECJ has considered 'covert discriminations' to be those differences in treatment which, without making express reference to nationality, produce the same result as an open discrimination.
179. With regard to the tax law cases on companies' freedom of establishment, see Case C-264/96, *ICI* [1998] ECR I-4711; the landmark 1999 Case C-307/97 *St-Gobain* ruling [1999] ECR I-6163 referred to in the text (below 1.4.2.a); Case C-141/99, *AMID* [2000] ECR I-11619; Joined Cases C-397/98 and C-410/98, *Metallgesellschaft and Hoechst* (below 1.4.2.b and c), [2001] ECR I-1727; Case C-436/00, *X and Y* [2002] ECR I-10829; Case C-324/2000, *Langhorst-Hohorst* [2002] ECR I-11779 (below 1.4.2.b); last, the landmark 2003 *Bosal Holding* ruling referred to in the text (above 1.3.1.c and below 1.4.2.c).
180. Case C-251/98, *Baars* [2000] ECR I-2787.
181. The case of more burdensome fulfilments for non-residents was at issue in Case C-250/95, *Futura* [1997] ECR I-2471, where double book-keeping was required to non-resident companies to prove that they met the requirement to benefit from the same tax benefit granted to resident companies. On this ruling, see below, 1.4.2.c. Tax provisions of the state of origin hindering the freedom of establishment in another Member State have been examined in Case C-9/92, *Lasteyrie du Saillant* [2004] ECR I-2409, concerning an 'exit tax' imposed on an individual wishing to transfer its tax resident to another Member State. On this ruling, see below 2.3.
182. Throughout the case law cited in notes 178 to 181.
183. Aspect stressed by M. Wathelet, note 176.
184. A significant example of the fact that, in practice, the distinction is doubtful was pointed out by M. Wathelet in his presentation, note 176, in Case C-484/93, *Svensson and Gustavsson* [1995] ECR I-3955.
185. See Appendix IV for a list of ECJ rulings.
186. Data evidenced by M. Wathelet, note 176.
187. In numerous cases concerning both companies and individuals: see *ICI*, *St-Gobain*,

Metallgesellschaft, *Langhorst-Hohorst*, note 179; *Bosal Holding*, note 122; Case C-35/98, *Verkooijen* [2000] ECR I-4073; Case C-136/00, *Danner* [2002] ECR I-8147, and Case C-422/01, *Skandia* [2003] ECR I-6817 on natural persons.

188. See note 187. In *Bosal Holding*, note 122, this justification was presented as the 'aim of avoiding an erosion of the tax base going beyond ... mere diminution of the tax revenue', but it was again rejected.
189. Case C-307/97, *St-Gobain* [1999] ECR I-6163.
190. *Avoir fiscal*, note 178.
191. Case C-279/93, *Schumacker* [1995] ECR I-225.
192. See note 179. As regards the possible application of the *Schumacker* ruling by analogy, see Wouters, note 177, p. 105.
193. As in Case C-175/88, *Biehl* [1990] ECR I-1779, and in the *Schumacker* case, with regard to rules of fiscal procedure, and in Case C-107/94, *Asscher* [1996] ECR I-3089, with regard to the progressive scale of taxation.
194. Case C-253/03, *CLT-UFA*, OJEC C200/12 [2003], ruling delivered on 23 February 2006 (not yet reported), OJEC C131/4 [2006]. On this ruling, see Szudoczky, R. (2006), 'EC update', *European Taxation*, 5 (46), 17–18.
195. See *Avoir fiscal*, note 178, para. 19 of the ruling, where the 'certain circumstances' were left undefined.
196. See *Schumacker*, note 191, paras 33 and 34 of the ruling.
197. See *St-Gobain*, note 189, para. 48 of the ruling.
198. See *CLT-UFA*, note 194, paras 19 to 25 of the ruling.
199. See *CLT-UFA*, note 194, paras 26 to 29 of the ruling.
200. *St-Gobain*, note 189, paras 58 and 59 of the ruling.
201. *Avoir fiscal*, note 178, para. 26 of the ruling.
202. *St-Gobain*, note 189, para. 42 of the ruling; *CLT-UFA*, note 194, para. 17 of the ruling.
203. Case C-324/2000, *Langhorst-Hohorst* [2002] ECR I-11779.
204. Case C-204/1990, *Bachmann* [2002] ECR I-249. In this case, Belgium did not allow the deduction of life insurance premiums paid abroad. The relevant national law offered two choices: either deducting premiums but taxing future benefits, or not deducting premiums and having future benefits exempted; and the cohesion of that system required the certainty to tax the benefits if the premiums had been deducted: from the viewpoint of the Belgian tax authority, this certainty did not exist if the benefits were paid in another Member State.
205. See above, note 179.
206. See below 1.4.2.c.
207. *Baars*, note 180, *Verkooijen*, note 187 and *Asscher*, note 193.
208. Such as income tax and corporation tax.
209. Case C-80/94, *Wierlockx (NL)* [1995] ECR I- 2508.
210. This position has been consistently taken by the ECJ (see cases cited above note 179).
211. See *ICI*, note 179, para. 26 of the ruling.
212. See *Langhorst-Hohorst*, note 179, para. 37 of the ruling. Another ruling, *X and Y*, note 179, also affirmed that tax evasion or avoidance cannot be presumed for the establishment of the parent company or of a subsidiary abroad.
213. See *Schumacker*, note 191, Case C-254/97, *Baxter* [1999] ECR I-4811, and Case C-55/98, *Bent Vestergaard* [1999] ECR I-7643.
214. Cases cited in note 213.
215. See *Langhorst-Hohorst*, note 179, para. 32 of the ruling. The importance of this innovative finding of general character is also emphasized by Gutmann, D. and L. Hinnekens (2003), 'The *Langhorst-Hohorst* case: the ECJ finds German thin capitalization rules incompatible with freedom of establishment', *EC Tax Review*, 2 (13) , 90–97, at 93.
216. See above 1.4.2.a.
217. Already referred to above 1.3.1.c as regards the case law on the Parent-Subsidiary Directive.
218. See Commission Report on *Company Taxation in the Internal Market*, note 89, at p. 27; Communication (COM (2003)726 final), note 96, at p. 9; Communication 'Tackling the corporation tax obstacles of small and medium-sized enterprises in the internal market:

outline of a possible Home State Taxation pilot scheme' (COM (2005)702 final) p. 6. A 1991 Commission proposal to allow cross-border loss off-set had to be withdrawn (COM (90) 595 final, OJEC C53/30 [1991]).
219. See above 1.4.1, note 181.
220. See above 1.4.1, note 179.
221. Mentioned above 1.4.2.b.
222. See *ICI*, note 179, para. 29 of the ruling; *Bosal Holding*, note 122, paras 29 to 32 of the ruling.
223. Mentioned above 1.4.2.b.
224. See *Metallgesellschaft*, note 179, para. 57 of the ruling and *ICI*, note 179, para. 26 of the ruling.
225. See *Bosal Holding*, note 122, paras 33 to 39 of the ruling; *Keller Holding*, note 123, paras 39 to 44 of the ruling. According to M. Wathelet (see the presentation cited in note 176), in *Bosal Holding* the ECJ closed the door to the territoriality principle 'that had been slightly opened in *Futura Participation* (1997)'.
226. Case C-446/03, *Marks & Spencer*, OJEC C304/18 [2003], ruling delivered on 13 December 2005 (not yet reported); OJEC C36/5 [2006].
227. See *Marks & Spencer*, note 226, paras 34, 39 to 51 and 55 of the ruling.
228. The comparative overview indicated in the text is drawn from the Commission's Working Document (SEC (2005) 1785), p. 43, Annex to Communication (COM (2005) 702 final), note 218.
229. See above 1.4.2.b and c.
230. The 2001 Report on *Company Taxation in the Internal Market*, note 89.
231. Convention 436/1990, OJEC L225/10 [1990].
232. As shown by the ECJ findings: see for example 1.3.1.b. See also the Report, note 89, p. 286.
233. See above 1.1.2, 1.1.4, 1.1.8 and 1.2.
234. See Communication (COM (2004) 297 final), and Commission Press Release IP/05/1403, 10 November 2005.
235. See Commission Communications 'Towards an internal market without tax obstacles: a strategy for providing companies with a consolidated corporate tax base for their EU-wide activities' (COM (2001) 582 final), pp. 15–16; (COM (2003) 726 final), note 96, p. 4; 'The contribution of taxation and customs policies to the Lisbon strategy' (COM (2005) 532 final), p. 5; 'Implementing the Community Lisbon Program: progress to date and next step towards a Common Consolidated Corporate Tax Base (CCCTB)'(COM (2006) 157 final), p. 8.
236. EP Report, 'Motion for a Resolution on the Commission Communication to the Council, the European Parliament and the Economic and Social Committee on tax policy in the European Union: priorities for the years ahead (COM/2001) 260-C5-0597/2001-2001/2248 (COS)' (AS-0048/2002) of 22 February 2002, statement 2, p. 6. Also, Schon, W. (2002), 'The European Commission's Report on company taxation: a magic formula for European taxation?', *European Taxation*, 8 (42), 278.
237. And that, as a consequence 'Tax competition is compatible with the completion of the internal market because it entails an area without internal frontiers in which the free movements of goods, persons, services and capital is ensured (Articles 14 and 3, EC Treaty), and hence not a total levelling out of competitive conditions, and in particular those relating to taxation, in each country': EP Report, note 236, p. 11. See also Commissioner Bolkestein, F. (2002), 'The future of European tax policy', *EC Tax Review*, 1 (12), 20.
238. See Bolkestein, note 237, who concludes 'since taxation is only one of the factors in any location decision, in my opinion, the study [the Report] does not demand Community action on tax rates'.
239. Commission Communication, 'Towards tax co-ordination in the European Union: package to tackle harmful tax competition' (COM (97) 495 final).
240. The Code of Good Conduct was definitively adopted on 3 June 2003 (IP/03/787), as part of the 1997 'tax package' (see above note 239), including also the Interest-Royalties

Directive (retro, par. 1.2.) and a Directive concerning the taxation of savings income (Directive 2003/48/EC). The Council had been continuing discussions since then on the basis of an outline that it agreed in December 1997 (Conclusions of the ECOFIN Council Meeting on 1 December 1997 concerning taxation policy, Resolution of the Council and the Representatives of the Governments of the Member States, meeting within the Council of 1 December 1997 on a Code of Good Conduct on business taxation, in OJEC C002/1-6 [1998]). The Code of Good Conduct has in practice been operating since 1998, when the Council meeting on 9 March 1998 (OJEC C99/1-2 [1998]) established a Code of Conduct Group to assess the tax measures that may fall within the Code of Conduct, although extensions for limited periods of time have been allowed for certain business tax measures considered as having harmful features.

241. In a Report of November 1999, the Code of Conduct Group identified a total of 66 tax measures with harmful features, which have then been revised by Member States.
242. Hamaekers, H. (2003), 'Taxation trends in Europe', *Asia-Pacific Tax Bulletin* 2, 46. See also Appendix I.
243. Martin Jiménez, note 87, p. 320.
244. Case C-311/94, *Ijssel-Vliet v. Minister van Economische Zaken* [1996] ECR I–5023; see para. 41 of this ruling.
245. As Schon, note 236, stresses at p. 278, 'The Commission Study gives the reader the impression that the Commission could not express all it wanted to say'.
246. See *Marks & Spencer*, note 226, paras 50 and 51 of the ruling.
247. See below 4.2.1.

2. Latest ECJ rulings on the freedom of establishment in the context of EC company law developments

2.1 DEVELOPMENTS OF EC COMPANY LAW REGARDING COMPANIES GOVERNED BY THE LAWS OF MEMBER STATES: OVERVIEW

Like EC corporate tax law and, in general, all areas of EC law, EC company law has been developed, on the one hand, by the Community institutions' legislative action, on the other hand by the case law of the ECJ. Most of the EC legislation in the area has assumed the form of Directives, based on a provision contained in the Treaty's Chapter on the right of establishment (Article 44, second paragraph, let. (g)) which requires the EC institutions to coordinate to the necessary extent the safeguards required by Member States for the protection of companies' members and others, with a view to making such safeguards equivalent throughout the Community. The Directives issued for the purpose and aimed, ultimately, at facilitating the exercise by companies and firms governed by the law of any Member States of the right of establishment within the Community granted by Articles 43 and 48 of the Treaty, have affected several areas of national company laws. A First Directive, issued in 1968[1] and covering public limited companies, private limited companies and some limited partnership forms,[2] dealt with disclosure, validity of obligations entered into by a company and nullity of a company; a Second Directive issued in 1976[3] and covering public limited companies dealt with their formation and with the maintenance and alterations of their capital; a Third Directive in 1978,[4] covering public limited companies, regulated their mergers within a single Member State; a Fourth Directive issued in 1978,[5] covering public limited companies, private limited companies and general and limited partnerships when all their members with unlimited liability are limited liability companies, governed their annual accounts; a Sixth Directive issued in 1982[6], covering public limited companies, dealt with their divisions within one Member State; a Seventh Directive in 1983,[7] on consolidated accounts, covers the same categories of companies as the Fourth Directive; an Eighth Directive in 1984, replaced by a new Directive in 2006,[8] dealt with the qualifications of auditors of annual and consolidated accounts of the categories of companies included in the scope of the Fourth and of the Seventh Directives; an Eleventh Directive, in 1989,[9] set out the disclosure requirements in respect of branches opened in a Member State by public and private limited companies governed by the law of another state; a Twelfth Directive, also issued in 1989,[10] covered private limited companies and dealt with single member companies. Last, a Directive issued in 2004[11] deals with take-over bids for publicly traded securities of companies governed by the laws of Member States, and a Directive issued in 2005[12] governs cross-border mergers of limited liability companies. Together with these Directives, Regulations have been issued in 1985 to introduce a scheme intended to facilitate various forms of cooperation between companies of different Member States – the European Economic Interest Grouping[13] – and, in 2002–2003, to achieve transparency and comparability of financial reporting of publicly traded companies,[14] whereas 'soft-law' instruments such as Recommendations have dealt, from 2000 to 2005, with other aspects affecting the interests of third parties.[15] On the whole, the legislative effort by the Community has contributed to ensure legal certainty in core areas of company law within individual Member States: the ECJ, in rulings concerning mainly the interpretation of the First and Second Directives, has stated, in substance, that their purpose is clearly defined, that they must be interpreted strictly and their prescriptive provisions have direct effect, so that they can be relied upon by all potentially interested individuals (or companies) against Member States in case of improper (or lack/delay of) implementation.[16] However, the most important contribution to the realization of companies' free movement from one Member State to another, which is the key goal of the Treaty's Chapter on the right of establishment and, ultimately, of EC company law, has been offered by the ECJ's company law judgments on the application of Articles 43 and 48 EC. Three recent company law rulings – the 2002 *Uberseering* ruling,[17] the 2003 *Inspire Art* ruling[18] and the 2005 *SEVIC Systems* ruling[19] – together with the company law implications of tax rulings, are of crucial importance.

2.2 THE *UBERSEERING* RULING

The *Uberseering* ruling directly dealt with an issue, of fundamental importance for the business community, which had drawn the attention of legal commentators ever since the 1980s, when the ECJ began its case law on the freedom of secondary establishment[20] and of primary establishment:[21] whether or not the conflict of laws, existing within the EC as regards the connecting factor for identifying companies' nationality is to be considered as resolved by Articles 43, 48 and 293[22] of the Treaty on companies' right of establishment.

Whereas most Member States in continental Europe have been identifying companies' nationality on the basis of the 'real seat criteria', other Member States – the United Kingdom, Ireland, the Netherlands, Denmark, Finland and Sweden – had been following the 'incorporation' principle: a company is governed by the law of the state of its head office ('real seat') and must maintain this head office in the same state as the registered office, according to the real seat criteria; by contrast, it can transfer its head office to another state and it remains governed by the law of the state of the registered office, according to the incorporation principle.[23] If the only criteria accepted under EC law were the incorporation principle, companies formed in any Member State would be free not only to create agencies, branches and subsidiaries in other Member States (the 'right of secondary establishment') but also to transfer their head office to another Member State (the 'host State'), where they would be entitled to recognition while retaining the legal status as entities formed in accordance with the law of the state of incorporation (that is, to benefit from the 'freedom of primary establishment'). Nevertheless, in the light of the ECJ case law prior to *Uberseering*, which had dealt with only one case of primary establishment,[24] and with others of secondary establishment,[25] the extent to which the incorporation system was to be regarded as accepted was rather controversial.[26]

Against this background, in *Uberseering* the ECJ had to examine the situation of a company incorporated under Netherlands law, Uberseering BV, which, after the acquisition of all its shares by two German nationals, had sued for damages a German company (NCC), before the relevant German courts but had seen its action dismissed on the ground that it could not bring legal proceedings in Germany. The reasons underlying this position taken by the German courts were that: (a) due to the acquisition by German nationals, under German law Uberseering was deemed to have transferred its real seat to Germany; and (b) as a company incorporated under Netherlands law, it did not have in Germany legal capacity, defined as the capacity to enjoy rights and to be the subject of obligations, unless it reincorporated under German law (which at that time adopted the real seat criteria).[27] Consequently, the ECJ had to decide whether Articles 43 and 48 EC preclude a host Member State from denying the legal capacity of a company which had moved the real seat to its jurisdiction,[28] that is whether the conflict of laws between the real seat and the incorporation systems was resolved in favour of the latter: it provided a positive answer, by adopting the arguments which Uberseering's supporters[29] opposed to those of the German company sued by Uberseering and of the German, Spanish and Italian Governments.

In the previous ruling on the right of primary establishment, the 1987 *Daily Mail* ruling, dealing with the case of a company incorporated in the United Kingdom and wishing to move its head office to the Netherlands, the ECJ had considered companies as creatures of national law and had concluded, with general statements, that the Treaty's Articles on the right of establishment cannot be interpreted as conferring on companies incorporated under the law of a Member State a right to transfer their head office to another Member State while retaining their status under the legislation of the first Member State.[30] These conclusions, according to Uberseering's opponents, ought to be applied also to the relations between a company validly incorporated in one Member State and the host Member State, due to the general wording of the ECJ's statements in *Daily Mail,* to the lack of Directives regarding the transfer of a company's seat and to the absence of a Convention on the mutual recognition of companies pursuant to Article 293 EC. To the contrary, Uberseering's supporters basically submitted that *Daily Mail* was concerned with a different situation and that reference had to be made, to find a solution, to the 1999 *Centros* ruling:[31] here, the ECJ had held that the host Member State, without imposing its own substantive law, in particular the rules on share capital, must allow a company validly incorporated in another Member State, where it has its registered office, to register within its jurisdiction another establishment (in that case, a branch) from which this company may develop its entire business.[32] De facto, this enables the company to achieve the same outcome which would be secured by the transfer of the real seat to the host Member State, and the Commission submitted that the position must be the same where, as in *Uberseering*, the host Member State invoked the real seat criteria, which in that case would have entailed the refusal to recognize the company's legal capacity, unless Uberseering had decided to reincorporate under German law.

To reach its conclusions, the ECJ used three main arguments, each following on from the other. First, it found that the rules which a Member State applies to a company, which is incorporated in another Member State and which moves the head office to its jurisdiction, do not fall outside the scope of EC law, on the grounds that Article 293 EC, when calling for Member States to conclude a Convention on the mutual recognition of companies, did not reserve legislative competence to Member States, and that Articles 43 and 48 EC, which entitle companies to carry out their business in another Member State, have been directly applicable since the end of the transitional period. Secondly, the Court stated that the *Daily Mail* ruling, despite the general statements formulated there, only concerned the relations between a company and a Member State under whose law this company had been incorporated in a situation where the company wished to transfer its head office to another Member State while retaining its legal personality in the state of incorporation.[33] Thirdly, and as a consequence, the ECJ observed that Uberseering was entitled under Articles 43 and 48 EC to exercise its freedom of establishment in Germany given its existence as a company validly incorporated in the

Netherlands and having its registered office there.[34] Last, the ECJ rejected the German justification for the restriction on freedom of establishment caused by the application of the real seat criteria. In the German view, such restriction was in fact not discriminatory, because of the application of the real seat criteria both to foreign companies moving their head office to Germany and to German companies which transferred their head office abroad, and was also justified by overriding requirements relating to the general interest. Such requirements were identified by the German Government in the enhancement of legal certainty, and in the protection of creditors offered by the required minimum share capital for companies having the principal place of business in Germany, and in the protection of minority shareholders, of employees as well as of the taxation authorities.[35] Once again, the ECJ accepted the submissions of Uberseering's supporters, whereby the restriction in question was not justified, on the ground that, in particular, the aim of protecting creditors was also unsuccessfully invoked by the authorities concerned in *Centros* and it was not certain that requirements associated with a minimum amount of share capital were an effective way of protecting creditors.

Consequently, the ECJ concluded that the refusal by a host Member State to recognize the legal capacity of a company incorporated in another Member State and moving its head office to the host Member State constitutes a restriction on freedom of establishment which is, in principle, incompatible with Articles 43 and 48 EC.[36] In reaching this conclusion, the ECJ accepted that overriding requirements relating to the general interest, such as the protection of the interests of creditors, minority shareholders, employees and even the taxation authorities, may, in certain circumstances and subject to certain conditions, justify restrictions on freedom of establishment.[37] Nevertheless, it stated that these objectives cannot justify denying the legal capacity of the company involved, since such a measure, deriving from the application of the real seat criteria, is tantamount to an outright negation of the freedom of establishment conferred on companies by Articles 43 and 48 EC.[38]

Globally considered, the *Uberseering* ruling, as shown by the comparison with *Daily Mail*, did not affect the application of the real seat criteria by a state from which a company wishes to transfer its seat. It recognized the incorporation system as the general rule solely for the host Member States, which only by way of exception, in case of alleged overriding requirements of general interests, were left free to apply restrictions to the freedom of establishment. These restrictions, as well as their circumstances and conditions, were defined neither on their own nor in a general criteria to identify them: in fact, the ECJ stressed that creditors' protection was not in that case a proper ground for the restriction, but avoided examining whether other reasons indicated by the German Government, that is the protection of the interests of minority shareholders, of employees, of the taxation authorities and the claim that the restriction was proportionate to the objective pursued, might justify the restriction in the circumstances of that specific case. However, as regards the margins left to the host Member States, it could be noted that the overriding requirements mentioned by the ECJ, and justifying in certain circumstances and under certain conditions restrictions on freedom of establishment, were the same arguments put forward by the German Government to justify the application in Germany up to that time of the real seat criteria (which in turn, in that case, led to the denial of legal capacity), and on which that system had typically found its justification in the states adopting it. All this suggests that, in the ECJ's reasoning, the application of the real seat criteria by the host Member States may be justified, in exceptional circumstances, provided it does not deny legal capacity (as in *Uberseering*) but results in other restrictions on the freedom of establishment of companies involved. This interpretation is, indirectly, confirmed by the fact that the ECJ ignored a claim that the real seat criteria is being made obsolete by an international, computerized economy in which the physical presence of decision-makers becomes increasingly unnecessary,[39] and that, in the ECJ's conclusions, the same refusal of recognition of the legal capacity was defined first as a restriction then as a negation of the freedom of establishment. The ECJ ruling raised a further question in that respect: can a possible type of legitimate restriction acceptable in exceptional circumstances be identified?

In this connection, it can be noted that the object of the dispute was whether or not Uberseering's legal capacity – defined as the capacity to enjoy rights and be the subject of obligations – ought to be recognized in Germany but the ECJ, throughout the ruling, and in particular when comparing the situation in *Daily Mail* with that in *Uberseering*, used the terms 'legal capacity' and 'legal personality' interchangeably.[40] Nevertheless, there are Member States, including some of those traditionally following the real seat criteria, where the two concepts do not coincide, and where the equivalent to the English word 'company' also indicates partnerships,[41] which latter enjoy there legal capacity as defined in *Uberseering*. In such jurisdictions, the concept of legal personality refers to corporate entities and thus implies one more component (the limited liability of the members of a company) than the concept of legal capacity, so that the recognition of the legal personality of a company formed under the law of another Member State would necessarily imply the recognition of the legal capacity too, but the recognition, vice versa, of the legal capacity might not entail the recognition of the (foreign) legal personality.[42] In the light of this difference, if all parts of the ruling are read together the interchangeable use by the ECJ of the terms 'legal capacity' and 'legal personality' appears to indicate that the recognition of the legal capacity of a company without the legal personality, by a host Member State, is not allowed in principle,[43] despite some arguments to the contrary.[44] In fact, the

ECJ, in addition to considering the comparison with *Daily Mail* (in which a transfer with the retention of the legal personality was involved) to be noteworthy, stated that the issue was whether the freedom of establishment requires that a company's legal capacity is to be determined according to the law of the state where the company is incorporated[45] and, in the Netherlands, Uberseering had legal capacity as a corporate entity. It follows that the recognition of legal capacity alone may only be admissible, in exceptional circumstances, as a legitimate restriction to the freedom of establishment.

Ultimately, *Uberseering* can be regarded as the ruling which has made it possible, to corporate entities formed in a Member State, to benefit from the right to have their legal personality recognized in any other Member State if transferring the head office to the extent, in ultimate analysis, to which the national law of the Member State of formation enables them to make such a transfer. *Uberseering* thus marked a key step in making available to companies new expansion strategies throughout the EC. Suppose that a company is formed under the law of a Member State A which follows the incorporation system and which provides, by assumption, the most favourable company law. This company may decide either to establish from the outset or to move after its setting up (and by fulfilling the conditions, if any, required by Member State A) its head office to Member State B, offering, by assumption, the most favourable corporate taxation regime. Unless exceptional circumstances justified restrictions to its freedom of establishment, the company, after *Uberseering,* is deemed to be unconditionally recognized as a corporate entity in Member State B. Whenever, according to the DTC between Member State A and Member State B and to the law of Member State B, the presence within the jurisdiction of this latter state of the head office determines the fiscal residence of the company[46] and its being subject in Member State B to unlimited tax liability, such company can ultimately achieve the result of combining the choice of the most favourable company law with that of the most favourable taxation regime, that is the outcome of being openly allowed by EC law to add, in the formulation of its international tax planning strategies within the EC, the comparative analysis of company law provisions. On the other hand, *Uberseering*'s contribution to the tax competition among Member States may also turn out to be strong. The Member States traditionally adopting the incorporation system currently tend to be, within the EC, those characterized by a liberal company law and, at the same time, by the most favourable tax regimes in various respects:[47] for this reason, the greater the extent to which any host Member State which would prefer to adopt the real seat criteria will be forced by the ECJ's case law to recognize legal persons which for any reason move their head office to that state, the greater the incentive which such host state may have, to protect at least its revenue interest, to design a corporate tax regime capable of being even more competitive than that of the state of origin of these companies. This would be intended to induce companies incorporated abroad to establish their fiscal residence in the state's jurisdiction (which would increase the number of taxpayers) while continuing to be regulated, from the company law viewpoint, by the more favourable law of the state of formation.[48] The host state under consideration may add the 'company law dimension' to its tax competition strategies (that is may try to compensate for its 'company law disadvantage' as a location for businesses) in many different ways, as regards both the aspects and/or the combinations of the aspects of the companies' tax systems (all of which will have to be weighed by businesses in their cost-benefit analysis) to be reshaped to strengthen its overall competitive position.

2.3 THE ECJ'S FINDINGS IN *INSPIRE ART*

The ECJ's conclusions in *Uberseering,* and in the previous case law, in particular, in the *Centros* case, dealing with the freedom of secondary establishment, are fully consistent with those reached in the 2003 *Inspire Art* ruling.[49] The situation examined by the ECJ in this case was substantially the same as in the *Centros* case: a private limited company, formed under English law by a Dutch national, carried on from the outset all its business through a branch in Amsterdam. The Dutch legislation in question recognized this company and allowed the registration in the Netherlands of the branch through which the entire business was carried on. However, it considered this company as a 'formally foreign' one (FFC), and imposed on it obligations designed to prevent it from evading overriding rules of national company law. Amongst these obligations, some of which concern the implementation in domestic law of disclosure requirements laid down by the Eleventh EC Company Law Directive, there are requirements going beyond the disclosure requirements provided for by the Directive. Specifically, the company had to add to its registration in the commercial register the indication of its status as an FFC, which, in turn, would entail the obligations to record the date of first registration in the foreign business register and to satisfy the minimum capital requirements applicable under Dutch law at the time of its registration and during all the company's existence: the joint and several liability of directors and of persons actually conducting the company's activity was attached, as a penalty, to non-compliance with these obligations. The ECJ had thus to solve three issues: (a) whether the harmonization brought about by that Directive was exhaustive; (b) in the affirmative case, whether the obligations going beyond those contemplated by the Directive impeded the freedom of establishment; (c) in the case of a positive response to this second question, whether those measures were justified.

The interest of the ruling lies in the latitude recognized to the freedom of establishment and in its ultimate potential effects. In fact, after finding that the requirements indicated by the Eleventh Company Law Directive were exhaustive[50] and could not justify the further obligations imposed by Netherlands law, the ECJ concluded that the imposition on the FFC of certain conditions provided for in domestic company law in respect of company formation, relating to minimum capital and directors' liability, was in breach of Articles 43 and 48 EC.[51] In this regard, the ECJ rejected a key argument, put forward by the Netherlands Government and by other Governments supporting its view.[52] In addition to questioning whether, with regard to FFCs, branches ought not actually to be regarded as principal establishments, these Governments argued that the freedom of establishment was not infringed because Dutch law recognized foreign companies and did not refuse the registration of a branch, but merely set a few limited preventive measures, consisting of a number of additional obligations, because of the location of the actual activity of the company in the Netherlands. The Commission, the UK Government and the company involved, by relying on the formal classification of a branch as a secondary establishment adopted by the ECJ in *Centros*,[53] objected that the use of the actual activity of a company as a connecting factor in order to attach to it a number of additional rules mandatory in the host Member State did not correspond to any of the criteria indicated in Article 48 EC. Although those rules were justified by the Netherlands by invoking the protection of creditors and not the real seat system, the ECJ attached importance to their ultimate effect, which was that of impeding the exercise of the freedom of establishment of foreign companies wishing to carry on their activity (almost) exclusively through a branch in the Netherlands, and for this reason found that the obligations at issue constituted a restriction of the freedom of establishment, prohibited by Articles 43 and 48 EC.[54]

A first, crucial 'lesson' to be drawn by Member States from *Inspire Art* is thus the following: the latitude of freedom of establishment is such that it prohibits any provisions of the host Member State which, without mentioning the real seat system, generate the effect, similar to that deriving from the application of this system, of making its national rules (other than those deriving from the only requirements set out by the Eleventh Directive) applicable to an establishment (even if this constitutes a branch from a purely formal viewpoint) of a company validly incorporated in another Member State. A further indication can be drawn if reading *Inspire Art* together with *Uberseering*. Although the recognition of the legal capacity was not directly at stake in *Inspire Art,* the 'preventive measures' imposed by the Netherlands and regarded by the ECJ as in breach of the Treaty did substantially coincide with those requirements (concerning, in particular, the minimum capital) which *Uberseering* would have had to fulfil according to German law had it decided to reincorporate to obtain German legal personality. Moreover the sanctions of joint and several liability of directors and persons who actually conduct the company's activity for non-compliance with Netherlands legislation are also comparable to the effects of what would have been a recognition, in Germany, of Uberseering's legal capacity without its legal personality, because the joint and several liability of some or all members in any case contrasts with a foreign status, that of private limited company, which excludes such liability. Accordingly the interpretation of the *Uberseering* ruling, whereby the freedom of establishment requires, as a general rule, the recognition of both legal capacity and foreign legal personality[55] seems to be confirmed by the ECJ's first finding in *Inspire Art*.

Moreover, the Court considered the company's incorporation in another state and its carrying out of the activities solely in the Member State of establishment to be immaterial for the purposes of the right of establishment, save where the existence of an abuse is established on a case-by-case basis, in which case Member States are free to take measures to prevent it.[56] After stating that none of the justifications submitted by the Netherlands – the aims of protecting creditors, of combating improper recourse to freedom of establishment, of protecting both effective tax inspections and fairness in business dealings – fell within the ambit of different treatments allowed by the Treaty under Article 46 EC, the ECJ found that none of the four conditions laid down in its case law for restrictions imposed by national provisions to be accepted were fulfilled in the case of the Netherlands provisions.[57] The four conditions were non-discriminatory application, imperative requirements in the public interest, suitability to achieve the objective and proportionality. With regard to the protection of creditors, the ECJ considered as sufficient for this purpose the fact that the company involved held itself out as a company governed by English law, which gave creditors sufficient notice that it was governed by a legislation other than that of the Netherlands and offered them the protection of the Fourth and Eleventh Directives. As for the improper use of the right of establishment, the Court recalled its findings in *Centros,* whereby the fact that a company did not conduct any business in the Member State in which it had its registered office and pursued its activity only or principally in the Member State where the branch was established was not sufficient to prove an abuse. As regards the protection of fairness in business dealings and efficiency of tax inspections, it stated that no evidence had been produced to prove that the Netherlands provisions met the required efficacy, proportionality and non-discrimination criteria.

The second key lesson from *Inspire Art* is therefore that the existence of an abuse, as well as the suitability of measures to combat this, must always be proved by the interested Member States: this conclusion by the ECJ would seem thus to have given the most restrictive answer to the question, left open by *Uberseering*, concerning the certain circumstances in which restrictions to the freedom of establishment may be justified. Accordingly, this ruling could strengthen the incentive, already offered by *Uberseering*, for companies to combine the choice of the most favourable company law with that of the most favourable taxation regime, and for host Member States to compete with each other in designing the structural aspects of their corporate taxation regimes. Having to accept within their jurisdiction (the primary or the formally secondary establishments of) companies regulated by more liberal company laws than their national ones, these states may be induced to try to attract these companies through their tax legislation. It can be noted that the ECJ's conclusion in *Inspire Art,* whereby the abuse is to be proved on a case-by-case basis, is perfectly in line with that reached in the case law concerning tax restrictions to the freedom of establishment: wholly artificial arrangements designed to circumvent national tax legislation must also be proved.[58] Ultimately, the ECJ thus accepted that abusive forum shopping practices, whether in company law or in tax law, create a distortion in the EC market, but the inability of Member States to presume their existence will not discourage businesses from undertaking them.

In fact, although a typical forum shopping practice such as that at stake in the situations examined by the ECJ in *Segers*,[59] *Centros* and *Inspire Art* (the creation of a company in Member States offering the most favourable laws by nationals of other Member States wishing to exercise all the business activity through secondary establishments of the company in the latter states) cannot on its own, according to the ECJ's decisions, constitute evidence of abuse,[60] it can certainly be arranged, in the business world, for the unique, ultimate purpose of circumventing national provisions at the expense of other stakeholders. However difficult to prove, this outcome may well be reached and it would be, for the ECJ, abuse (and distortion).

Last, it was submitted that *Uberseering* and *Inspire Art* could also have, as a tax implication, that of bringing about the full realization of the freedom of establishment from the viewpoint of the state of origin, through the removal of restrictions such as 'exit taxes'.[61] The extent to which this may hold true for companies is particularly important after the ECJ *Lasteyrie du Saillant* tax ruling,[62] which may also generate a key company law implication.

2.4 A KEY COMPANY LAW IMPLICATION FROM A TAX RULING

In its 2004 *Lasteyrie du Saillant* ruling, concerning a French national transferring its tax residence to Belgium, the ECJ held that Article 43 EC precludes a Member State from taxing, in order to prevent a risk of tax avoidance, as yet unrealized increases in value where a taxpayer transfers his tax residence outside that state.[63] A typical 'exit tax' (the taxation of latent increases in value) was thus banned by the ECJ.

Although this ruling concerns natural persons, it can immediately be noted that Article 48 of the Treaty equates companies and firms governed by national laws of Member States with natural persons.[64] Consequently, whereas there can be no doubt that this ruling is deemed to apply to companies formed in Member States adopting the incorporation system,[65] the key question is whether it may also be considered applicable to companies formed in jurisdictions adopting the real seat criteria. As these companies could be unable to benefit from the removal of exit taxes on the transfer of their head office to another Member State as long as the state of origin does not allow them to operate the transfer, the positive response would imply, from the company law viewpoint, that the real seat criteria should be definitively given up by the state of origin.

In other words, *Lasteyrie du Saillant* may have two interpretations. The first would be that it can only apply to companies formed in countries adopting the incorporation theory, because the ECJ in *Uberseering* has reconciled its finding[66] with its previous statement in *Daily Mail* that companies are creatures of national law. In this case, the adoption of the incorporation system only from the viewpoint of the state of destination in *Uberseering* and *Inspire Art* would limit the scope of *Lasteyrie du Saillant*. The second interpretation[67] would be that this ruling goes further than *Uberseering* and *Inspire Art*, that is that it completes such ECJ judgments by imposing the adoption of the incorporation theory from the perspective of every state of origin, at least where no abuse motivating the transfer of the head office to another Member State can be proved. This reading seems more acceptable, on the following grounds: (a) Article 48 EC, which does not distinguish according to the Member States of formation of companies; (b) the ECJ reference, in *Lasteyrie du Saillant*, to 'a taxpayer', without distinction between individual and corporate taxpayers; (c) the possibility of interpreting the *Daily Mail* finding that companies are creatures of national law as meaning that, once created by national laws, their existence cannot be subject to obstacles incompatible with EC law; (d) the realization that the first interpretation would lead to a striking difference of treatment between companies within the Community: companies formed in Member States adopting the incorporation theory would not only be able to move their head office to other Member States but would enjoy the additional advantage of doing so without exit taxes; companies formed in other Member States would still remain unable to make the transfer and to benefit from the lack of exit taxation.[68]

Arguments for this second interpretation of *Lasteyrie du Saillant* can also be drawn from the 2005 *SEVIC Systems*[69] company law ruling.

2.5 AND A COMPANY LAW RULING WITH TAX IMPLICATIONS

In *SEVIC Systems*, concerning the compatibility of the refusal of registration of a cross-border merger in the national commercial register with Articles 43 and 48 EC, the ECJ dealt with the substantive contents of freedom of establishment and the methods of exercising it, and it reached a conclusion with potentially far-reaching implications from the viewpoint of both company law and company taxation.

A German public limited company, SEVIC Systems, who had concluded a contract for a merger by acquisition of a Luxembourg-based public limited company, was refused registration of this operation in the national commercial register in Germany on the ground that the relevant German provisions, contained in a Law on company transformations, only governed mergers between companies established in Germany. The merger contract between SEVIC and the Luxembourg-based company provided for the dissolution without liquidation of this second company and the transfer of the whole of its assets to SEVIC, without any change in the latter's company name. This type of merger, had it taken place between companies based in Germany, would have been regarded as a way of transforming companies, expressly allowed by the German Law on company transformation and governed by detailed provisions concerning the procedure, the effects of registration and the protection of third parties, particularly creditors.

Interestingly, in its preliminary observations the ECJ assumed also the standpoint of the Luxembourg company. In fact, it stated that the issue to be resolved was whether Articles 43 and 48 EC preclude, in a Member State, a refusal of registration in the national commercial register of the type of merger under consideration where one of the two companies is established in another Member State.[70] With this premise, the ECJ found, first, that Articles 43 and 48 EC cover all measures which permit or even merely facilitate access to another Member State by participating 'in the economic life of the country effectively and under the same conditions as national operators',[71] and that cross-border mergers, like other company transformation operations, 'constitute particular methods of exercise of the freedom of establishment, important for the proper functioning of the internal market.'[72] In assessing whether German law, due to the lack of provisions for registration of cross-border mergers, created a restriction, the ECJ analysed the economic advantages of a merger, such as that implemented by SEVIC, making it possible, within the framework of a single operation, to pursue a particular activity in new forms and without interruptions.[73] On those grounds, the ECJ stated that, in so far as recourse to such a means of company transformation was not possible where one of the companies was based in a Member State other than Germany, the difference in treatment between companies according to the internal or cross-border nature of the merger is likely to deter the exercise of the freedom of establishment and thus creates a restriction of this freedom.[74] In its conclusive findings, the ECJ ruled that the possible justifications of a restrictive measure – a legitimate objective compatible with the Treaty, imperative reasons in the public interest, proportionality with the objectives to be pursued – did not apply to this restriction. In contrast to the German and the Netherlands Governments' submissions that cross-border mergers presuppose a harmonization of the legislation relating to these operations, the ECJ stated that, whilst Community harmonization rules are useful for facilitating cross-border mergers, such rules could not be made a precondition for the implementation of the freedom of establishment. It recognized that cross-border mergers pose specific problems and, in that respect, it held again, as in *Uberseering*, that imperative reasons in the public interest relating to the protection of third parties may, under certain circumstances and under certain conditions, justify a measure restricting the freedom of establishment. The protection of interests of creditors, of minority shareholders and of employees, the effectiveness of fiscal supervision and the fairness of commercial transactions, which were indicated by the German and by the Dutch Governments as justifications for the refusal of registration of cross-border mergers, were admitted by the ECJ as imperative reasons in the public interest. Nevertheless, a general refusal of registration of cross-border mergers, which would prevent such mergers even when these interests were not threatened, was found to go, in any event, beyond what was necessary to protect them (and thus was found to fail the proportionality test).[75]

Given the reasoning of the ECJ, the ruling has several company law implications. First, the classification of cross-border mergers and of other company transformation operations as particular methods for exercising the freedom of establishment, and the assessment of the effectiveness of a cross-border merger operation for this purpose, seem to express a general principle. The ECJ, in referring to company transformation operations, moved from the German provisions applicable to internal operations, according to which legal entities can be transformed, in addition to the change of legal form, by merger, by demerger (that is by division) and by transfer of assets: thus, as a general principle each of the corresponding types of cross-border operations, as a particular method of exercise of the freedom of establishment, can be implemented by companies irrespective of whether or not national provisions of the Member State(s) involved regulate these cases, provided the structure of the operations is such as to enable the interested parties to pursue a particular activity in new forms and without interruptions (as stated by the ECJ). In fact, the case of interruptions of the activity and liquidations would fall outside the scope of the freedom of establishment, to the extent that a company would cease to exist and could thus not exercise this freedom. When this is not the case, the possibility for companies to implement cross-border mergers, divisions and transfers of assets irrespective of the presence of national provisions governing these operations applies both to the state of 'destination' and to the state 'of origin': in *SEVIC Systems*, Germany would have been the state of destination for the Luxembourg-based company, whose assets, including any of those located in Luxembourg, were to be transferred to the German acquiring company, and the state of origin for the German (receiving) company, who, by means of the operations, would have been able to acquire a branch in Luxembourg (including any assets of the acquired company located there). Member States would need to accept these cross-border restructuring operations under their own rules applying, in the same types of domestic operations, to transferring companies (in the case of the state of origin) and to the receiving companies (in the case of the state of destination). Secondly, the circumstance that EC company law harmonization measures can only serve to facilitate these operations implies that, although the 2005 Directive on cross-border mergers of limited liability companies[76] only covers one type of operation, all other types of intra-EC operations falling outside the scope of this new Directive on cross-border mergers are also legally possible. In this respect, companies interested in implementing cross-border operations governed neither by the domestic provisions dealing with the corresponding types of internal operations nor by EC harmonization measures would need to design such operations in such a way as to indicate that the interests of all third parties are being considered and safeguarded, in order not to fall within the certain circumstances and the certain conditions under which restrictive measures could be enacted by Member States. For this purpose, an effective way to demonstrate that the interests of third parties are all spontaneously safeguarded by the companies concerned, in structuring the operations, could lie in the spontaneous fulfilment of all procedural requirements laid down for the corresponding types of domestic operations, and other strategies such as, for example, the payment of creditors, the notice to and consultation of employees or the clearance of any pending tax liability. Thirdly, although in the *SEVIC Systems* ruling the acquiring and the acquired companies were both public limited companies, the fact that all such cross-border operations are considered as methods of exercising the freedom of establishment implies that they can also be implemented by all other types of entities (partnerships and so on) that are not covered in the 2005 Directive but are implicitly included in Article 48 EC amongst the beneficiaries of this freedom.

These company law outcomes inevitably have tax consequences. In fact, some Member States,[77] which did not provide for cross-border merger and divisions operations in their national laws, avoided implementing that part of Directive 434/90/EC dealing with the tax relief for cross-border mergers and divisions, on the ground of the lack of EC company law provisions making these operations possible. After *SEVIC Systems*, no Member State could any longer be able to invoke this justification, at least when companies structure the operations in such a way as to show that all third parties' interests are safeguarded: the fact that EC secondary legislation provisions may only serve to facilitate these operations (and are not a condition for making them legally possible) makes it possible to deduce that a cross-border restructuring operation, which is not (yet) facilitated from the company law viewpoint by a Community harmonization Directive, cannot certainly, for this reason, be hampered by the refusal to grant a tax relief provided for by a Community corporate tax harmonization Directive.

Furthermore, the ECJ's reasoning in the *SEVIC Systems* ruling, if read together with the tax rulings in *Lasteyrie du Saillant*[78] and in *Marks & Spencer*,[79] can provide companies formed in any Member State with important arguments when designing their strategies for cross-border expansion and restructuring throughout the Community. The fact that cross-border restructuring operations which do not result in the liquidation of the acquired company constitute a method of exercise of the freedom of establishment of this company strengthens the interpretation of the *Lasteyrie du Saillant* ruling according to which the application of the 'real seat' criteria is to be abandoned also by the Member State of origin, except for the case of exceptional circumstances. In fact, a company A formed in Member State A, which is absorbed through a restructuring operation by a company B resident in Member State B, can no longer be regarded as having its real seat (primary establishment) in Member State A, which latter cannot, in principle, oppose the operation. Moreover the absorption of company A would imply that those tax losses incurred by this latter in the accounting year of the operation have no possibility of being taken into account in Member State A because of the operation itself, and, according to the *Marks & Spencer* ruling, can thus be off-set by company B in Member State B.

Ultimately, to the extent that it may be seen as complementing *Uberseering* and *Inspire Art*, by strengthening the interpretation of *Lasteyrie du Saillant* according to which the real seat criteria must also in principle be given up by the state of origin, and as suggesting to companies a strategy for benefiting from the *Marks & Spencer* tax ruling, *SEVIC Systems* could certainly strengthen the incentive for national legislators to compete with each other to encourage the creation and the maintaining of the tax residence of companies within their jurisdictions.

NOTES

1. Directive 68/151/EEC of 9 March 1968, OJEC L65/8 [1968].
2. The limited partnership forms, such as the French *sociétés en commandite par actions*, the German *Kommanditgesellschaft auf Aktien* or the Italian *società in accomandita per azioni*, included in the scope of the First Directive are generally regarded as belonging to the same category of limited liability companies.
3. Directive 77/91/EEC of 13 December 1976, OJEC L26/1 [1977].
4. Directive 78/855/EEC of 9 October 1978, OJEC L295/36 [1978].
5. Directive 78/660/ EEC of 25 July 1978, OJEC L222/11 [1978], as subsequently amended. See note 2 as regards the limited partnership forms included.
6. Directive 82/891/EEC of 17 December 1982, OJEC L378/47 [1982].
7. Directive 83/349/EEC of 13 June 1983, OJEC L193/1 [1983], as subsequently amended.
8. Directive 84/253/EEC of 10 April 1984, OJEC L126/20 [1984], replaced by Directive 2006/43/EC on statutory audits of annual accounts and consolidated accounts of 17 May 2006 in OJEC L157/87 [2006].
9. Directive 89/666/EEC of 21 December 1989, OJEC L395/96 [1989].
10. Directive 89/667/EEC of 21 December 1989, OJEC L395/40 [1989].
11. Directive 2004/25 EC of 21 April 2004 on take-over bids, OJEC L142/12 [2004].
12. Directive 2005/56/EC of 26 October 2005 on cross-border mergers of limited liability companies, OJEC L310/1 [2005].
13. Regulation 2137/85/EEC of 25 July 1985 on the European Economic Interest Grouping (EEIG), OJEC L199/1 [1985].
14. Regulation 1606/2002 of 19 July 2002 on the application of international accounting standards, OJEC L243/1 [2002]. In accordance with this Regulation, the Commission has adopted certain international accounting standards by means of Regulation 1725/2003 of 29 September 2003, OJEC L261/1 [2003] and other subsequent amending Regulations.
15. Commission Recommendation of 15 November 2000 on quality assurance for the statutory audit in the EU: minimum requirements, OJEC L91/91 [2001]; Commission Recommendation of 30 May 2001 on the recognition, measurement and disclosure of environmental issues in the annual accounts and annual reports of companies, OJEC L156/33 [2001]; Commission Recommendation of 16 May 2002 on statutory audit independence in the EU: a set of fundamental principles, OJEC L191/22 [2002]; Commission Recommendation of 15 February 2005 on the role of non-executive or supervisory directors of listed companies and on the committees of (supervisory) boards, OJEC L52/51 [2005].
16. See inter alia Case C-106/89 *Marleasing* [1990] ECR I-4135, paras 9 to 13; Joined Cases C-19 and C-90, *Karella* [1991] ECR I-2691, paras 16 to 36; Case C-381/89, *Syndesmos* [1992] ECR I-2111, paras 25 to 43; Case C-97/96, *Daihatsu Deutschland* [1997] ECR I-6834, paras 22 and 23; Joined Cases C-387/02, 391/02 and C-403/02, *Berlusconi and others* [2005] ECR I-3565, paras 56 to 65. In the literature, see inter alia Tridimas, T. (1994), 'The case-law of the European Court of Justice on corporate entities', *Yearbook of European Law*, (13), 347–360. Because this case law does not directly concern restrictions imposed on companies created in one Member State and wishing to exercise their freedom of establishment in another, and it has not changed the conclusions reached by the literature on the limits of the company law harmonization programme, which derive from the underlying legislative choices (see below 3.1), it will not be dealt with in this work.
17. Case C-208/00, *Uberseering* [2002] ECR I-9919. On the *Uberseering* ruling, in the literature, see inter alia, Baelz, K. and T. Baldwin (2002), 'The end of the seat theory (*Sitztheorie*): the European Court of Justice decision in Üeberseering of 5 November 2002 and its impact on German and European company law', *German Law Journal*, 12 (3), www.germanlawjournal.com, 1 December; Wooldridge, F. (2003), 'Uberseering: freedom of establishment of companies affirmed', *European Business Law Review,* 3 (14), 227–235; Cerioni, L. (2003), 'The *Uberseering* ruling: the eve of a "revolution" for the possibilities of companies' migration throughout the European Community?', *Columbia Journal of European Law*, 1 (10), 117–137.

18. Case C-167/01, *Inspire Art* [2003] ECR I-10155.
19. Case C-411/03, *SEVIC Systems*, OJEC C289/13 [2003], ruling delivered on 13 December 2005 (not yet reported), OJEC C36/5 [2006].
20. In addition to the tax case law, which started with the *Avoir fiscal* case (Case C-270/83 [1986] ECR 273: above 1.4.2.a), the ECJ case law on the freedom of establishment also included company law rulings on the right of secondary establishment: Case 79/1985, *Segers* [1986] ECR 2375; Case C-212/1997 *Centros* [1999] ECR I-1459.
21. Case 81/1987, *Daily Mail* [1988] ECR 5483.
22. Article 293 of the Treaty, referred to below, states that Member States will enter negotiations with a view to ensure, so far as necessary, the mutual recognition of companies and the retention of legal personality in the event of transfer of their seat from one country to another.
23. The issue of the conflict of laws between the real seat and the incorporation theory has been widely discussed in the literature: see, inter alia, Cath, I.G.F. (1986), 'Freedom of establishment of companies: a new step towards completing the internal market', *Yearbook of European Law*, 247–261; Frommel, S.N. (1988), 'EEC companies and migration: a setback for Europe?', *Intertax*, 409–414; Loussouarn, Y. (1990), 'Le droit d'etablissement des societés', *Revue trimestrelle de droit europeen*, 227–239; Reindl, A. (1990), 'Companies in the European Community: are the conflict of law rules ready for 1992?', *Michigan Journal of International Law*, 1270–1293.
24. *Daily Mail*, note 21.
25. *Segers* and *Centros*, note 20.
26. See, inter alia: Tridimas, T. (1994), 'The case-law of the European Court of Justice on corporate entities', *Yearbook of European Law*, (13), 336–360; Cerioni, L. (1999), 'The barriers to the international mobility of companies within the European Community: a re-reading of the case-law', *Journal of Business Law*, 59–79; Roussos, A. (2001), 'Realising the free movement of companies', *European Business Law Review*, 1 (12), 7–25; Merkt, H. (2001), 'Centros and its consequences for Member State legislatures', *International and Comparative Corporate Law Journal*, 1 (3), 119–147; Cerioni, L. (2000), 'A possible turning point in the development of EC company law: the Centros case', *International and Comparative Corporate Law Journal*, 2 (2), 165–195; Xanthaki, H. (2001), 'Centros: is this really the end for the theory of the siege reél?', *Company Lawyer*, 21, 2–8.
27. For the description of the facts, see *Uberseering*, note 17, paras 6 to 9 of the ruling.
28. See ibid. para. 22 of the ruling.
29. The Commission, the Netherlands Government, the UK Government and the EFTA Surveillance Authority.
30. See *Daily Mail*, note 21, para. 24 of the ruling.
31. On the ground that the dispute in *Centros* concerned, as in the *Uberseering* case, the treatment in the host Member State of a company incorporated under the law of another Member State: *Centros*, note 20. The different parties' arguments have been described in more depth in Cerioni, note 17.
32. See *Centros*, note 20, para. 39 of the ruling.
33. See *Daily Mail*, note 21, para. 70 of the ruling.
34. See *Uberseering*, note 17, paras 80 and 81 of the ruling.
35. See ibid. paras 87 to 90 of the ruling, where the ECJ recalled one by one these justifications submitted by Germany.
36. See ibid. para. 82 of the ruling.
37. See ibid. para. 92 of the ruling.
38. See ibid. para. 93 of the ruling.
39. Put forward by the EFTA Surveillance Authority: see ibid. para. 51 of the ruling.
40. See ibid. paras 3 and 61 to 70 of the ruling.
41. This is the case, for example, in Germany and Italy.
42. In the text, the word company is used as synonymous of both entities with and without legal personality, to maintain the coherence with the legal terminology of the country (Germany) in which this case arose.

43. For a different interpretation, see Mock S. (2002), 'Harmonization, regulation and legislative competition in European corporate law', *German Law Journal*, 12 (3), www.germanlawjournal.com/ 1 December.
44. These might be: the formulation of Article 293 EC, where legal personality and the mutual recognition of companies are mentioned as separate goals, although the latter would be implicit, by definition, in the former if legal personality were intended in the sense of corporate personality; the ECJ's statement that it is not necessary for the Member States to adopt a convention on the mutual recognition of companies in order for companies indicated by Article 48 EC to enjoy the freedom of establishment (*Uberseering*, note 17, para. 60 of the ruling); the inclusion in Article 48, second paragraph, for the purpose of the freedom of establishment, of all profit-making entities (with or without legal personality).
45. See *Uberseering*, note 17, para. 21 of the ruling.
46. Which is the normal case, because the almost universally-adopted OECD Model for DTCs states that, in this situation, a company is resident 'only of the State in which its place of effective management is situated' (Article 4) and the head office, that is the central administration, can reasonably be supposed to coincide with the place of effective management.
47. This is, in particular, the case of Cyprus (with its 10 per cent corporation tax rate), of Ireland (12.5 per cent corporation tax rate) and of the United Kingdom.
48. Germany, which drastically reduced in 2000 the corporate income tax from one of the highest – 40 per cent – to one of the lowest – 25 per cent – levels within the EC, offers a striking example of a Member State characterized by stricter company law provisions than others, and trying to gain a competitive position as a business location through changes in the companies' taxation regime.
49. *Inspire Art*, note 18. In the literature, see, inter alia, Rebberg, M. (2004), '*Inspire Art*: freedom of establishment for companies in Europe between "abuse" and national regulatory concerns', *European Legal Forum*, 1 (4), 1–8; and Deininger, R. (2004), 'Case comment: impact of the ECJ *Inspire Art* decision', *The European Legal Forum* 1 (4), 17–19.
50. See *Inspire Art*, note 18, paras 65 to 71 of the ruling. This interpretation of the Eleventh Company Law Directive is consistent with the case law on the interpretation of the company law Directives, in particular of the First and the Second Directive: see note 16.
51. See *Inspire Art*, note 18, para. 143 of the ruling.
52. The German, the Austrian and the Italian Governments.
53. See *Centros*, note 20, paras 21 to 29 of the ruling.
54. See *Inspire Art*, note 18, paras 100, 101 and 105 of the ruling.
55. As regards the distinction between legal capacity and legal personality in some jurisdictions, see above 2.2.
56. See *Inspire Art*, note 18, paras 95 to 105 and 143 of the ruling. Member States' right to take appropriate measures to combat abuse had already been recognized in previous rulings: see *Segers*, note 20, para. 17 of the ruling and *Centros*, note 20, para. 26 of the ruling.
57. See *Inspire Art*, note 18, paras 131 to 142 of the ruling.
58. See above 1.4.2.b. Assume that a Member State A has the most liberal company law but a less favourable tax system than another Member State B, which may have stricter company law provisions but may create a more favourable tax regime. If a company established in Member State A decided either to move the primary establishment or to create, as in *Centros* and *Inspire Art*, a formally secondary establishment in Member State B, neither of the two Member States would thus be allowed to assume, from the sole circumstance of the establishment in Member State B, that the company wanted to circumvent the national tax legislation (in the case of Member State A) or the national company law provisions (in the case of Member State B).
59. See *Segers*, note 20.
60. See *Inspire Art*, note 18, para. 96; *Segers*, note 20, para. 16; *Centros*, note 20, para. 18.
61. Commission Communication, 'An internal market without company tax obstacles: achievements, ongoing initiatives and remaining challenges' (COM (2003) 726 final), at p. 8.
62. Case C-9/02, *Lasteyrie du Saillant* [2004] ECR I-2409.

63. The national provisions in question established the principle that, on the date on which a taxpayer transfers his tax residence outside France, tax is to be charged on increases in value of company securities; such increase was determined by the difference between the value of those securities at the date of that transfer and their acquisition price.
64. See Article 48, first paragraph EC.
65. Which are allowed by their national legislations to transfer the head office while retaining their legal status: the application of *Lasteyrie du Saillant* is obvious, as their situation in the event of transfer of the head office to another EC country turns out to be entirely comparable to that of the French national wishing to migrate to another Member State (without changing his nationality because of the migration).
66. By requiring, as a rule, the application of the incorporation theory by the state of destination: see above 2.2.
67. Taken for granted by some German academic commentators: Deininger, note 48, p. 18.
68. Which would increase the difference of treatment in the state of formation, left by *Daily Mail* and *Uberseering*.
69. Case C-411/03, *SEVIC Systems*, OJEC C289/13 [2003], ruling delivered on 13 December 2005 (not yet reported), OJEC C36/5 [2006].
70. See ibid. para. 15 of the ruling.
71. See ibid. para. 18 of the ruling.
72. See ibid. para. 19 of the ruling.
73. See ibid. para. 21 of the ruling.
74. See ibid. paras 22 and 23 of the ruling.
75. See ibid. paras 24 to 31 of the ruling.
76. Referred to above 2.1.
77. Belgium, Germany and the United Kingdom: see above 1.1.6.
78. See above 2.4.
79. On *Marks & Spencer,* see above 1.4.2.c.

3. From the limits of the EC company law harmonization programme to the 'limited supranationality' in the SE

Along with the Directives aimed at approximating national company laws, the Community's legislative effort in this area has resulted in the European legal forms recently introduced, the SE and the SCE. This chapter will, however, demonstrate with particular regard to the SE (the main legal instrument) that, from the company law viewpoint, they evidence strong limitations in respect of their objectives, which, together with some envisaged developments, have far-reaching implications on the legal competition between Member States.

3.1 REVIEW OF THE RESULTS OF THE COMPANY LAW HARMONIZATION PROGRAMME AND ENVISAGED DEVELOPMENTS

The literature identified two substantial limits in the company law harmonization programme consisting of the Directives introduced from 1968 to 1989:[1] (a) the differences which the programme has allowed to remain between the company laws of Member States are significant; (b) the range of companies affected, which has been influenced by compromise and by the choices granted to Member States, turns out to be narrow in relation to the economic reality of businesses within the EC. A key reason lies behind both limits: the existence as between Member States of deep-rooted differences about the conception of the role of company law, which has caused the Directives to be fitted into existing structures rather than to induce fundamental structural changes in national legal systems.[2] The first limit has resulted, with regard to the first two Directives, characterized by an apparently prescriptive nature, from the fact that Member States used the derogations allowed by the Directives, interpreted the Directives' provisions and their objectives in different ways and some Member States 'entered the Community later, therefore having a different response to those Directives',[3] whereas the other Directives (such as the Fourth and the Seventh Directives, moving towards flexibility and allowing many more options to Member States) have led to the accommodation of Member States' differences rather than to harmonization.[4] The EC institutions have shown an awareness of this limit of the harmonization programme, at least as far as the 'second generation' Directives (such as the Fourth and the Seventh Company Law Directives, on annual and consolidated accounts) are concerned. In fact, Regulation 1606/2002 on the application of international accounting standards (IAS/IFRS) expressly recognizes that the reporting requirements set out in the Fourth and Seventh Directives (a striking example of the movement in the harmonization programme toward flexibility) 'cannot ensure the high level of transparency and comparability of financial reporting' and sets itself the objective of ensuring 'a high degree of transparency and comparability of [all] financial statements and hence an efficient functioning of the Community capital market and of the Internal Market'.[5] This Regulation, however, does not overcome the limitations of the two Directives at issue and it does not appear capable of achieving its objective: in fact, it governs only consolidated accounts of publicly traded companies, whereas it leaves Member States the choice whether to permit or require the preparation, according to IAS/IFRS, of the annual accounts, which are the only financial statements for publicly traded companies having no subsidiaries. Moreover, publicly traded companies, despite their importance, represent only a minority of all companies operating in the EC internal market, where more than 90 per cent of businesses within the EC are SMEs having fewer than ten employees and usually choose the legal forms of either private limited liability company or partnership.[6] Consequently, this Regulation also mirrors the second limit which, to date, the literature has noted in the harmonization programme in terms of restriction of the scope of the harmonization Directives.

In this context, the Commission published, in 2003, an Action Plan on Company Law and Corporate Governance in the EU (APCLCG), which clearly identifies the objectives of the EC company law policy in the strengthening of shareholders' rights, of third party protection and in the efficiency and competitiveness of EC businesses, and indicated several initiatives regarding corporate governance and companies' formation, financial disclosure obligations and restructuring.[7] Whereas in the subarea of corporate governance these initiatives, in the form of new Directives, would enhance disclosure requirements, facilitate an effective involvement of all shareholders in companies' decision-making process, strengthen the responsibility of board members and allow all listed companies the choice between a monistic or a dualistic type of board structure, in the other mainstream areas of company law they would introduce, together with new obligations, new possibilities for companies and new margins for national laws. Specifically, the company law initiatives have currently led to the adoption of the 2005 Directive on cross-border merger of limited liability companies and of the 2006 Directive on statutory audits of annual and consolidated accounts, tightening the standards on independent external auditing in terms of ethics, public oversight and rotation.[8] Moreover, they have resulted in proposals for other Directives, which would: (a) simplify the Second Company Law Directive, by making it easier for public limited companies to take procedural steps that affect the structure, size and ownership of their capital; (b) strengthen shareholders' rights, by removing barriers to shareholders' involvement in listed companies; (c) amend the Fourth and the Seventh Directives, by strengthening directors' responsibilities for financial and non-financial information, in particular in all listed companies which would have to provide a corporate governance statement in an annual report; (d) allow the transfer of the registered office as a form of restructuring, by means of a Fourteenth Directive, and possibly, in the medium term, simplify the Third and the Sixth Company Law Directive on internal mergers and divisions of public limited companies. The proposed revision of the Fourth and Seventh Directives, and the simplification of the Second Directive, have been approved by the European Parliament (EP) and are awaiting formal adoption.[9]

Neither the latest adopted Directives nor the new initiatives would overcome the limits of the company law harmonization programme. The 2004 Directive on take-over bids, despite its purpose of coordinating Member States' legislation and practices relating to takeover bids for securities traded on a regulated market, leaves some of the most important aspects of corporate control take-over as options for Member States, and the EC Commissioner on the Internal Market admitted that its text would be bound to be unable to create a level playing field for corporate control acquisitions within the Community.[10] The 2005 Directive on cross-border mergers of limited liability companies (which, for private limited companies, is the only EC legislative measure dealing with mergers) is expressly based on the principle that, save as otherwise provided, a company taking part in a cross-border merger remains subject to the provisions and formalities of the national law which would be applicable in the case of a domestic merger.[11] Although it was supposed to facilitate cross-border merger operations, this choice inevitably leaves space, in the event of transnational mergers involving private limited companies (which have not been affected by the Third Directive on internal mergers), to the possibility of considerable differences in the necessary fulfilments from one Member State to another.

In turn, the new initiatives, to the extent that they are deemed to impact mainly on larger companies, would leave a margin for considerable differences between the Member States particularly as regards the regulatory framework on SMEs, and thus for the greatest majority of EC businesses; even the proposed amendments to the Fourth and to the Seventh Directives would allow Member States to exempt SMEs from certain disclosure requirements. Amongst the new intended measures, the suggested Fourteenth Directive on the transfer of the registered office from one Member State to another with the change of applicable law, considered a restructuring operation, would facilitate the freedom of companies to move within the EC to the Member State whose domestic legislation best suits their particular needs. A company incorporated, say, in Germany could thus move its registered office to the United Kingdom or to Ireland by changing its legal form from that of a 'GmbH' (German private limited company form) to that of a 'Ltd' (a situation which could be compared with that of a natural person wishing to transfer to another Member State and to change his nationality). The survival of significant differences between national company laws such as to motivate this type of intra-EC migration, despite the 'harmonization' programme, becomes thus a precondition for this proposed Directive.

Globally considered, the company law harmonization programme carried out to date and the next envisaged developments are sufficiently evidence, therefore, that a limited contribution has been offered to the achievement of the ambitious goal of creating a similar regulatory environment and thus a level playing field within the EC for all companies which can enjoy the right of establishment under the Treaty.

3.2 MAIN EC LAW 'SUPRANATIONAL' INSTRUMENT: THE SE

After over 30 years of discussions, during which the project of introduction of a European form of public limited company (SE) had switched from the original idea (1970) of a self-sufficient regulation deemed to govern all aspects of the SE to a much less ambitious version (1989–1991) composed of a draft Regulation leaving large space to national laws and of a draft Directive on the participation of employees in the management of the company, the SE was finally introduced on 8 October 2001 by Regulation 2157/2001 concerning the European Company Statute (ECS) and by Directive 2001/86/EC on employee involvement, completing the Statute.[12] The ECS, in force since 8 October 2004, has three basic objectives, connected to each other and clearly stated in the Preamble to the Regulation: (1) to make possible, through restructuring and reorganization on a Community scale, the formation of 'companies with a European dimension, free from the obstacles arising from the disparities and the limited territorial application of national company law'; (2) to release companies governed by different legal systems from the obligation to choose a form of company governed by a particular national law; (3) as a result, to 'ensure as far as possible that the economic and legal unit of business in

Europe coincide'.[13] Nonetheless, the enthusiastic expectations of the Commission, in the aftermath of the approval of the ECS, about the impact of the SE form in facilitating businesses' restructuring and reorganization operations on a Community-wide scale[14] have so far been disappointed. In addition to a delay by most Member States in the introduction of the necessary implementing laws, by May 2006 only some 40 companies throughout the Community territory had adopted the SE form or planned to do so, and few others expressed an interest.[15] This limited appeal in the business community frustrates the objectives of the SE vehicle, which are important for the proper functioning of the internal market and for the global competitiveness of the EC economy. The current situation therefore makes it essential to identify the areas of the ECS where, in view of these objectives, the Commission might, under Article 69 of the Regulation, propose improvements after five years of application of the current ECS, that is after October 2009. These areas will coincide with those aspects where the 'supranational' character in the current version of the ECS can mostly be called into question and where interpretative uncertainties may arise: in fact, businesses wishing to expand and restructure within the Community would certainly be interested in the reduction of administrative and legal costs that could be made possible by a (supranational) set of rules as much unrelated as possible, without interpretative uncertainties, from national laws. In the identification of the possible areas of improvement, the criticism that the academic literature, prior to the approval of the current version, had addressed to the 1989–1991 draft needs to be reconsidered. That draft had in fact been seen as an illustration of the difficulties encountered by the company law harmonization programme and as the possible source of a legal vehicle whose supranationality (and practical utility for businesses) could be called into question, owing to the great number of options open to Member States and to the gaps left by the (then) draft Regulation in crucial areas to be filled by national laws and capable of resulting, for this reason, in many different national types of SE rather than in a truly supranational legal instrument.[16] Accordingly, a comparison between the ECS currently in force and the previous 1991 draft[17] can identify the aspects where the current ECS fails to overcome the limits already pointed out by the academic literature. These aspects can be found in the general provisions of the Regulation, in the Directive on employee involvement and in the Regulation provisions on the formation and working of the SE, which together have been affecting the outcome of Member States' choices in the implementation process.[18]

3.2.1 The Regulation's General Provisions: A Real Attempt to Recover Supranationality?

Unlike the revised 1991 text, whose legal base was in the former Article 100A

EC[19] dealing with the approximation of national laws for the draft Regulation, and in the former Article 54 EC[20] in the Treaty Chapter on the freedom of establishment for the complementing draft Directive, both the current Regulation and the accompanying Directive find their base in Article 308 of the Treaty, which is the same general provision (formerly Article 235)[21] which constituted the base for the original 1970 Commission's proposal too. This choice suggests that, despite all efforts made in harmonizing national company laws,[22] the creation of a supranational instrument has returned to being a priority for meeting those objectives, in terms of business reorganization and growth on a Community scale, which could be achieved neither through new measures based on other Treaty provisions (such as those concerning the approximation of national laws and the freedom of establishment),[23] nor through measures taken by Member States so that, in the light of the subsidiarity principle,[24] EC measures based on Article 308 EC were the only way for introducing this new company law tool 'side by side with companies governed by a particular national law'.[25]

This importance of the objectives of the SE vehicle in terms of distinctive contribution to the completion of the internal market, recognized in the Preamble,[26] makes this legal form not comparable to national forms.[27] It also requires an assessment as to whether the ECS in force attempted at the outset,[28] or has the potential,[29] to recover the supranational character[30] which is the key element in achieving the objectives.[31]

Article 9, specifying the hierarchy of applicable laws, states that the SE shall be governed in the first instance by Regulation 2167/2001 and, where expressly authorized by the Regulation, by the provisions of its statutes, or in the case of matters not regulated by the Regulation or, where matters are partly regulated by it, of those aspects not covered by it, by the provisions of national laws adopted in implementation of Community measures relating *specifically* to SEs.[32] This specific source of law, not indicated in the 1991 version, must take priority over the provisions of Member States' laws which would apply to a public limited company 'formed in accordance with the law of the Member State in which the SE has its registered office'[33] which by contrast were mentioned in the 1991 draft as the first source in the absence of specific provisions in the company's statutes (for issues not directly covered by the Regulation). This hierarchy seems to indicate an attempt to recover supranationality. In turn, the Preamble to the Regulation states that 'work on the approximation of national company law has made substantial progress, so that where the *functioning* of an SE does not need uniform Community rules, reference may be made to the law governing public limited-liability companies in the Member State where it has its registered office',[34] whereas, under the second paragraph of Article 9,[35] the provisions adopted by Member States specifically for SE's must be 'in accordance with Directives applicable to public limited-liability companies'.[36] Considered together, the Preamble and Article 9 would suggest that, in the Commission's view, the areas where uniform EC law rules are not necessary for the working of the SE are those in which the approximation of national company laws has made substantial progress and that, for this reason – thus for preventing relevant differences between Member States – the provisions specifically adopted for SEs must be in accordance with the Directives applicable to public limited companies.[37]

Nevertheless, three observations can be formulated. First, the literature[38] has consistently stressed that, despite the substantial work carried out on it, the harmonization programme has overall achieved limited results: this would have made it necessary to exactly identify the areas (if any) where the SE, for achieving its stated goals, does not actually need uniform Community rules. Secondly, the choice made in Article 9 ultimately links a good deal of the supranationality of the SE to future EC measures specifically relating to it, to their national implementation and to the (general) requirement whereby the consequent provisions of Member States must be 'in accordance' with Directives on public limited companies. Thirdly, the text of the Regulation, by referring to EC measures to be implemented by Member States, appears to suggest that (at least part of) these measures may consist of Directives rather than Regulations and, if these Directives adopted the minimalist approach of some of the company law harmonization Directives,[39] the survival of noticeable differences between national laws (a result which has occurred for the harmonizing Directives)[40] would also characterize the measures on the SE. This would inevitably continue to undermine both the supranationality of the SE and the possibility of being considered a valid alternative to national company law schemes.

3.2.2 Possible Participation of Companies with Head Office Outside the EC in the Formation of the SE: Key Issues

Article 2 of the Regulation allows four routes of formation of an SE: by merger of public limited-liability companies (listed in Annex I); formation of a holding SE on behalf of public and private limited-liability companies (listed in Annex II); constitution of a subsidiary SE by companies and firms falling within the second paragraph of Article 48 of the Treaty; and transformation of a public-limited-liability company.

In addition to establishing these four routes of formation of an SE, this Article 2, unlike the 1991 draft, offers Member States the option of allowing a company, the head office of which is not in the Community, to participate in the formation of an SE provided that company is formed under the law of a Member State, has its registered office in that State and has a real and continuous link with a Member State's economy, a link which is regarded to exist in particular 'if the company has an establishment in that Member State and conducts operations therefrom'.[41]

This option has been exercised by some Member States generally adopting the incorporation system (the United Kingdom, Denmark, Sweden, Finland) and by the Czech Republic and Poland, whereas it has not been implemented in Germany, Austria, France and the Netherlands.[42] Companies formed in one of the Member States implementing the option find no legal obstacle in participating in the formation of an SE having its seat in their own state, whose national implementing provisions literally repeat the requirement, laid down by the Regulation, whereby the interested companies to be eligible must have a 'real and continuous link with a Member State's economy'.

Nevertheless, this requirement lends itself to different interpretations: it could be interpreted as meaning that companies whose head office is outside the Community should have an economic link with the state of location of the registered office which is presumed to be real and continuous when they maintain an establishment there, or, as the literal wording of the provision as a whole[43] may perhaps suggest, it could be seen as applying solely to companies having their registered office within the state of origin, in which case such companies would need to have a (secondary) establishment in another Member State for meeting the condition of an economic link with that other state. In the latter hypothesis, the doubt arises as to whether companies finding themselves in the situation envisaged in the 1999 *Centros*[44] and in the 2003 *Inspire Art*[45] rulings (thus formed in a Member State adopting the incorporation theory and maintaining only the registered office there, while formally having a secondary establishment (branch) in another Member State) could take part in the formation of an SE if their head office, instead of coinciding with the formally secondary establishment, were located outside the Community. In the event of a company having solely its registered office in a Member State such as the United Kingdom or Ireland, a secondary establishment in another Member State (from which almost no operation is conducted) and its head office outside the Community, it may thus be questioned whether such a company may take part in the formation of an SE, because the wording of the provision does not clarify how real the link should be with the economy of the state of location of the secondary establishment, that is which part of the company's overall operations should be conducted from there. The negative answer would seem to contrast with the literal wording of the provision, whereas the positive one may induce companies incorporated in one such Member State, maintaining there no more than the registered office and having the head office outside the EC, to create almost pseudo-secondary establishments[46] in other Member States, merely for the purpose of participating in the setting up of an SE. Moreover, in this second sense, the requirement examined turns out to be discriminatory among different groups of domestic companies of the states in question according to whether these companies have such establishments,[47] and risks generating practical effects contrary to the intention, as stated in the Preamble,[48] to make the resort to the SE accessible to SMEs too, these latter being less likely than larger companies to have PEs in other Member States.[49] Alternatively, the provision at issue could be intended as covering both the two cases, so that the ECJ will have the task, in the event of litigation between companies and Member States, to clarify the exact meaning of the requirement under consideration, which is certainly not immaterial from the viewpoint of the range of potential beneficiaries of the possibility of taking part in the formation of an SE.

A further issue is the interpretation of the option granted by the Regulation in relation to the *Uberseering* ruling,[50] following which the incorporation system must be adopted under EC law, as a general rule, by a Member State of destination. In effect, after this ruling, Member States such as Germany which had up to that time adopted the 'real seat' criteria have now accepted that companies created, for example in the United Kingdom, could move their head office into their jurisdiction and exercise all activities there while remaining governed by the UK legislation.[51] However, states such as Germany or France which, consistently with their traditional acceptance of the real seat criteria, have not exercised the option may argue that, as a result of the ECJ case law, the real seat criteria must be given up only with regard to transfers of the head office from one state to another within the Community, but not for transfers to/from outside the Community. Consequently, assuming that a company having its registered office in the United Kingdom and its head office outside the EC wishes to set up an SE by means of a merger with a French or German partner, the question arises as to whether this company would find any legal obstacle if the SE was to be located in France or Germany. The answer, which needs to be in the negative,[52] supposes that, in the case at issue, the UK company would find no problem in being recognized under the applicable French or German law as a legal person capable of being part of the (legally binding) agreement to be concluded in France or Germany with the local partner for the formation of the SE. This appears to be necessary if Articles 15 and 18 of the Regulation are read together:[53] in fact, each company involved is to be governed by its national provisions applying to mergers of public limited companies (under Article 15), and the formation of the SE, which inevitably implies a legally binding (and enforceable) agreement as between the partners, is to be regulated by the applicable law of the state of registered office of the SE (under Article 18).

Any possible contrast would be overcome if the incorporation system were to be adopted by EC law with no exceptions (given the absence, to date, of a multilateral Convention on the mutual recognition of corporate entities). On the contrary, it may well be asked whether the conflict of laws between the two systems still exists for the case under consideration: in *Uberseering*, the ECJ did not exclude the possibility that in certain circumstances and subject to certain conditions, overriding requirements relating to the general interest[54] may justify restrictions on freedom of establishment, such as the application of the real seat criteria. This makes it debatable whether the case under examination, in which the company at issue would need to have its legal personality recognized in France or Germany to the same extent as it would have been if it moved its head office to one of these countries, may fall within such circumstances. If so, France or Germany, if they wish to continue to apply the real seat criteria towards companies with a head office outside the Community, might argue that the company is a national neither of the third country where it has its head office nor of the United Kingdom, and may thus refuse to recognize its legal personality.[55] A possible solution, in the light of the 2003 *Inspire Art* ruling,[56] may be that the condition allowing these states to refuse to recognize the company's legal personality is the existence of an abuse, which would however need to be demonstrated on a case-by-case basis.[57]

In addition, the requirement that a company maintaining its head office outside the Community should have a continuous link with the economy of a Member State, if interpreted as referring to the case of a company solely maintaining its registered office in the state of formation, and as requiring such companies to have an economic link with another Member State,[58] can give rise to the doubt as to whether or not the state with whom the company should have the real and continuous link must be the same state in which its partner company is formed and in which, by hypothesis, the SE ought to be formed. In the above example, the question would be whether or not the UK company in question should have the PE in either France or Germany in order to be recognized, under the applicable French or German law, as a legal person capable of entering a contract for the formation of an SE. The literal wording of Article 2[59] does not offer any answer, for it merely sets the conditions which the interested company should meet to be allowed by its state of formation (if it wishes to take such option) to participate in the formation of an SE. Nevertheless, the above-mentioned statement of the ECJ in *Uberseering*, whereby there may be under certain conditions certain circumstances in which the application by a Member State of the real seat criteria, with its implications in terms of recognition of foreign legal persons, can be justified by overriding requirements relating to the general interest (read together with the previous case law on the right of establishment[60] and with *Inspire Art*) would seem again to make the answer entirely dependent, on a case-by-case basis, on the arguments put forward by the relevant authorities of the Member State (that is, those adopting the real seat criteria) in which the SE is to be formed. The outcome could be the risk of originating within the EC, for de facto identical situations, differences of treatment from one of the Member States in question to another, against which the companies involved would find no protection under EC law.

In ultimate analysis, the exercise of the option of allowing companies having their head office outside the Community to participate in the formation of an SE by some Member States and not by other Member States, together with the ambiguous formulation of Article 2, requires the unconditional acceptance, on behalf of Member States which have not exercised this option, of all possible solutions offered by jurisdictions adopting the incorporation system to companies formed in accordance with their national law[61] and in which this option has been exercised. In the absence of this, companies having their head office outside the Community may well be discouraged from participating in the formation of SEs to be located in most continental Europe Member States.

3.2.3 Is the SE Disadvantaged in Comparison with National Companies?

Title I of the Regulation, containing 'General Provisions', shows in Articles 2 and 7 other important differences in comparison with the 1989–1991 draft.

Instead of requiring interested companies to have their central administrations in different Member States, as did the 1989–1991 version, Article 2 sets the condition that at least two of the companies involved must be '*governed by the law* of different Member States'.[62] This wording clarifies that companies formed in Member States adopting the incorporation system, and remaining governed by the law of these states when having their head office in another Member State[63] even if under the formal label of a branch, may participate in the formation of an SE together with local partners, which is in line with *Uberseering* and *Inspire Art*.[64]

Nonetheless, Article 2 introduces a restriction, absent in the 1989–1991 draft, with regard to the formation of an SE holding, of a subsidiary SE and of an SE by way of transformation of an existing public limited company: it requires that each of at least two of the businesses involved in forming an SE holding or a subsidiary SE has for at least two years had a subsidiary governed by the law of another Member State or a branch in another Member State,[65] and that a transformation of an existing public limited company into an SE is possible if this company has for at least two years had a subsidiary governed by the law of another Member State.[66] In the case of two or more companies governed by the law of a Member State and wishing to create an SE holding or a subsidiary SE in other EC countries, the requirement could be interpreted, in the light of the freedom of establishment throughout the EC, as meaning that the holding or subsidiary SE could be located either in the same Member State where the subsidiary or branch is situated[67] or in another Member State. The ratio of these restrictive provisions may thus be found in a willingness to ensure that an SE is being created by businesses already integrated into the economy of more than one Member State, which would not have been the case had the 1991 draft been approved.[68]

Article 7 adopts the real seat criteria for the SE, by requiring that the registered office of an SE shall be located in the same Member State as its head office: this makes the SE subject to a more restrictive regime than that of companies formed in states adopting the incorporation system and, probably, of all companies regulated by national laws (depending on the interpretation of *Lasteyrie du Saillant*).[69] In addition, it grants Member States a further option, according to which a Member State may impose on SEs registered in its territory the obligation of 'locating their head office and their registered office in the same place'.[70] This option has been exercised by Austria, Denmark and Latvia,[71] which have interpreted the expression 'the same place' as meaning either the same municipality[72] or the same location,[73] although no similar restrictions exist for companies governed by their national law. This ends up placing the SE at a disadvantage in comparison with national companies, so that the Member States concerned risk not complying with their obligation, under the Regulation, not to discriminate against the SE and not to impose disproportionate restrictions on its formation.[74]

3.2.4 A Legal Paradox: Seat Transfer as an Extraordinary Event in the Life of a 'Supranational' Company Law Vehicle

Article 8 allows an SE, without dissolution of the company, to transfer its registered office from one Member State to another, which transfer, by virtue of the real seat arrangement adopted by Article 7, must be accompanied by the transfer of the head office. This Article, in governing the operation, imposes obligations on the organs of the SE and confers powers to the national authorities of the state of 'departure' which were not envisaged by the 1989–1991 draft.[75]

In detail, Article 8 makes the transfer of the SE registered office subject to a rigorous and time-scheduled procedure: the preparation of a transfer proposal by the management or administrative organ, and its publication in the manner laid down in the national laws in accordance with the First Company Law Directive as well as in compliance with any additional forms of publication provided for by the state of departure;[76] the drawing up, by the management or administrative organ, of a report on the operation, explaining and justifying the legal and economic aspects of the transfer and explaining its implications for shareholders, creditors and employees;[77] the right of shareholders and creditors to examine the transfer proposal and the report on the operation, at the SE's registered office, at least one month before the decision on the transfer (length of time which is supposed to be sufficient in order for them to formulate their opinion on the project);[78] the decision on the transfer by the general meeting of the SE, at least two months after publication of the proposal;[79] the issue of a certificate attesting the completion of all acts and formalities by a national authority of the state of 'departure';[80] the new registration in the state of 'destination', from the date of which the transfer takes effect; the notification from the registry of the new registration to the registry of the old registration; the new registration; the deletion of the old registration and the publication of both in the two Member States concerned.[81]

The same procedure is laid down by the draft Fourteenth Company Law Directive on the transfer of the registered office of companies governed by national laws[82] and it is also similar to those imposed by the Third[83] and by the Sixth Company Law Directives[84] for internal mergers and divisions.

As the proposal for a Fourteenth Company Law Directive, the Third and the Sixth Company Law Directives all regulate restructuring operations, which can take place in extraordinary times during the life of a company, it can be noted that the transfer of the registered office of an SE has also been regarded as an extraordinary operation, although, from the viewpoint of businesses, one of the main reasons for choosing to form an SE (in comparison with national law companies) should be, by definition, the possibility of moving from one state to another without the creation of a new legal person. Moreover, Article 8 left Member States some options significantly affecting the procedure as regards the degree of protection of interests of minority shareholders and creditors, and capable of making the transfer easier from some Member States than from others.

As regards minority shareholders, Member States may, in the case of SEs registered within their territory, adopt provisions designed to protect minority shareholders who oppose the transfer.[85] This option has not been exercised in the United Kingdom (where the SE is however required to notify in writing any shareholder of the right to examine the transfer proposal and the report), in the Netherlands or in Sweden,[86] whereas numerous other Member States – Germany, France, Austria, Denmark, Finland, Czech Republic, Spain, Latvia and Poland – have implemented it. In these states, the common manner of protection for shareholders opposing the transfer consists of a possibility of withdrawing from the company and receiving compensation in cash in the amount equivalent to the value of their shares, although with different mechanisms, exemplified by their right, in Germany, to receive from the company an offer of acquisition of their shares;[87] in Denmark or in Latvia, to demand the redemption of their shares or compensation from the SE within four weeks or one month of the general meeting;[88] in France, to obtain under certain conditions the redemption of their shares,[89] but the implementing law in Poland goes farther. Under Polish law the shareholders concerned may, in fact, even claim the cancellation or declaration of invalidity of the transfer decision[90] (a choice which appears to be disproportionate in relation to the purpose of the option left by the Regulation).

In addition, the decision of transfer, exactly as the decisions concerning the amendments to the SE statutes, is to be taken by the general meeting with a majority of two-thirds of votes cast, unless otherwise provided by Member States' national legislation applicable to public limited-liability companies or decided by national legislators for the SE.[91] As a result of this provision, even the approval by the general meeting is not always a sufficient condition: in France, the transfer proposal needs to be approved by an extraordinary general meeting with a majority representing specific percentages of shares entitled to vote and ratified by any particular category of shareholders in their own special meetings.[92]

The outcome of these differences is a legal context in which, at the moment of formation of the SE, an in-depth comparative examination of the relevant provisions of the potential Member States of location turns out to be a crucial factor for the choice of the place where the registered and head office of the company is to be situated, in order to enjoy, during the life of the SE, the possibility to (more) easily move to another Member State whenever the various business situations may make such a choice appropriate.

With regard to the protection of the interests of creditors, the Member State 'of departure' maintains the fundamental task of laying down the requirements to be met in order to ensure this protection in respect of any liability arising prior to the publication of the transfer proposal. Article 8 allows Member States to extend these requirements to liabilities that arise or may arise prior to the transfer and this option has been exercised – except for the Czech Republic, Spain and Poland[93] – by all other Member States considered, giving rise to wide differences between the strictest implementing provisions and the most liberal ones: the former, which can be found in France, Germany and Denmark, allow creditors to obtain either the payment or specific guarantees of payment before the transfer;[94] the latter, in the United Kingdom, consider sufficient a statement of solvency made by all the members of the administrative or management organ of the SE.[95] Nonetheless, the interests of creditors are more directly protected by Article 8 than those of minority shareholders, to the extent that Article 8 sets the (minimum) condition that, before the issue of the certificate conclusively attesting the completion of the acts and formalities to be accomplished before the transfer, the SE must prove to such authority that the interests of creditors have been adequately protected in compliance with national law requirements.

The options of introducing provisions protecting minority shareholders and creditors would also be allowed by the Fourteenth Directive; moreover, both Article 8 and this draft forbids the transfer if proceedings for winding up, liquidation, insolvency or suspension of payments or other similar proceedings have been brought against the SE or the transferring company. As a further common feature, both Article 8 and the proposed Fourteenth Directive are interpreted as meaning that the interests of employees also need to be considered, because the transfer proposal must indicate the implications for employees and it is envisaged that employee involvement in the case of transfer of registered office of a company from one Member State to another would need to be governed by Directive 2001/86/EC, which should be amended to take into account the Fourteenth Directive.[96]

Nevertheless, Article 8, unlike the proposed Fourteenth Directive, allows national laws to provide that the transfer resulting in a change of applicable law shall not take effect if competent national authorities oppose it (subject to review by a judicial authority), on the sole grounds of public interest, within a period of two months after publication of the proposal, during which no decision to transfer may be taken.[97] This option has been exercised in the Member States considered, with the exception of Austria, of Germany and, for those companies which are not subject to the supervision of the Financial Supervisory Authority, of Denmark.[98] The national provisions do not state on which grounds the competent authorities may found opposition, consistently with the fact that Article 8 specifies neither the aspects of the change of applicable law which could justify opposition nor the public interest justifying it. However, in the light of the hierarchy of laws applicable to the SE laid down by Article 9, which includes national laws,[99] it seems logical to interpret the provision in the sense that opposition may be taken by the competent authorities of the Member State in which the SE is registered against the transfer resulting in the change of those applicable national provisions covering important aspects of the protection of stakeholders' interests in such a way that the authorities of the state of origin may consider the provisions of the proposed state of destination as offering a lower standard of protection. In other words, to the extent that what may be defined as a 'Community interest' to make the transfer possible will need to be reconciled with a national public interest, an assessment on a case-by-case basis, on behalf of national authorities, may become necessary to establish whether the transfer implies such a relevant change as to justify an opposition, if no less restrictive means exist to protect the interest at stake. Consequently, the ultimate outcome of the implementation of the option by Member States might be that their competent authorities could end up opposing the transfers to those states which, in their view, have made (widely) different choices, in comparison with their national ones, within the ambit of all the options left by the Regulation. This would make the transfer easier as between groups of Member States. If the Fourteenth Directive were introduced without this option for Member States, the outcome would paradoxically be the risk of making the transfer of a registered office of the SE, which would keep its 'European' legal personality in this transfer, more difficult than the transfer of the registered office of a company governed by a national law which would change its national legal personality.

Moreover, the SE must comply with national legislation 'concerning the satisfaction or securing of payment to public bodies'.[100] This gives rise to the question if, amongst the reasons of public interest, the authorities of Member States can invoke the (not yet occurred) payment of tax liabilities. This problem concerns the possible taxation arising out of the transfer: as indicated in Chapter 1, according to the amended Merger Directive,[101] the state of 'departure' must not tax, at the time of the transfer, the capital gains relating to those of its assets becoming effectively connected with a PE of the SE in that state; moreover, the new formulation of the anti-abuse clause allows Member States not to apply this tax relief when the transfer of the registered office can be presumed to have tax evasion or tax avoidance as one of its principal objectives, which may occur if transfer is not related to restructuring or rationalization of the activities. As a result, if the condition requiring the assets to become effectively connected with a PE of the SE will not be met, or if the transfer will show no connection with a restructuring or rationalization of the activities, the tax provided for by the national legislation of this state will be levied and secured to national budget. Accordingly, in such cases the national authorities of the Member States which have implemented the option may well be induced to put forward anti-avoidance and anti-evasion purposes as grounds of public interest to oppose the transfer until the settlement of tax liabilities.

This possible scenario, together with the real seat arrangement for the SE, would risk placing the SE at a further disadvantage in comparison with domestic companies. It can be noted again that the ECJ case law, after requiring any state of destination to accept the formal transfer to its jurisdiction of the head office, without the registered office (*Uberseering)*, or the de facto transfer of the head office under the label of a secondary establishment (*Centros*, *Inspire Art*), seems to have eliminated those obstacles to the freedom of establishment created by 'exit taxes' of any state of departure (*Lasteyrie du Saillant*) imposed on companies regulated by national laws, and thus to have made the application of the real seat criteria even by the state of departure in principle incompatible with Articles 43 and 48 EC.[102] If this were definitively confirmed by future ECJ rulings, so that the transfer of the head office alone (not allowed for the SE) would be recognized, except for certain circumstances, as an ordinary operation with no exit taxes for companies governed not only by the law of Member States traditionally adhering to the incorporation system but by the law of any Member State, the regulation of the SE as regards seat transfer and its tax treatment would be even more obsolete[103] than it currently is if compared with the treatment of domestic companies formed in countries traditionally adopting the incorporation system. It was thus properly argued that no condition for the lack of exit taxation should have been imposed on the SE,[104] although this outcome will be difficult to achieve if the overall tax regime of the SE is left to the greatest extent to national legislators (as occurs with the inclusion of the SE in the scope of the Tax Directives).

Lastly, the prohibition of the transfer in case of insolvency proceedings is consistent with the choice not to cover, amongst others, the area of insolvency law, expressly excluded from the scope of the Regulation[105] and in which no harmonization Directive has been enacted. Nevertheless, the lack of a specific Directive in the field, in the light of the choice to rely on national law in areas where the progress of harmonization is supposed to have made substantial progress,[106] might have been a reason for providing an ad hoc insolvency procedure for SEs. Moreover, the prohibition of transfer for companies against which procedures for insolvency have been brought does not seem to consider Regulation 1346/2000, governing insolvency procedures, with which the choice whether or not to allow the transfer ought to have been coordinated. Under Regulation 1346/2000, in fact, the procedure is regulated by the applicable law of the state where it has been commenced, the decision to commence the procedure, once made by a judicial authority of a Member State and taking effect in such state, is recognized in all other EC countries and, as a consequence, the decision to commence an insolvency procedure implies in any other Member State, with no additional formalities, the effects established by the law of the state where the procedure commenced,[107] which cannot be called into question. Accordingly, if the transfer of registered office of an SE against which insolvency proceedings have commenced had been allowed, the transfer would neither have prevented the interested SE from escaping the effects of the procedure nor, in itself, affected creditors' protection (given both the maintaining of the effects of the procedure and the provisions of Article 8 aiming at safeguarding the interests of creditors existing prior to the transfer). This, together with the entry into force of Regulation 1346/2000 well before Regulation 2167/2001[108] ought to have reasonably suggested a solution different from the (absolute) prohibition of the transfer, such as a solution considering the economic reasons behind the insolvency and the potential effects of the transfer, in the specific case, on the possibility of recovery of the company business.[109]

3.2.5 Other 'National Solutions' for the SE

In governing other issues, Title I of the Regulation confirms an increase, rather than a reduction, of the space left to national law if compared with the 1989–1991 draft. In this regard, Title III of the previous draft,[110] dealing with the capital of the SE and with all aspects of its maintenance and changes[111] and providing for particular procedures aiming at protecting the interests and rights of creditors and minority shareholders,[112] has been totally eliminated. Article 5 provides that, subject to its being expressed in Euros and to its amounting to at least 120 000 Euros,[113] the capital of an SE, the maintenance of and changes thereto, together with its shares, bonds and other similar securities, is governed by national laws applicable to public limited companies. The maintenance of and changes to the capital of public limited companies are the object of the Second Company Law Directive, imposing detailed obligations on Member States[114] and, consequently, the choice of relying on national laws may be seen as coherent with the statement in the Preamble recognizing that, due to the progress of the harmonization work, in some areas uniform rules are not needed for the functioning of the SE.[115] Nevertheless, the same does not apply to all other possible issues concerning shares, bonds and other similar securities, thus to an equally important sector of company law in which, to date, no approximation Directive has been issued. Accordingly, the reliance on national laws in this field, directly concerning the way of financing of any SE, at least with regard to the shares, seems to go beyond the intention, stated in the Preamble,[116] to apply national provisions governing public limited companies who make resort to public savings and to negotiation of securities to the formation of the SE through the resort to public savings and to SEs willing to use financial instruments. This adds a further element to be considered, by means of an in-depth comparative study of national provisions of the countries of possible location of the SE to be created, even by companies interested in forming an SE with no intention to resort to particular categories of securities.

Moreover, Article 3, after specifying that an SE may itself set up one or more subsidiaries in the form of SEs, and offering thus the possibility of forming single-member SEs, implicitly suggests that this particular form is entirely regulated by the national law of the Member State of the registered office applying to public limited-liability companies finding themselves with a single member, as well as by that state's provisions, *mutatis mutandis*, concerning single member private limited companies. Given the complexity and importance of issues deriving from all shares being concentrated in the hands of a single member – whether, when and/or under which conditions the single member should be jointly and/or unlimitedly liable for the obligations of the company, whether the insolvency of the company should also imply consequences for the single member[117] – the reliance on national company laws in this area indicates the giving up, at EC level, of any attempt at regulating in detail the creation of a subsidiary SE by another SE.

3.2.6 Solution to the Issue of Labour Co-determination and Results of the Directive's Implementation in Member States: Overview

According to the 1991 draft, an SE could only be registered after the choice of a model, amongst those contemplated by the proposed complementing Directive, aiming at ensuring employee participation in the management of the company,[118] and the difficulty of reaching an agreement between the Member States on the controversial rules on labour co-determination had been, ever since the first formulation of the proposal, one of the major obstacles to its approval. Article 12 of the Regulation shows that the solution adopted to reach agreement has been that of side-tracking the problem, by shifting from the concept of 'participation in the management of the company' to a much broader concept of 'involvement'. This is defined by Article 2 of Directive 2001/86/EC, as 'any mechanism, including information, consultation and participation, through which employees' representatives may exercise an influence on decisions to be taken by the company'. Unlike the 1991 draft, Article 12 of the Regulation and the Directive are based on two basic principles: (a) free determination of the manner of involvement of employees by means of negotiations between their representatives and the management organs, and, in the absence of negotiation and of any decision to rely on rules on information and consultation of employees, application of 'standard rules' laid down by Member States; (b) no need for employee participation in the management of the SE if none of the companies involved in the formation of the SE was governed by rules on employee participation. These key principles result from the provisions of Article 12 of the Regulation, of the key Articles 1, 2, 3, 4, 5 and 7 of the Directive and of the standard rules laid down in an Annex to the Directive. Article 12 of the Regulation sets three alternative requirements.[119] The first is the reaching of an agreement between the competent organs of the participating companies and a special negotiation body (SNB) representing employees which must be created under Article 3 of the Directive. The agreement must specify all details indicated by Article 4 of the Directive concerning employee involvement through a permanent representative body.[120] The second is a decision, by such SNB, not to open or to terminate negotiations and to rely on the rules on information and consultation of employees in force in the Member State where the SE has employees. The last is the effort to reach an agreement within the period of six months, which may be extended up to one year, from the establishment of the SNB. In the event of no agreement being reached and of no decision to rely on the rules concerning information and consultation in force in the Member States where the SE has its employees, Article 7 requires the application of the 'standard rules' laid down by the relevant Member State. These standard rules must satisfy certain provisions, detailed in an Annex to the Directive which deals in Part 1 with the composition of a permanent body representative of the employees, in Part 2 with standard rules on information and consultation and, in Part 3, with standard rules for participation. Such provisions, while describing the composition of the representative body and, in Part 2, its rights and competence, specify in Part 3 of the Annex that 'If none of the participating companies was governed by participation rules before registration of the SE, this latter shall not be required to establish provisions for employee participation'.[121] Consequently, the Directive is quite prescriptive in its core requirements (such as those concerning the SNB, the contents of the agreement, the composition of the representative body) but largely flexible in the ultimate outcome which is left open as a result of its implementation. Within the Community, wide differences exist regarding employee participation rights at company board level: widespread participation rights, in both private and state-owned companies, can be found in Germany, Austria, the Netherlands, Luxembourg, the Czech Republic, Slovakia, Slovenia, Hungary, Denmark, Sweden and Finland; limited participation rights, mainly in state-owned or privatized companies, exist in France, Spain, Ireland, Portugal, Poland, Greece and Malta; no or very limited participation rights exist in Belgium, in Italy, in Cyprus, in Lithuania, in Latvia and in Estonia, in addition to the United Kingdom where participation rights have always been extraneous.[122] In this context, a comparison between some national legislations implementing the Directive shows that Member States, although they have introduced very similar or identical provisions to the Articles of the Directive to comply with the parts of it which are of a prescriptive nature, have taken benefit from any aspect not dealt with by the Directive either to minimize the practical effects of rules that could be unfamiliar to businesses in their own jurisdictions, or to minimize the differences in respect of established national practices.

The most significant example of the first approach seems to be offered by the UK implementing legislation, in at least three respects. In the event that the SNB is not set up or is not set up properly, the enforcement of the obligation to establish it depends entirely on the initiative of an interested party (employees, would-be members of the SNB, the competent organ of a participating company) who may lodge a complaint with the Central Arbitration Committee (CAC). Secondly, the standard rules on information and consultation, which would apply after the expiry of the six months period, after establishing the duty of information upon the competent organ of the SE, state that this organ shall meet with the employees' representative body at least once a year, to discuss the progress of the business of the SE and its prospects, if this body so desires. Thirdly, the assessment as to whether a participating company is misusing or intending to misuse the SE for the purpose of depriving employees of involvement rights (misuse which, under Article 11 of the Directive, must be prevented by Member States) is left entirely to employees or their representatives, who may have recourse to the CAC if they believe there is misuse.[123] In a context in which both employee participation rights and employee involvement on a regular basis, in the form of information and consultation, are familiar neither to businesses nor to employees themselves,[124] as a result of these provisions an 'unofficial agreement' of no effective involvement on a regular basis may end up being possible. From the viewpoint of businesses considering the setting up of a local SE which would have employees, this could result in a cost-benefit analysis between the choice of a national form of company and that of waiting six months to be able to register an SE, despite the obligation for Member States, under the Regulation,[125] to apply in case of infringements the sanctions applicable to public limited companies governed by its law. In fact, the sanctions on the competent organ of the SE would end up not being applicable to the extent to which employees would not attach importance, for example, to regular meetings with the competent organ of the SE, and the situation exemplified might not fall within the scope of the provisions of Articles 11 and 12 of the Directive (the first aimed at preventing the 'Misuse of Procedures' depriving employees of rights of involvement, the second at ensuring 'Compliance with this Directive')[126] to the extent to which employees would not, by definition, be deprived of rights of involvement.

The same outcome would not be possible under the implementing laws of Member States which have followed the second approach, such as Germany, the Netherlands or France, aimed at minimizing differences from pre-existing national practices of either participation or at least regular information and consultation. Contrary to the UK approach, the German, Dutch or French provisions do not leave express or implicit routes to avoid regular employee involvement: the setting up of the SNB is simply imposed; their standard rules require, without explicit or implicit possibilities of exceptions, at least yearly meetings between the management organs of the SE and the body representative of employees or, in the case of France, at least yearly meetings of a 'European company committee' having legal personality and composed of the company managers and of the employees' representatives; last, in the German case, where the stated purpose of the implementing law is to safeguard the acquired rights of employees in an SE to participate in company decisions, misuse of procedures is defined unequivocally as the situation in which, in the absence of any negotiations procedure, changes leading to employees being deprived or to such rights being withheld take place within one year following establishment of the SE.[127] The impossibility under these national implementing provisions, for businesses wishing to set up an SE, to avoid fulfilling effectively the requirement of involvement of the SE's employees is indicated also by the circumstance that only some SEs having no employees and created as 'shell companies' (that is, as companies not yet in operation) have been allowed to be registered without a form of employee involvement in Germany also.[128]

Ultimately, the Directive and Member States' tendency to adapt its implementation to existing national laws and practices have been paving the way for the creation of SEs not only with and without employees' participation – thus with different forms and degrees of employee involvement – but also with the possibility of effective information and consultation of employees on a regular basis in some Member States only. This outcome offers multinational groups with affiliated companies in many Member States and potentially interested in forming SEs the choice whether to create, at their discretion, SEs with worker participation or with more limited forms of involvement, according to the Member States in which the SE will establish its seat and will have its employees.

The historically controversial issue of employee participation, which had been opposed by Member States with no national provisions contemplating it, has thus been turned into an almost neutral element for businesses in the decision whether or not to prefer the form of SE to a company regulated by national laws. Nevertheless, with regard to the importance of this issue in the development of the company law harmonization programme, it was argued that, without an answer to the problem of employee participation, 'the future of the whole company law program is under threat':[129] it may thus be concluded that even the ECS has avoided giving an answer and has missed the occasion to indicate a way forward.

3.2.7 Critical and Unresolved Issues Relating to the Regulation's New Provisions on the Formation of the SE: Overview

The current version of the Regulation evidences important differences, compared with the 1991 draft, with regard to the formation, the working and the dissolution of the company, which are dealt with in Title II ('Formation'), Title III ('Structure of the SE'), Title IV ('Annual accounts and consolidated accounts') and Title V ('Winding-up, liquidation, insolvency and suspension of payments'). Globally considered, the major part of the Regulation (after Title I) is devoted to the formation of the SE, in Title II: just as with the general provisions, this Title is characterized on the one hand by the introduction of new possibilities (such as the formation of an SE through a merger by acquisition), which potentially broadens the number of interested companies, and, on the other hand, by the widening of the fields covered by national laws and by the increase of the number of options left to Member States, which, in contrast with the indication of the Preamble, extend to sectors not yet affected by the harmonization programme.

At the same time, interpretative questions of utmost practical interest for businesses arise, and attempts at a response may be made by way of coordination with other areas or measures of EC business law.

3.2.8 Intra-EC Mergers Leading to the Formation of an SE v. the 2005 Directive on Cross-border Mergers

With the entry into force of the ECS, the issue of the 2005 Directive on cross-border mergers of limited liability companies[130] and the *SEVIC Systems* ruling,[131] public limited-liability companies governed by the laws of two different Member States find two routes to implement intra-EC mergers: a merger leading to the formation of an SE governed by the ECS and a merger allowing them to maintain a form of company governed by national law. These latter, the only ones possible to private limited companies, as a result of the *SEVIC Systems* ruling, are legally possible irrespective of national provisions allowing them, but are bound to be facilitated by the 2005 Directive after its implementation in national systems, the deadline for which has been set as 15 December 2007.[132]

The ECS and the 2005 Directive allow the same operations: merger by acquisition,[133] including the case of acquisition of a wholly owned subsidiary,[134] and merger by formation of a new company;[135] and set out the same procedure for these operations.[136] Nevertheless, regarding one of the necessary steps of the procedure, the provisions of the 2005 Directive and of the ECS would seem to result in margins for different choices for national legislators. The Third Company Law Directive indicates some conditions under which, in a merger by acquisition, national laws need not require the approval by the general meeting of the acquiring company, and the 2005 Directive specifies that, if those conditions are fulfilled, national laws need not require the approval of the draft terms of merger by the general meeting of the acquiring company.[137] In contrast, the wording of Article 23 of the ECS, stating that 'the general meeting of each of the merging companies shall approve the draft terms of merger', does not seem to leave space for an exemption, even if the conditions laid down by the Third Company Law Directive were met. Consequently, national legislators might seem to be allowed to offer companies more flexibility, as regards the fulfilments that are necessary in a merger by acquisition, under the 2005 Directive than under Article 23 of the ECS.

Nevertheless, as the 'general provision' of Article 9 of the Regulation, whereby the provisions adopted by Member States specifically for the SE must be in accordance with the Directives applicable to public limited companies, suggests that all points of the ECS that are not clarified by its own provisions could be interpreted in the light of all these (past and future) Directives, the provisions of the ECS regarding the formation of the SE by merger could be read in the light of the 2005 Directive, applying to public limited-liability companies too. This would be consistent with the obligation on Member States not to place disproportionate restrictions on the formation of an SE as compared with public limited companies governed by national law,[138] which could be breached if more procedural requirements were placed on the formation of an SE than on the formation of a public limited company governed by national law. It may thus be argued that the 2005 Directive would need to be read as requiring, for cross-border mergers of public limited companies leading to a national form of company, the same fulfilments as required by the ECS for cross-border mergers of public limited companies leading to the creation of an SE, whereas it may allow national legislators to offer more flexibility in the case of cross-border mergers of private limited companies.

In effect, a further argument, concerning employee participation rights, suggests that the two pieces of EC legislation need to be read together while considering, at the same time, the scope of the 2005 Directive. This Directive, in providing as a general rule that the law of the Member State of the company resulting from the cross-border merger should apply, admits an exception when employees have participation rights in one of the merging companies and the national law of the Member State of the company resulting from the cross-border merger does not provide the same rights. In this case, the 2005 Directive states that Directive 2001/86/EC on employee involvement, and the SE Regulation, are deemed to serve as a base in governing employees' rights, subject to the modifications that are deemed necessary because the resulting company will be subject to national laws.[139] This suggests that, if the provisions of the ECS are to be taken as a model, subject to adaptations, in the area of employee involvement, they can also be read in interpreting the requirements set by the 2005 Directive concerning cross-border mergers of the same types of companies which can create an SE.

In addition, the reading of the ECS and of the 2005 Directive in the light of each other clarifies that, in the case of formation of the SE by merger, the publication of the draft terms of merger in the manner laid down in each Member State's law in accordance with the First Company Law Directive, indicated by the 1991 draft and not in the current ECS version,[140] remains necessary. This requirement, together with the reports by the management and by an independent expert, is laid down under Articles 32 and 37 of the current ECS,[141] in the two cases of formation of a holding SE and of conversion of an existing public limited company into an SE, which had not been indicated in the 1991 draft.[142] Article 31 specifies that the reports by the management and independent experts, in the formation of an SE through a merger by acquisition of an at least 90 per cent-owned subsidiary, are not needed if the national law governing one of the companies involved does not require them, which is the case in the United Kingdom, Denmark, Finland, Sweden, the Netherlands, Spain, Austria and in the Czech Republic.[143] Outside this exception for the reports by management and experts, the circumstance that all procedural requirements are set out by the 2005 Directive[144] makes it easy to consider them (including the publication of the draft terms of merger) as aspects (not covered by the Regulation) which Article 18 makes subject to the provisions of the Member States governing mergers of public limited-liability companies in accordance with the Third Company Law Directive, where these requirements are set out in clear and precise terms.[145] It is thus possible to deduce that, in cross-border mergers leading to the formation of an SE, a *tout court* application of the Third Company Law Directive equates the procedural requirements to those specified by the 2005 Directive.

From the tax viewpoint, after the extension of the Merger Directive to the SE, it is clear that intra-EC mergers leading to the creation of SEs can enjoy the tax benefit of this Directive, as well as intra-EC mergers resulting in companies governed by national laws which are going to be facilitated under the 2005 Directive. Nevertheless, some differences in the scope of application of the relevant tax and company law provisions may be noted. The 2005 amendments to this Tax Directive have maintained two requirements laid down by the original version: in the definition of merger for its purposes, the Merger Directive is still limited to the cases where any cash payment (that may accompany the issue of shares to the shareholders of the transferring or acquired company as a consideration for the transfer of assets and liabilities to the acquiring company or to the newly set up company) does not exceed 10 per cent; moreover, to be eligible for the tax relief, companies must not be considered to be resident for tax purposes outside the Community under the terms of a DTC concluded with a third state.[146] These requirements can both lead to the exclusion from the tax relief granted by the Merger Directive of mergers facilitated by the 2005 Directive and allowed by the ECS. On the one hand, the fact that mergers eligible to the tax relief may only be those operations where any cash payment does not exceed 10 per cent excludes those cross-border mergers without this limit which, when allowed by the law of Member States, may be carried out expressly under the 2005 Directive[147] and implicitly under the ECS.[148] On the other hand, the requirement that companies must not be considered tax resident outside the Community implies that these companies must maintain their head office within the Community: a situation where a company is considered to be tax resident outside the

Community corresponds to one where this company has its registered office in a Member State and its head office outside the Community, as the head office usually coincides with the place of effective management and control which, under the standard terms of a DTC, identifies the place of fiscal residence.[149] As a result, the implementation by some Member States of the option, left open by the ECS, of allowing companies with their head office outside the Community to take part in the formation of an SE, could cause mergers between these companies, even if resulting in an SE, not to benefit from the tax relief granted by the Merger Directive. This risk would also exist as regards cross-border mergers facilitated by the 2005 Directive, which extends its scope[150] to companies with their registered office in a Member State and their head office outside the Community exactly as in Article 48 of the Treaty[151] on the freedom of establishment, of which cross-border mergers represent a method of exercise (*SEVIC Systems* ruling).

Nevertheless, one of the purposes of the SE being that of releasing businesses from the need to choose a form of company governed by national law, the removal of tax obstacles (such as the obstacle created by the unavailability of the tax relief under the Merger Directive) needs to be extended to the full range of solutions possible under the ECS for the formation of an SE, including mergers as between companies having their head office outside the Community or in which one of such companies is involved, and this would be appropriate even before such obstacles are removed (as they need to be) for cross-border mergers resulting in company forms governed by national laws.

3.2.9 Creditors' Protection in the Event of an SE's Winding-up on Ground of 'Absence of Scrutiny of Legality of Merger': Which Solution?

Article 30 of the Regulation, in its first paragraph, specifies that a merger 'may not be declared null and void once the SE has been registered'. Moreover, as Articles 25 and 26 require an overall scrutiny of the legality of a merger leading to the formation of an SE, under the second paragraph of Article 30 the absence of this scrutiny may be a possible ground for winding-up of the SE. This marks a striking innovation in comparison with Article 29 of the 1991 version, which did allow the nullity of a merger which had already resulted in the creation of an SE to be declared, in the event of absence of the scrutiny of legality, when, under the legislation of the state of location of the seat of the SE, this ground for nullity could exist for public limited companies.[152] In fact, compared with the 1991 draft, which, had it been approved, would have led to the possibility of a different degree of 'legal stability' of SEs from one state to another in the case considered, the approved version offers a clear advantage both to the founding companies and to third parties entering into business relationships with the SE (after its registration). Owing to the impossibility of declaring the nullity of the merger concerned – and of the resulting SE – after the coming into legal existence of the SE, which under Article 27 coincides with the date of the registration,[153] third parties can in fact acquire the certainty that all obligations entered into by the SE, from its registration and until the time when such SE is wound up on the ground of absence of scrutiny of legality, remain valid and enforceable against the SE itself, which should provide them with an incentive to contract with an SE irrespective of whether the formation procedure by merger has been totally complied with.[154]

However, in turning the absence of scrutiny of legality from a possible ground for nullity into a possible ground for winding-up, the Regulation does not expressly deal with a key aspect, concerning the protection of third parties' interests. Obligations entered into by the SE before its winding-up may, in fact, not yet be satisfied at the time of the winding-up, as frequently occurs in the case of companies' winding-up and liquidation. Accordingly, creditors need to know in such a case who should be asked to meet such obligations – the liquidators, or the shareholders in proportion to their holdings in the dissolved SE – and, if so, when their right will expire. If Articles 24 and 63 are read together, they suggest that these aspects, strictly pertaining to the protection of creditors' interests, have been left to the national laws of the Member States.

Nonetheless, the SE under consideration (that is, one resulting from a merger which has taken effect without a scrutiny of legality and which has, for this reason, been wound up) may have creditors in more Member States and, in particular, in the Member States in which each of the merging companies used to have its seat. The usual business counterparts of each of the companies participating in the merger resulting in the SE are likely to continue their relationship with the SE, which, on the other hand, finds itself with a branch in the Member State of at least one of the participating companies. If companies A and B, based in Member States A and B, decide to merge to form the SE C, having its seat in Member State B, the formerly primary establishment of company A in Member State A (with its assets and liabilities) is bound to become a secondary establishment of C in Member State A, under the form of a branch, unless and until C decides to close it. Under Article 29, all the assets and liabilities of the merging companies 'are transferred to the SE'.[155] Similarly, if the same companies intend to form an SE through a merger by acquisition of company A on the part of company B, this latter (which, under Article 17, *ipso jure* becomes an SE)[156] automatically ends up having a branch (again, with all assets and liabilities previously belonging to company A) in Member State A. The question thus arises as to which national law should protect all the SE's creditors' interests in this hypothesis, that is which national law should safeguard the interests of those creditors based in the Member State of location of the branch of the SE, and who are probably involved in doing business with the branch, in the event of subsequent winding-up of the SE. The Regulation, in its literal wording, omits the answer to this question, of extremely practical importance. Whereas Article 24, which expressly refers to the protection of the interests of creditors of the merging companies (and thus of creditors who, in the case considered, are bound to become the creditors of the (branch of the) SE resulting from the merger) provides that the law of the Member State governing each merging company shall apply as in the case of a merger of public limited companies, 'taking into account the cross-border nature of the merger',[157] Article 63, which does not mention the protection of creditors' interests, states that, as regards winding-up, insolvency and other procedures, an SE shall be governed by the legal provisions of the Member State of location of its registered office applicable to a public limited company, including provisions relating to decision-making by the general meeting.

Consequently, in the case under examination, Article 24 would seem to suggest that the law of each of the states of location of the companies which had taken part in the merger, resulting in the subsequently wound-up SE, should apply to the protection of the creditors established in these states, in which case the interests of the creditors of the SE doing business with the branch would maintain the same legal protection they had before the merger (when dealing with company A, in the above example); on the contrary, Article 63 would indicate that the national law of the Member State in which the registered office of the SE is situated should apply to all creditors, however this interpretation may be called into question.[158]

The two provisions, read together, could reasonably be interpreted in the sense that, although the creditors of each of the two merging companies are likely to become the creditors of the SE, their claims which arise in respect of the two (or more) companies involved in the merger and until the formation of the SE are safeguarded by the national law provisions of the Member States of location of each of the companies concerned, whereas their subsequent claims deriving from obligations entered into by the SE will be governed (even in the case of winding-up of the SE) solely by the provisions of the Member State of the registered office of the SE. Nevertheless, given the absence of any EC measure of general character harmonizing the national laws of obligations and contracts,[159] in this second case those creditors doing business with the branch of the SE (located in Member State A, in the above example) would find themselves subject to a national legislation different from that which would have applied had the merger not taken place and had they kept on dealing with company A. This situation may turn out to be acceptable, from their viewpoint, solely when the applicable law (the law of the Member State of the registered office of the SE) offers their interests a protection at least equivalent to that provided by their national legislation (the law which had been applicable in the absence of the merger, had they continued to deal with company A). In this case, the only issues to be solved through private international law rules and Convention between the Member States concerned would lie in the extra-territorial application of the law of the Member State of the registered office of the SE, thus in its enforcement in the Member State of location of the branch. By contrast, if the law of the Member State of the registered office of the SE did not offer their interests such equivalent protection, the creditors in question, located in a Member State different from that of the registered office, would prefer continuing to do business with company A and being safeguarded by the law of the Member State of location of this company in the event of winding-up, instead of dealing with the branch of the SE (and being subject to the law of location of the registered office of the SE in the case of winding-up). Irrespective of the problem of identifying the criteria to establish whether the protection offered by the law of the state of the registered office of the SE would be equivalent in the hypothesis of similar provisions, if this condition were not satisfied they would thus be induced, as creditors of one of the would-be merging companies or the acquired company (depending on the type of envisaged merger), to use any possibility allowed by their national law[160] either to oppose the merger or to claim the payment of all their existing claims before the merger itself, in order then to cease any business relationship with the SE. This would result in an obstacle either to the creation of the SE or to the development of its activity, and such an outcome would certainly be contrary to the objectives stated in the Preamble to the Regulation.[161] The absence of a clear answer to the question concerning the national law deemed to ensure the protection of those creditors of one of the companies taking part in the formation of the SE who become the creditors of (a branch of) the SE itself may therefore (due to wording of Articles 24 and 63 read together) give rise to legal uncertainty and to practical problems of utmost importance. To avoid them, further Community law and/or Member States' law specifically governing the SE, to be enacted pursuant to Article 9, let. (i)[162] and providing a response to these and the other unresolved issues, would certainly be desirable.

Last, under the second paragraph of Article 30, the absence of scrutiny of the legality of the merger may be included among the grounds for the winding-up of the SE, which leaves Member States this choice at least until the introduction of further Community legislation dealing with the matter. Most of the Member States considered, including the United Kingdom,[163] do not consider the absence of scrutiny of legality, but French implementing law includes it amongst the grounds for winding-up and establishes a length of time within which winding-up may be required.[164] Accordingly, the result of generating a different degree of 'legal stability' of the SEs within the Community in the case of absence of scrutiny of the legality of the merger (which, under the 1991 draft Regulation, would have been generated by the declaration of nullity and which has re-emerged in the current Regulation with regard to winding-up), contributes to defeating the objective of achieving the 'legal unit of business in Europe' stated in the Preamble.[165]

3.2.10 Legal Uncertainty and the Need for a Practical Solution in the Formation of a Holding SE

Article 32 of the Regulation, dealing with the 'Formation of a holding SE', in specifying the procedure to be followed, states that a company promoting this operation shall continue to exist and makes the procedure itself applicable, *mutatis mutandis*, to private limited companies.[166] In comparison with the 1991 draft, which omitted to specify this aspect,[167] the extension of the procedure to private limited companies is consistent with the inclusion of this category of companies amongst the beneficiaries of the possibility to create a holding SE, and avoids the uncertainty about the route to be followed by such companies which would have arisen had the 1991 draft been approved.

Article 32 also provides that[168] the general meetings of each company promoting the operation may reserve the right to make registration of the SE conditional upon its express ratification of the arrangements concerning employee involvement.[169] Nevertheless, as the SE comes into existence by acquiring its legal personality on the date on which it is registered, it may only ratify such arrangements as a legal person, as well as assume any obligations, after its registration.[170] Literally, Article 32 would thus produce the legal paradox of enabling the general meetings of each company to make the registration and the formation of the SE conditional upon an act, such as the ratification, which the SE, by definition, cannot accomplish before the registration, which makes no sense. No problem arises, in practice, should the SE, after coming into existence, ratify the arrangements. However, relevant legal (and practical) questions, which are given no answers, arise in the event of absence of ratification on behalf of the SE, when the only effect which appears to be certain would be the joint and unlimited liability of the natural persons, companies, firms or other legal entities which have entered into the arrangements for employees' involvement, in the absence of agreement to the contrary.[171] By contrast, there appears to be full uncertainty about the fate of the SE. From the wording of Article 32 it might be argued that, if each of the meetings of the companies involved were able to prevent the registration, and thus the coming into existence of the SE, in the event of absence of ratification, the intention of the drafters of the Regulation would be to ensure them the right to require the declaration of nullity of the registration of the holding SE which has not ratified the arrangements. Such a solution would however be (illogical and) in contrast with the fact that, under Article 12, even if no agreement on arrangements for employee involvement has been concluded (in which case, by definition, it cannot be ratified after the registration) the SE may register provided that one of the alternative conditions is met.[172] The hypothesis of a right for the meeting of the companies involved to require the declaration of nullity of the registration of the holding SE which has failed to ratify agreements on employee involvement might thus be seen only as an exception to the existence of alternative conditions for registration under Article 12.[173] Even in this case, it would be difficult to reconcile with the choice made in Article 30 with regard to the formation of an SE by merger.[174] A more reasonable interpretation may perhaps be that the drafters of Article 32 intended to confer on the meetings of each of the companies involved in the operation the right to decide the winding-up of the holding SE in the hypothesis considered. This solution, in turn, does not clarify when the winding-up should take place, although, given the absence in Article 32 of a deadline within which the SE should ratify the arrangements, it might perhaps be decided by the meetings of each of the companies promoting the operation shortly after the formation of the SE holding.

In any case, further EC and/or Member States' legislation on the SE, aiming at clarifying inter alia these issues, would be appropriate. In the absence of this, the only way to avoid all such uncertainties would be, in practice, from the viewpoint of the companies involved, that of securing in advance, before the formation of the holding SE, the ratification of the arrangements decided for employees' involvement. Such a result may be achieved by those shareholders of the companies concerned who do not intend to contribute their securities to the formation of the SE and who, therefore, will form the general meeting of each of the promoting companies but not the general meeting of the SE holding, by entering into a binding agreement with the shareholders who will form the general meeting of the SE. Obviously, no problem would arise (and no agreement would be necessary in advance) if either all shareholders of the promoting companies or the shareholders holding the majority in the general meeting of each of them decide to become shareholders of the SE holding.

3.2.11 New Options and New Issues in Search of Answers

Amongst the options left to Member States by the approved Regulation, which are new in comparison with the 1991 draft and which have found different 'responses' in Member States, there appear to be two most significant ones, which may potentially prevent the formation of an SE itself.

First, Article 19 grants Member States the option of preventing a domestic company from taking part in the formation of an SE by merger if any of that Member State's competent authorities opposes it, on grounds of public interest, before the issue of the certificate conclusively attesting the completion of the pre-merger acts and formalities, and specifies that this opposition is subject to judicial review. This option, not exercised in Germany, Austria, the Czech Republic, Finland or Sweden, has been implemented in the United Kingdom, France, Spain, the Netherlands, Poland and, only with regard to the largest companies subject to the supervision of the national Financial Supervisory Authority, in Denmark: however, neither the Regulation nor these national implementing provisions,[175] which are formulated in as general terms as the provision of Article 19, provide indications about the margins of discretion left to national authorities.

Because the provisions governing the SE, by their very objective of permitting the creation and management of companies with a European dimension[176] should contribute to the achievement of the general EC law key objectives in terms of proper completion of the internal market, there appears to be no doubt that national authorities' discretion is to be confronted with 'Community interest'. In particular, the ECJ's case law whereby cross-border mergers leading to a national form of company are a method of exercising the right of establishment and restrictions to the exercise of this right may only be justified by overriding reasons in the public interest and enacted through proportionate measures[177] offers a clear indication about the power of Member States' authorities legitimately to oppose the participation of a company governed by their national law in the formation of an SE by merger. Such opposition must thus be, in the individual case, a measure proportionate to the 'threat' to public interest, no other less impeding means should exist to achieve the same protection of the public interest and the opposition must be promoted by national authorities, under the same circumstances, against the participation of the company involved in the formation by cross-border merger of another company regulated by national law. This may also be clearly deduced from the obligation on Member States to ensure that the provisions applicable to SEs do not disadvantage the SE compared with national public limited companies and do not impose disproportionate restrictions on the formation of an SE or on the transfer of its registered office.[178]

As regards the matters on which the grounds of public interest might arise, the wording of Article 24, in recognizing the need to protect creditors of the merging companies, holders of bonds of these companies, holders of securities, other than shares, carrying special rights in the merging companies and minority shareholders who have opposed the merger, and leaving this protection to national laws, indirectly seems to indicate that, whenever the interests of one of these categories of stakeholders (and of others indicated by national laws) are genuinely and seriously threatened[179] by the merger, there may be in the specific cases 'public interest grounds'. These latter, if satisfying the test of proportionality imposed by the 'Community interest', may in turn lead national authorities to oppose (and the law of a Member State to prevent) the participation of a company governed by this law in the formation of an SE by merger. An hypothesis in which these conditions are met may be found in an infringement of the national provisions designed to protect such categories, which could also constitute a public interest ground to oppose an internal merger: Article 4 of Directive 2005/56/EC on cross-border mergers states that the law of a Member State enabling its national authorities to oppose a given internal merger on grounds of public interest shall also be applicable to a cross-border merger where at least one of the merging companies is subject to the law of that Member State. To the extent that Article 4 of the 2005 Directive ensures equal treatment between internal mergers and cross-border mergers leading to a company still governed by a national law, it also ensures equal treatment between an internal merger and an intra-EC merger leading to an SE, which under Article 9 is subject to provisions of Directives (amongst which the 2005 Directive) concerning domestic public companies and, for aspects not covered by the Regulation, to national laws applicable to these companies.

Given the similarity between the interests mentioned in Article 24 of the Regulation and those indicated in Article 8 as regards the transfer of the registered office, and the obligation on Member States not to impose disproportionate restrictions on the formation of an SE or on the transfer of its registered office, these conclusions about the proportionality test and the grounds of public interest appear to be, *mutatis mutandis*, applicable to the opposition to the transfer of the registered office dealt with by Article 8.[180]

In addition, in the event of merger, other grounds of public interest may derive from the need to prevent the coming into existence of businesses of such dimensions as to alter competition within the Community, as mergers leading to the formation of an SE can be carried out only in compliance with the rules of competition laid down in the Treaty.[181] In this hypothesis, the opposition to the participation of a national company in a merger leading to an SE would be made necessary by the 'Community public interest' itself and, as such, should be allowed by EC law (rather than by the national laws) and promoted by the Commission (rather than by national authorities). In any case, the wording of Article 19 (as well as that of Article 8), in the absence of future provisions clearly identifying the grounds of public interest justifying opposition by national authorities, may provide a relevant scope for litigation between the companies involved and national authorities; a case-by-case solution, suggested by the indicated interpretation and provided, in due course, by the ECJ rulings, may not sufficiently satisfy companies' need for legal certainty. To an even greater extent, this may also apply to another issue of utmost practical interest: whether, in the event of judicial rejection of the opposition from national authorities, the company concerned will be deemed to take part in the formation of the SE from the date of rejection of the opposition or, with retroactive effect, from the date when it originally started the related procedure. Given the absence in the Regulation of any mention of this issue and the general provision of Article 18 which makes national laws concerning public limited companies applicable to aspects not covered by the Regulation, the response is left, again, to national laws, and a different solution in each of the states of location of the (two or more) companies participating in the formation of the SE would result in the maximum of uncertainty for the companies involved.[182] To avoid this, either a further act of Community legislation regarding this important question or a coordination of the solutions provided by national laws would certainly be necessary.

Secondly, Article 34, dealing with the formation of a holding SE, grants a Member State the option to adopt provisions 'designed to ensure protection for minority shareholders who oppose the operation, creditors and employees'. This option, not exercised in the United Kingdom, has been implemented in France and in Germany.[183] The scope of the provisions which Member States are allowed to introduce by this option is similar to that of the provisions they are required to adopt to protect such interests in the case of a formation by merger, and the whole procedure established for the formation of an SE holding is also similar to that set out for the formation by merger. As a consequence, the question may arise as to whether the option granted by Article 19 (opposition on grounds of public interest) may be exercised, in the administrative practice of those Member States implementing Article 34, even in the case of the planned formation of a holding SE, although not expressly provided for. If the Member States decide to allow this possibility as a result of their national provisions implementing Article 34, litigation between the national authorities and those companies interested in forming an SE holding will provide the answer through the future case law of the ECJ.

3.2.12 Key Choices on the Operation and Dissolution of the SE

The comparison between the 1991 draft and the Regulation as regards the operation and the dissolution of the SE evidences three striking features: (a) the deletion from the latest text of entire parts governing important aspects, which has resulted in a Regulation containing in the relevant Titles just one-third of the provisions (Articles 38 to 70) which had been included in the 1991 proposals (Articles 38 to 134); (b) the reliance on national laws in the regulation of those aspects for which the provisions contained in the 1991 version have been deleted; (c) the granting to Member States in the remaining provisions of a much greater number of options; in particular, it must be noted that almost every provision contained in Title III ('Structure of the SE'), Title

IV ('Annual accounts and consolidated accounts') and Title V ('Winding-up, liquidation, insolvency and suspension of payments') offers Member States an option. By contrast, with only the exception of the possibility of converting, after two years, into a public limited-liability company governed by the law of the Member State in which its registered office is situated, allowed by Article 66,[184] companies have been granted no additional option to those allowed by the 1991 text.

Basically, those businesses potentially interested in forming SEs still have the option between two systems for their structure[185] which would have been allowed had the 1991 version been approved, but the three key choices made by the drafters of the Regulation seem to have left little space for 'uniform rules' aimed at regulating the new instrument in a manner different from the corresponding aspects of national companies. On the whole, the matters deemed to be governed by the Regulation or by the company's statute, with neither options for Member States nor resort to national legislation, are limited to some aspects of the features and the tasks of the company's organs and of the working of the annual general meeting. Only a few basic requirements, in fact, do not admit of different choices or national variations: a structure of the SE comprising a general shareholders' meeting and either an administrative organ (one-tier system) or both a management and a supervisory organ (two-tier system) depending on the form adopted in the statute; the appointment of members of the supervisory organ by the shareholders' meeting, the duty of the management organ to report to the supervisory organ and the prohibition on the supervisory organ exercising the power to manage the SE, in a two-tier system; the maximum length of the term of office of the members of companies' organs; the rules relating to quorum and decision-taking in SE organs, where there is no employee participation; the powers of shareholders holding at least 10 per cent of the subscribed capital to require the convocation of the general meeting, the rules concerning the votes cast and the separate approval of every decision by the general meeting, in an SE having two or more classes of shares, by each class of shareholders whose rights are affected thereby.[186]

Accordingly, if the 'General Provisions' and Title II have 'sacrificed' supranationality to an even greater extent than the 1991 draft, with regard to the operation and dissolution of the SE, the creation of a body of rules unrelated to national laws has almost entirely 'surrendered' to the desire of Member States to retain as much freedom as possible in regulating this new company law vehicle.

3.2.13 And the Response by Member States

In essence, the setting up of an SE offers businesses the possibility of choosing in their statutes either a two-tier system or a one-tier system even in Member

States where only one of the two systems would be possible to domestic company forms. Nevertheless, in exercising the options granted to them, Member States have been duplicating to a considerable extent the regulation of national law companies. This is exemplified on the one hand by the use of key options allowed by the Regulation regarding the corporate governance mechanisms, on the other hand by the approach followed. Two options appear to be most significant in relation to the internal working of the SE: the option, in the case of both a two-tier and a one-tier system, to regulate the responsibility of managing directors for the current management under the same conditions as for national public limited companies, which has been exercised by all Member States considered, except for the United Kingdom;[187] the option, in a two-tier system, to require or permit the statutes to leave the appointment and removal of members of the management organ to the general meeting under the same conditions as for national public limited companies, rather than to the supervisory organ as provided in principle by the Regulation, which has resulted in the entrustment of this role to the general meeting in Denmark, the Czech Republic, Finland, the Netherlands, Poland, Sweden and France within the limits already indicated by the national legislation.[188] As regards the approach followed in using these options, some Member States have chosen a *tout court* extension to the administration and management of the SE, as well as to the working of the general meeting, of pre-existing provisions concerning national companies, except for those parts which have been regarded as not in line with the Regulation.[189]

An alternative course of action by Member States, such as that of making the same choices in using the options available, by coordinating with each other in implementing them and, in so doing, of deciding to regulate aspects of the SE in a manner different from that of companies (entirely) governed by their national laws, would have been needed to allow the SE to acquire more distinctive features in respect of national company forms.

3.2.14 Conclusions: A 'Key Challenge' for the Future of the SE

The success of any company law 'supranational' instrument introduced by the EC is inevitably bound to depend, in practice, on the extent to which businesses throughout the Community find the resort to it more convenient than the use of company schemes governed by particular national laws. From their viewpoint, such convenience cannot but lie in its capacity to represent a clear and valid alternative in comparison with national law companies, and therefore in the concrete possibility of its offering different, more effective and efficient solutions to all issues concerning the formation, the management and the dissolution of the business enterprise: clear and unambiguous provisions providing better response to these issues, flexibility for the founding partners, absence of disadvantages in comparison with national law companies and unconditional recognition in all Member States' jurisdictions are essential 'ingredients' of this capacity to be a true alternative.

The experience of extra-EC jurisdictions of federal states, such as Canada and Australia, shows that truly supranational company law vehicles having the above features and enabling businesses choosing them to carry out their activities throughout the territory of the Federation, as do those existing in these countries,[190] prove to be quite 'competitive' and are usually chosen by foreign investors. In addition, it reveals that a key component of supranationality is the possible choice of the legal form in question by both natural and legal persons wishing to create a new corporate entity: however, direct creation by natural persons wishing to carry on business throughout the EC has never been contemplated as a possible route to the formation of the SE. It might be submitted that, the SE being intended to facilitate restructuring and reorganization, direct creation by natural persons would go further than is necessary and, perhaps, that as the EC still lacks some of the institutional features of a Federation, it could not yet introduce a vehicle comparable to the Canadian or Australian supranational company law schemes (which is why the original 1970 proposal of the ECS had to be given up). However, the SE would in any case need to offer businesses wishing to reorganize on a Community scale a better alternative than national forms, in order to fully achieve its goal[191] of releasing (all) companies governed by different legal systems 'from the obligation to choose a form of company governed by a particular national law'. From this perspective, the comparison with the 1991 draft clearly indicates that, on balance, the current ECS, from the company law perspective, presents none of the features needed to be a successful alternative to company law schemes governed by national legislation. The legislative technique used by the Regulation and by the accompanying Directive in leaving wide margins to national laws, together with the differences which the national implementing acts have created between the overall SE regulation in the various Member States, have led to a company law form which is a hybrid one: supranational in its stated objectives and in its basic features but still national in numerous rules relating to its functioning. This 'limited supranationality' reduces the advantages which would have been offered to businesses, including in terms of reduction of administrative and legal costs, by a wholly supranational vehicle and makes unsurprising the scarce appeal of the SE vehicle two years after the entry into force of the ECS.

Accordingly, while awaiting possible amendments that the Commission might propose after October 2009,[192] these limitations from the company law viewpoint imply that the main possibility for the ECS currently in force to attract more interest amongst business circles lies in those aspects not covered by the Regulation. Amongst these aspects, the taxation regime is certain to be the key element for the future of the SE instrument in the business world, given the sensitivity of businesses to tax aspects which, generally, affect a great many of their decisions.[193] This circumstance, together with the new statement that, in sectors such as tax law, the provisions of Member States and of EC law will have to be applied,[194] sets for the EC institutions, if they wish to try to make resort to the SE in its current version more attractive to businesses from all Member States, a key challenge, which goes beyond the current inclusion of the SE in the body of EC tax legislation and amongst those forms which could benefit from the CCBT.[195]

3.3 A 'SLIGHTLY MORE SUPRANATIONAL' FORM: THE SCE: OVERVIEW

The Preamble of Council Regulation 1435/2003, which introduces the SCE and is supplemented by Council Directive 2003/72 on employee involvement in the management of the SCE,[196] expressly states that the SE 'is not an instrument which is suited to the specific features of cooperatives' and that the Community should provide cooperatives (which are generally recognized in all Member States) 'with adequate legal instruments capable of facilitating the development of their cross-border activity'.[197] With these premises, the SCE form (available from 18 August 2006) shows distinctive features which reflect those of cooperatives regulated by national laws: (a) variability of the number of members and of the capital without amendments of the statutes; (b) legal personality but lower minimum subscribed capital (30 000 Euros) than the SE; (c) satisfaction of its members' needs and/or development of their economic and social activities; (d) possibility of distribution of a dividend to members in proportion to their business with the SCE, or to the services they have performed for it; (e) democratic control by its members; (f) distribution of net assets and reserves, on winding-up, to another cooperative pursuing similar aims or general interest purposes.[198]

Apart from these necessary features, the overall regulation of the SCE is shaped around that of the SE with regard to most of the key issues: hierarchy of applicable laws;[199] formation;[200] participation of a 'legal body' with head office outside the EC in the formation of a SCE;[201] real seat criteria;[202] transfer of the registered office from one Member State to another;[203] negotiation-based solutions or standard rules for employee involvement;[204] one-tier or two-tier management structure;[205] and, as does the regulation of the SE, it leaves Member States extensive options. This regulation of the SCE along the same lines as that of the SE has been to some extent adapted to cover only those aspects which have been regarded as suitable for the specific form: the Preamble considers applicable by analogy the provisions adopted by the

Member State where the SCE has its registered office in implementing not all company law harmonization directives (unlike the case of the SE) but just the First, Fourth, Seventh, Eighth and 11th Directive;[206] amongst the formation routes, a holding SCE and a joint-subsidiary SCE are not contemplated.[207]

However, there are two interesting differences in comparison with the ECS, because the regulation of the SCE: (a) allows it to be formed either by natural persons resident in different Member States or by natural persons together with companies or firms within the meaning of the second paragraph of Article 48 of the Treaty (provided there are at least five founders in both cases);[208] and (b) governs some more aspects related to the structure and working of the SCE (Articles 36 to 63) than the ECS (Articles 38 to 60) does for the SE.[209] As a result, it may be observed that the SCE evidences a somewhat greater possibility of providing cooperative enterprises wishing to structure across the EC with an alternative to national forms, than the SE may manage to be for all other enterprises. On the other hand, the possibility of seat transfer from one state to another and in general of carrying out cross-border activity, guaranteed to cooperative enterprises by the choice of the SCE, could also be open to cooperatives choosing the national forms. The case law on the free movement of companies formed under national law (*Centros*, *Uberseering*, *Inspire Art*)[210] could in fact be expected to apply by analogy to cooperatives (at least to the extent that national laws allow them to carry out their activity in a Member State other than that of constitution), for this category is also listed amongst the beneficiaries of the right of establishment under the second paragraph of Article 48 EC.

Most of the observations formulated on technical details on the SE thus turn out to be applicable, *mutatis mutandis,* to the SCE, except that the SCE appears to be slightly more supranational from the company law viewpoint. While awaiting the entry into force of the Statute of the SCE, of the implementation by Member States of the options left open to them and a specific ECJ case law on the free movement of cooperative enterprises regulated by national laws, which will determine how competitive the SCE alternative will become for the category of cooperative enterprises, the conclusion reached above on the need for an appropriate tax regulation for the SE in order to make it a valid alternative to national company law forms seems thus applicable, although to a minor extent, to the SCE too.

3.4 FINAL OBSERVATION

After the harmonization programme based on Directives whose limits have been widely highlighted by the academic literature, the development of company law at EC level has created, by introducing the SE, what was defined as the 'flagship of European Company law'.[211] It was argued that the internal market concept underlying the ECS relies on 'competition between different locations and legal systems' in all jurisdictions of possible location of the SE, so that the ECS also 'relies on competition elements and opens the door for competition between national company law systems'[212] and between the SE and national legal forms of company in each state. According to this reasoning, the absence of a specific tax regime for the SE is to be welcomed since the SE is a 'European legal form of business organization rather than an individual tax planning tool'.[213] However, the effect of leaving open or creating competition between different national company laws had already arisen, before the introduction of the SE, from the limits of the harmonization programme,[214] and it is also generated by the ECJ case law on the freedom of establishment.[215] The comparison between the choices made in different Member States shows that national legislators have also in fact been competing with each other in implementing the ECS: for example, an SE created in the United Kingdom may be seen as more flexible than an SE created in Germany to the extent that the United Kingdom, unlike Germany, has not implemented the options allowing the introduction of provisions for the protection of minority shareholders in case of transfer of the registered office or of formation of either of an SE by merger or of a holding SE, and due to the United Kingdom approach to the employee involvement Directive; nevertheless, these aspects ought to be weighed against the circumstance that Germany, unlike the United Kingdom, has not introduced provisions allowing national authorities to oppose the transfer of the registered office or the participation of a company in the creation of an SE by merger on ground of public interest, so that the German version may appear more 'enabling' in these respects. Ultimately, this creates further scope, in addition to differences between national forms of companies, for an overall 'company law engineering' based on the legal aspects to which businesses attach most importance rather than to location choices based on economic efficiency and market considerations, and may thus increase what the Commission regarded as distortions hindering the achievement of a system of undistorted market competition and the 'Lisbon objective'.[216]

Consequently, in order to contribute effectively to the level playing field within the EC and to fully achieve its goal of enabling (all) businesses which do not satisfy purely local needs to reorganize on a Community scale without using company forms governed by national laws,[217] the introduction of the SE should have resulted in an alternative instrument more attractive than any national forms irrespective of the location in one jurisdiction or in another: an alternative which, through its availability in all Member States, would have contributed to eliminate these distortions. That the current company law features can be regarded as representing more an illustration of the difficulties which have marked the history of the harmonization programme than such an alternative makes it appropriate to continue the search for a supranational solution relating at least to the tax regime and capable of allowing the SE to play this role.[218]

NOTES

1. These Directives have been listed above 2.1. In the literature, see, inter alia, Dine, J. (1989), 'The Community company law harmonisation program', *European Law Review*, 14, 322–332; Wooldridge, F. (1991), *Company Law in the United Kingdom and the European Community: Its Harmonisation and Unification*, Athlone Press, London; Villiers, C. (1996), 'Harmonisation of company laws in Europe, with an introduction to some comparative issues', in Geraint G. Howells (eds), *European Business Law*, Aldershot, Ashgate/Dartmouth, pp. 169–195. Villiers, C. (1998), *European Company Law: Towards Democracy?*, Aldershot, Ashgate/Dartmouth, p. 161, affirms that 'Although the company law program has been extensive and has led to many reforms in company laws of Member States, the remaining differences are strong enough to expose the company law program to the charge that it has failed to achieve harmony'. A different view seems to be taken, from the Commission's viewpoint, by Edwards, V. (1999), *EC Company Law*, Clarendon Press, Oxford, UK, p. 412 which concludes that 'A review of the harmonization program in the light of the Commission's recent consultation suggests that ... the achievements have been not only many but necessary and largely appreciated'.
2. This is evident in the history and the features of the Directives, widely described by the literature cited in note 1. Villiers (1996), note 1, evidences this feature both in a comparative analysis of the implementation of Directives in two Member States, the United Kingdom and Spain (p. 188) and in a general conclusion (p. 194).
3. Quoted from Villiers (1998), note 1, p. 162.
4. Du Plessis J.J. and J. Dine (1997), 'The fate of the draft Fifth Directive on Company Law: accommodation instead of harmonisation', *Journal of Business Law*, 23–47.
5. Regulation 1606/2002 of 19 July 2002, OJEC L243/1 [2002], Preamble, recital (3) and Article 1.
6. The data on the overwhelming majority of SMEs within all EC businesses are cited in Drury, R. and A. Hicks (1999), 'The proposal for a European private company', *Journal of Business Law*, 429–451, at 430. Partnerships only fall in the scope of the Fourth and Seventh Directives on annual and consolidated accounts when all their members with unlimited liability are limited liability companies: see above 2.1.
7. Commission Communication, 'Modernising company law and enhancing corporate governance in the European Union: a plan to move forward' (COM (2003) 284 final), pp. 7–22 and Annex 1, pp. 24–26.
8. See Directive 2005/56/EC of 26 October 2005 on cross-border mergers of limited liability companies, OJEC L310/1 [2005], mentioned above 2.1 and 2.5, and Directive 2006/43/EC of 17 May 2006 on statutory audits of annual accounts and consolidated accounts, OJEC L157/87 [2006], mentioned above 2.1.
9. See The Law Societies, Joint Brussels Office, The Brussels Office Law Reform Update Series, *Company Law and Financial Services*, May 2006, on the progress of the initiatives (the simplification of the Second Company Law Directive, the draft Fourteenth Directive and so on) included in the APCLCG.
10. Directive 2004/25/EC of 21 April 2004 on take-over bids, OJEC L142/12 [2004], mentioned above. 2.1. As regards the key options left to Member States, see Articles 5, 7 and 12 of the Directive; the concerns expressed by the EC Commissioner and, in general, the limits of the Directive are referred to by Johnston, A. (2004), 'The European Takeover Directive: ruined by protectionism or respecting diversity?', *The Company Lawyer*, 9 (25), 270–276, at 274.
11. Directive 2005/56/EC, Preamble, recital (3) and Article 4.

12. Regulation 2167/2001 of 8 October 2001 on the Statute for a European Company, OJEC L294/1 [2001] ('the Regulation') and Directive 2001/86/EC of 8 October 2001 supplementing the Statute for a European Company with regard to the involvement of employees, OJEC L294/22 [2001].
13. See Preamble, recitals (3), (4), (6) and (7). These advantages could certainly have been brought about by a self-sufficient Regulation deemed to govern all aspects of such intended supranational instrument, as it stood in the original 1970 Commission's proposal. See proposal for a Council Regulation of 24 June 1970 on the Statute for a European Company, OJEC C124/1 [1970]. This proposal, in turn, first emerged from the Council of Europe in the 1950s, was then taken up at the 57th Congress of French Notaries in 1959 and by Prof. P. Sanders of Rotterdam from 1959 onwards (Sanders, P. (1960), 'Naar een Europese N.V.?' in T. Willinke (ed.), *Aussenwirtschaftdienstdes Beetriebsberaters*, Zwolle, Netherlands). See also proposal for a Council Regulation of 25 August 1989 on the Statute for a European Company (COM (89) 268 final, SYN 218), OJEC C263/41 [1989], and amended proposal for a Council Regulation of 16 May 1991 on the Statute for a European Company (COM (91) 174 final, SYN 218), OJECC 176/1 [1991].
14. Commissioner F. Bolkestein stressed the advantages of the SE, in his speech 'The new European Company: opportunity in diversity', address to a Conference, University of Leiden, 29 November 2002, as follows: 'The benefits of this concept of a true *Societas Europaea,* organised under a supra-national European law rather than the law of an individual Member State, are evident ... there is no longer a need for setting up a costly and complex network of subsidiaries. There will be substantive reductions in administrative and legal costs [that are] estimated to be up to 30 billion Euros per year'.
15. See (2006), 'SEs in Europe: announced, in preparation, announced interest and failed', www.seeurope-network.org/, 31 May.
16. See, inter alia, Burnside, A. (1991), 'The European company re-proposed', *Company Lawyer*, 11 (12), 216–220; Wenz, M. (1993), *Die Societas Europaea (Se)*, Ducker & Humblot, Berlin, Germany and New York, US, pp. 10–17. In addition, it was stressed that the project was a response to the perception of the primary needs of large businesses throughout the Community in the 1970s, but that nowadays their priorities have changed and, as a result, a vehicle like the SE would no longer be best suited to meet them: Drury and Hicks, note 6, p. 429.
17. Proposal for a Council Regulation of 25 August 1989 on the Statute for a European Company (COM (89) 268 final, SYN 218), OJEC C263/41 [1989] and amended proposal for a Council Regulation of 16 May 1991 on the Statute for a European Company (COM (91) 174 final, SYN 218), OJEC C176/1 [1991]. An earlier version of the comparison between the ECS and the 1991 draft, before the start of the national implementation, was published in Cerioni, L. (2004), 'The approved version of the European Company Statute in comparison with the 1991 draft: some first remarks from the General Provisions and from the Directive on employees' involvement' (Part I), *The Company Lawyer* 8 (25), 228–242 and 'The approved version of the European Company Statute in comparison with the 1991 draft: some critical issues on the formation and the working of the SE and the key challenge' (Part II), *The Company Lawyer* 9 (25), 259–269.
18. The basic choices have been highlighted, from a comparative perspective, in *Investing in Europe: Modernisation of Company Law in Europe*, EUR-LAW, publication for the European Area of Freedom, Security and Justice, 2/2005, pp. 6–13 ('the Survey').
19. Renumbered as Article 94.
20. Renumbered as Article 44.
21. Which empowers the Council to take action when, in the absence of a specific provision in the Treaty, a Community initiative turns out to be necessary for the achievement, in the working of the common market, of one of the EC objectives.
22. See above 2.1 for the list of adopted Directives.
23. Regulation, Preamble, recital (3).
24. Article 5 of the Treaty and Regulation, Preamble, Recital (29).
25. Preamble, recital (6). Article 308 EC is the legal base of both the ECS and the SCE, introduced by Regulation 1435/2003 complemented by Directive 2003/72/EC: as regards

the SCE, the suitability of Article 308 as a legal base was unsuccessfully challenged by the EP in Case C-436/03, *Parliament v. Council* OJEC C289/16 [2003], ruling delivered on 2 May 2006 (not yet reported) OJEC C143/4 [2006]. In particular, the EP argued that the concept of 'harmonization' in Article 95 is a broad one, which includes measures aimed at overcoming the territorial boundaries of national laws, and that the SCE is not a new form of company divorced from national laws because its regulation is not exhaustive but merely governs the SCE's structure and systematically refers to national laws. Nevertheless, the ECJ found that Article 308 is the proper legal base, on the ground that several provisions of Regulation 1435/2003 (conditions for formation, transfer of the registered office) make it clear the purpose of creating a new legal form in addition to national forms and that the referral to national laws is merely of subsidiary nature: see *Parliament v. Council*, above, paras 23 to 26 and 38 to 46 of the ruling. The provisions of Regulation 1435/2003 from which the ECJ drew its arguments are very similar to provisions of Regulation 2167/2001, and the Regulation merely governs the structure of the SE just as Regulation 1435/2003 governs the structure of the SCE: thus, the ECJ reasoning in this ruling can be read as applying to the SE too. This confirms that the choice to base the ECS on Article 308 EC can be taken as an indication of the different purpose of the SE in respect of national vehicles, and of its non-comparability with national forms.

26. Regulation 2167/2001, Preamble, in particular recitals (1) and (4).
27. None of which has a distinctive role concerning the internal market.
28. In the legislative choices already made by the Regulation and the accompanying Directive.
29. In the overall legal structure.
30. Mostly missing from the 1991 draft.
31. As implicitly recognized in the Preamble, recital (7).
32. Article 9, first paragraph, let. (c) (i). Emphasis added.
33. Article 9, first paragraph, let. (c) (ii).
34. Emphasis added. The sentence repeats the analogous sentence contained in the Preamble to the 1989–1991 version.
35. Absent in Article 7 of the 1989–1991 draft.
36. That is, with the measures adopted to approximate national company laws.
37. Which, to date, have been introduced in many important areas of company law but have not always managed to approximate all important aspects in these areas (see above 3.1).
38. See above 3.1.
39. See above 3.1 regarding those Directives leading to 'accommodation' instead of harmonization.
40. See above 3.1.
41. Preamble, recital (23).
42. See the Survey, note 18, p. 8, the UK European Public Limited Liability Company Regulations 2004, and SI 2004/2326, Part 4, reg. 55, the Danish Act on the European Company, Part 2, art. 4. These national implementing acts are available at www.seeurope-org.net
43. Regulation, Article 2, fifth paragraph: 'formed under the law of *a* Member State … registered office in *that* State … a real and continuous link with *a* Member State's economy' (quotation of the key passages, emphasis added).
44. Case C-212/1997, *Centros* [1999] ECR I-1459: see above 2.2 and 2.3.
45. Case C-167/01, *Inspire Art* [2003] ECR I-10155: see above 2.3.
46. A branch from which almost no operation is conducted.
47. In a Member State adopting the incorporation system and implementing this option, two companies, A and B, both having the registered office in this state and the head office outside the Community, would end up being treated differently, for if A had a 'real and continuous link' with the economy of another Member State and B had not, A could take part in the formation of an SE established in the state concerned, B could not.
48. Regulation 2167/2001, Preamble, recital (13).
49. Which might be the case even if an SME managed under the form of a company having its registered office in a Member State following the incorporation system could, for various reasons depending on the concrete case, find it useful to maintain the head office outside the Community.

50. See above 2.1.
51. In Germany, the Federal Court of Cassation first gave up the real seat criteria with a ruling issued on 13 March 2003, where a Netherlands company that had moved its head office to Germany was recognized as having legal capacity and the capacity to be part of legal proceedings with no need to be reincorporated under German law.
52. In order for all eligible companies from each Member State to benefit from the possibility of setting up an SE with partners from any other Member State.
53. See Article 15, first paragraph and Article 18.
54. See above 2.1.
55. In fact, according to the real seat criteria the (foreign) legal personality of a company wishing to carry on operations within the territory of these states would only be recognized when the company maintain the real seat in the state of the registered office, as a consequence of their choice of the connecting factor for identifying the nationality of a company: Goldman, B. and A.L. Caen (1983), *Droit Commercial Européen*, Paris, France: Dalloz, pp. 130–131. This could remain true, after *Lasteyrie du Saillant* (above 2.4), when the head office is located outside the EC.
56. See above note 45.
57. As stated by the ECJ in *Inspire Art*: see above 2.2.
58. See above.
59. Article 2, fifth paragraph: see above note 43.
60. In which the ECJ, in line with *Uberseering*, when examining cases of formally secondary establishment (such as in the *Segers* and *Centros* cases), had already offered commentators the occasion to argue that the incorporation theory should be the rule under EC law without openly declaring that the real seat criteria was unlawful, and without denying Member States the right to take appropriate measures to combat any possible abuse (although this latter may be difficult to prove): see above 2.2 and 2.3.
61. In other words, it requires that the doubts left by *Uberseering* and *Inspire Art* about the 'certain circumstances' and 'certain conditions' (see above 2.2 and 2.3) be definitively clarified.
62. Emphasis added; see Article 2 first paragraph; second paragraph, let. (a); third paragraph, let. (a); fourth paragraph.
63. Which was the situation examined in the *Centros* and *Inspire Art* rulings of the ECJ, notes 44 and 45. See also above 2.3.
64. See above 2.1 and 2.2.
65. See Article 2, second paragraph, let. (b) and third paragraph let. (b).
66. See Article 2, paragraph 4.
67. Two companies governed by the law of Member State A and wishing to create an SE in other EC countries may be in the following situations: (a) they both have a subsidiary or branch in Member State B; (b) one of them has a subsidiary or branch in Member State B, another has one in Member State C. In the first case, they may wish to set up an SE either in Member State B or in a third Member State; in the second case, they may wish to form an SE either in Member State B or in Member State C, or in a third Member State.
68. See Article 2 of the 1991 draft, which would have allowed the formation of an SE immediately after setting up a subsidiary or a branch in another Member State.
69. See above 2.4. The real seat criteria was also adopted by Article 5 of the 1991 draft ('The registered office of an SE shall be situated at the place specified in its statutes. It shall be the same as the place where the SE has its central administration'), but, at the time, the ECJ case law had not yet reached the current phase of development on the free movement of companies (see Chapter 2 and below 3.2.4).
70. See Article 7.
71. See the Survey, note 18, p. 8.
72. See the Danish Act on the SE, Part I, art. 3, available at www.seeurope-org.net
73. In the case of Austria and Latvia: see the Survey, note 18, p. 8 and the Latvian Law on the SE, ch. II, s. 6, available at www.seeurope-org.net
74. See Regulation, Preamble, recital (5).
75. See Article 5bis of the 1991 draft.

76. Article 8, second paragraph and Article 13.
77. Article 8, third paragraph.
78. Article 8, fourth paragraph.
79. Article 8, sixth paragraph.
80. Article 8, eighth paragraph.
81. See Article 8, seventh to fourteenth paragraphs.
82. See Articles 3 to 10 of the draft Fourteenth Directive (draft XV/D2/6002/97-EN-REV2).
83. Directive 78/855 EEC of 9 October 1978, OJEC L295 [1978], Articles 5 to 9.
84. Directive 82/891 EEC of 17 December 1982, OJEC L378 [1982], Article 3 onwards.
85. Article 8, fifth paragraph.
86. See the Survey, note 18, p. 8 and the UK European Public Limited Liability Company Regulations 2004, SI 2004/2326, Part 4, reg. 56.
87. See s. 3, art. 12 of the German Act on the introduction of the European Company (SEEG), in *Official Gazette of the Federal Republic of Germany (BGBI)*, 29 December 2004, I 2004, pp. 3675–3686.
88. See Part 3, art. 6, first paragraph of the Danish Act on the SE, and ch. III, s. 9 of the Latvian Law on the SE.
89. See Article L. 229-2, third paragraph of the Code of Commerce as amended by Law 2005-842 implementing the ECS.
90. See the Survey, note 18, p. 8.
91. Article 8, sixth paragraph and Article 59, first and second paragraph.
92. See Article L. 229-2, second paragraph of the Code of Commerce as amended by Law 2005-842 implementing the ECS, and Article L. 225-96 of this Code.
93. Article 8, seventh paragraph, and the Survey, note 18, p. 8.
94. See Article L. 229-2, sixth paragraph, of the French Code of Commerce as amended by Law 2005-842 implementing the ECS; s. 3, art. 13, of the German SEEG; Part 3, art. 7, first paragraph of the Danish Act on the SE.
95. See the UK European Public Limited Liability Company Regulations 2004, SI 2004/2326, Part 5, reg. 72.
96. For a complete comparison between Article 8 and the draft Fourteenth Directive, see Johnson, M. (2004), 'Does Europe still need a Fourteenth Company Law Directive?', *Hertfordshire Law Journal*, 3 (2), 18–44, at 34–36.
97. Article 8, 14th paragraph.
98. See the Survey note 18, pp. 8–9; UK European Public Limited Liability Company Regulations 2004, SI 2004/2326, Part 4, reg. 58; Article L. 229-4 of the French Code of Commerce as amended by Law 2005-842 implementing the ECS; ch. III, s. 11 of the Latvian Law on the SE; Part 3 and Part 7, art. 19, first paragraph of the Danish Act on the SE; s. 3 of the German SEEG and s. 2 of the Austrian Law on the SE (in *Official Gazette of the Federal Republic of Austria* No. 2004/67), which contain no reference to Article 8, 14th paragraph of the Regulation.
99. Article 9, first paragraph, let. (c). See also above 3.2.1.
100. Article 7, third paragraph.
101. See above 1.1.4.
102. See above 2.4: as the ECJ has removed barriers created by exit taxes for natural persons in *Lasteyrie du Saillant*, its application to companies, given the wording of Article 48 of the Treaty, would appear quite logical.
103. Werlauff, E. (2003), 'The SE company: a new common European company from 8 October 2004', *European Business Law Review*, 1 (14), 85–103, at 97, also expresses the view that the SE Regulation appears to be obsolete as regards seat transfer. See also Thommes, O. (2004), 'EC law aspects of the transfer of seat of an SE', *European Taxation* 1 (44), 22–27, 27.
104. Roch, M.T.S. (2004), 'Tax residence of the SE', *European Taxation* 1 (44), 13–16.
105. Regulation, Preamble, recital (20).
106. Preamble, recital (9). See above 3.2.1.
107. Regulation 1346/2000, Article 4, OJEC L160/1 [2000].
108. Whereas Regulation 2167/2001 entered into force on 8 October 2004, the date of entry into force of Regulation 1346/2000 was May 31 2002.

109. Which recovery, if facilitated by the transfer in the concrete case, would benefit the creditors existing prior to the decision to commence proceedings, as well as its employees.
110. See 1991 draft, Articles 38 to 56.
111. See 1991 draft, Articles 38 to 45bis.
112. See 1991 draft, Articles 46 to 49.
113. Required by Article 4.
114. See, however, above 3.1 as to the plan to simplify this Directive.
115. Preamble, recital (9): see above 3.2.1 and 3.2.4.
116. Preamble, recital (12).
117. These issues are dealt with by national company laws, with different solutions.
118. See 1991 draft, Article 8, third paragraph.
119. See Regulation, Article 12, second paragraph.
120. See Directive 2001/86/EC, Article 4, second paragraph, let. (a) to (f).
121. Directive, Part 3 of the Annex, second paragraph.
122. Comparative information available at www.seeurope-network.org/, 28 April 2006.
123. See UK European Public Limited Liability Company Regulations 2004, SI 2004/2326, Part 3, ch. 2, reg. 22, Sch. 4 para. 30, ch. 6, art. 35.
124. Of which the United Kingdom has traditionally been regarded as the typical example as concerns the ordinary companies' decisions, because, in decisions concerning company restructuring, which may imply important alterations to activity or collective redundancies, employee involvement is in fact common, although with major variations, to all countries. This is highlighted by a comparative study by the European Industrial Relations Observatory (EIRO) of the European Foundation for the Improvement of Living and Working Conditions, *The Involvement of Employees and Collective Bargaining in Company Restructuring*, 2002.
125. Regulation, Preamble, recital (18).
126. See the wording of Articles 11 and 12 of the Directive.
127. See Part 1, art. 1, Part 2, art. 4, Part 3, arts 23 and 28 and Part 4, arts 43 and 44 of the German Law on the participation of employees in a European company, in *Official Gazette of the Federal Republic of Germany (BGBI)* I 2004 S 3686; ch. 2, art. 2:2 and ch. 3, art. 3:8 of the Dutch Involvement of Employees Act; s. 2, arts L 439-26, L 439-31, L 439-33 and s. 3, subsection (1), in particular arts L 439-35 and L 439-39 of the French Code of Labour as amended by Law 2005-842 implementing the ECS.
128. See 'SEs in Europe: established, in preparation, announced interest and failed', www.seeurope-network.org:/, 28 April 2006.
129. Villiers (1998), note 1, p. 232. A study by the Involvement and Participation Association (IPA), *Sharing the Challenge: Employee Consultation: A Guide to Good Practice*, published in 1998, highlighted that, in practice, the difference between the UK model of labour relations (typified as flexible, voluntarist, favouring communication over consultation, company-driven and retaining 'management's right to manage') and the Continental model tends to be reduced through the resort, by big companies, to a combination of models.
130. Directive 2005/56/EC of 26 October 2005, OJEC L310/1 [2005] ('2005 Directive'). The Directive is based on a proposal submitted in 2003 by the Commission (IP/03/1564, 8 November 2003).
131. Case C-411/03, *SEVIC Systems*, OJEC C289/13 [2003], ruling delivered on 13 December 2005 (not yet reported), OJEC C36/5 [2006], where the ECJ regarded a refusal of registration of a cross-border merger in a national register as a restriction to the freedom of establishment in breach of Articles 43 and 48 of the Treaty: see above 2.5.
132. Article 19 of the 2005 Directive.
133. See Article 17, second paragraph, let. (a) of the Regulation, and Article 2, second paragraph, let. (a) of the 2005 Directive.
134. See Article 18 of the Regulation and Article 24 of the Third Company Law Directive, read together, regarding the merger by acquisition of a wholly owned (intra-EC) subsidiary, leading to the formation of an SE; and Article 2, second paragraph, let. (c), of the 2005 Directive.

135. See Article 17, second paragraph, let. (b) of the Regulation, and Article 2, second paragraph, let. (b) of the 2005 Directive.
136. See Articles 5 to 13 of the 2005 Directive; Articles 17 to 28 of the Regulation.
137. See Article 8 of the Third Company Law Directive, and Article 9, third paragraph of the 2005 Directive.
138. 2005 Directive, Preamble, recital (5).
139. See ibid. Article 16, first to third paragraphs, and Preamble, recital (13).
140. See Articles 19 and 20 of the 1991 draft, together with Articles 17 to 20 of the current version.
141. See Regulation, Article 32, second to fourth paragraphs and Article 37, fourth to sixth paragraphs.
142. See Articles 31, 31bis and 34 of the 1991 draft.
143. See Regulation, Article 31, second paragraph, and the Survey, note 18, p. 11.
144. See Articles 6 and 7 of the 2005 Directive.
145. Articles 6, 9 and 23 of the Third Company Law Directive.
146. See Article 2 of the Merger Directive and above 1.1.4 on this Directive in its 1990 version and on its amendment.
147. See Article 3 of the 2005 Directive.
148. See Articles 9, second paragraph and 18 of the Regulation and Article 30 of the Third Company Law Directive.
149. See OECD Model, Article 4.
150. See Article 1 of the 2005 Directive.
151. See Article 48, first paragraph of the Treaty.
152. See Regulation, Article 29, first paragraph of the 1991 draft.
153. Regulation, Article 27, first paragraph.
154. As Article 27, second paragraph prevents registration of an SE before the formalities provided in Articles 25 and 26 have been completed, the absence of scrutiny of legality seems to have been considered to be an infrequent case.
155. Regulation, Article 29, first paragraph, let. (a).
156. Ibid. Article 17, second paragraph, let. (a).
157. Ibid. Article 24, first paragraph.
158. The literal wording of Article 63 would in fact have been clearer had it expressly included the protection of the interest of all SE creditors in each of the listed procedures, that is if it had stated 'an SE shall be governed by the legal provisions which would apply to a public limited-liability company formed in accordance with the law of the Member State in which its registered office is situated, including provisions relating to decision-making by the general meeting *and provisions regarding the protection of creditors of the SE*'. Emphasis added.
159. At least until the implementation of a European Civil Code, which could be the final outcome of an ongoing process of consultation and discussion launched by the Commission in 2001 and strengthened in 2003 by means of an Action Plan presenting possible ways forward, about the way in which problems resulting from divergences between national contract laws within the EC should be dealt with at European level: Communication on European contract law (COM (2001) 398 final), and in particular Communication on 'A more coherent European contract law: an action plan' (COM (2003) 68 final), pp. 7–45, set out the options for a systematic approach after several EC Directives, already issued, applying to particular commercial situations.
160. Article 13 of the Third Company Law Directive on internal mergers, which is made applicable by Article 17 of the Regulation, requires Member States to introduce an adequate system to safeguard the interests of creditors of the merging companies with regard to claims deriving from obligations entered into before the publication of the draft terms of merger and which have not yet been satisfied at the time of the publication.
161. Regulation, Preamble, recitals (3) to (7). See above 3.2.1.
162. Which refers, amongst the 'hierarchy of laws' governing the SE, to 'provisions of laws adopted by Member States in implementation of Community measures relating specifically to SEs'. See above 3.2.1.

163. UK European Public Limited Liability Company Regulations 2004, SI 2004/2326, Part 4 and the Survey, note 18, pp. 3 and 11.
164. Article L. 229-3, second paragraph of the French Code of Commerce as amended by Law 2005-842 implementing the ECS.
165. Regulation, Preamble, recital (6). See above 3.2.1.
166. Ibid. Article 32, first paragraph and seventh paragraph.
167. See Article 31 of the 1991 draft.
168. See Regulation, Article 32, sixth paragraph.
169. Pursuant to the supplementing Directive: see above 3.2.6.
170. The English formulation of the provision may perhaps give rise to a doubt as to whether the wording 'its express ratification' refers to the general meetings of each of the companies promoting the operation rather than to the SE, but the formulation in other languages clarifies that the express ratification is required from the SE.
171. Regulation, Article 16, second paragraph. To assume the obligations arising out of such acts after its registration would mean, on behalf of the SE, to ratify such acts. Article 16 thus confirms that, before registration, there may only be other subjects acting in an SE's name and that, only after registration can such SE ratify the acts they have accomplished.
172. These conditions are either a decision by the SNB not to open or to terminate negotiations, or the expiry of the period of negotiations without an agreement having been concluded, given the application, in these cases, of 'standard rules': see above 3.2.6.
173. That is, a specific exception for the case of formation of a holding SE.
174. Whereby the merger cannot be declared null and void once the SE is registered: see above 3.2.9. Although Article 30 refers to the case of formation by merger, nothing in either the Preamble or text of the Regulation seems to suggest that the drafters intended to make in the case of formation by merger a treatment of nullity different from the case of formation of a SE holding and of the two other routes to the creation of the SE.
175. See, in particular, the UK European Public Limited Liability Company Regulations 2004, SI 2004/2326, reg. 60; Title II, book II, ch. IX, art. L. 229-4 of the French Code of Commerce as amended by Law 2005-842 implementing the ECS; Part 7, art. 19 of the Danish Act on the SE.
176. Regulation, Preamble, recital (8).
177. According, in particular, to the *SEVIC Systems* ruling, note 131. This finding is consistent with the conclusions reached by the ECJ in the area of natural persons' free movement. In Case 41/1974, *Van Duyn* [1974] ECR II-1346, on public policy, the ECJ ruled that Member States have an area of discretion within the limits imposed by the Treaty (see para. 18 of this ruling), and in Case 67/1974, *Bonsignore* [1975] ECR I-306 on public policy and public security, it held that 'departures from the rules concerning the free movement of persons constitute exceptions which must be strictly construed' (see para. 6 of this ruling).
178. Regulation, Preamble, recital (5).
179. On analogy with the case law cited above note 177.
180. See above 3.2.4.
181. See Regulation, Preamble, recital (2). Compliance with competition rules laid down in the Treaty implies compliance with EC secondary legislation adopted thereunder, which, again, is in line with Article 4 of the 2005 Directive specifying that its provisions shall not apply to the extent that Article 21 of Merger Regulation 139/2004 (on the control of concentrations between undertakings) is applicable.
182. Suppose that companies A and B, located respectively in Member States A and B, wish to merge to create an SE, to be located in one of these two Member States. The national authorities of both states, on grounds of public interest, oppose the participation of companies A and B in the formation of the SE, but their opposition is rejected. If the national law of Member State A provides that the participation of company A takes effect from the time of the judicial rejection of the opposition, whereas the law of Member State B provides that the participation of company B takes effect from the time at which the two companies initially started the procedure, an evident conflict of laws problem would arise. To affirm simply that the SE could not be formed until the law of Member State A enables the participation of company A to take effect would not appear an adequate solution, since

the interests of the shareholders of company B and of third parties in both states are also involved.

183. See the UK European Public Limited Liability Company Regulations 2004 SI 2004/2326, Part 4 compared with ch. IX, art. L. 229-5 of the French Code of Commerce as amended by Law 2005-842 implementing the ECS, and with s. 2, arts 9 to 11 of the German SEEG; exact information not available as regards other countries.
184. Regulation, Article 66, first paragraph. See also above 3.2.8. In turn, the procedure for conversion laid down by the subsequent paragraphs of Article 66 reflects that required by the Third and Sixth Company Law Directives.
185. Regulation, Articles 38 to 51.
186. Article 38 (structure); Article 40, first paragraph (role of the supervisory organ); Article 41, first and second paragraphs (management organ's duty to report to the supervisory organ); Article 46, first and second paragraphs (appointment of members of company organs); Article 49 (duty of confidentiality on the members of the SE organs); Article 50, first and second paragraphs (rules relating to quorums and decision-taking in SE organs); Article 55 (power of a minority of shareholders to require convocation of the general meeting); Article 58 (votes cast) and Article 60 (case of two or more classes of shares).
187. Regulation, Articles 39 and 43, and the Survey, note 18, p. 11.
188. Regulation, Article 39, second paragraph; and the Survey, note 18, p. 11.
189. Approach well exemplified by ch. IX, arts L. 229-7 and 229-8 of the French Code of Commerce as amended by Law 2005-842 implementing the ECS, by Part 4, art. 8 of the Danish Act on the SE and by ch. IV, s. 12 of the Latvian Law on the SE.
190. In the case of Canada, the supranational company law vehicle provided by federally incorporated companies (companies incorporated under the Canada Business Corporations Act (1985)) represent a successful alternative to companies incorporated under the law of the individual 'Provinces' (that is, of the individual states) which are Members of the Federation, and, in Australia, the same applies to the Australian companies established under the Corporations Act (2001).
191. Regulation, Preamble, recital (3).
192. See ibid. Article 69.
193. As evidenced by the circumstance that 'Governments around the world are scrabbling for scarce corporate taxes' and 'OECD countries cut corporate tax rates by nearly seven percentage-points between 1996 and 2003. Some have cut aggressively' (see 'A taxing battle', *The Economist*, 31 January–6 February 2004, pp. 59–60).
194. Regulation, Preamble, recital (20). This new statement is substantially different from the corresponding recital of the Preamble to the 1991 draft, which simply stated that in the tax field the SE must be subject to the national legislation of its Member State of residence.
195. See below 3.4.
196. Regulation 1435/2003 of 22 July 2003, OJEC L207/1 [2003], and Directive 2003/72 of 22 July 2003, OJEC L207/25 [2003].
197. Regulation 1435/2003, Preamble, recital (6).
198. Ibid. recitals (7) to (10) and Articles 1, 3, 65, 66 and 75.
199. Ibid. Article 8 as compared with Article 9 of Regulation 2157/2001.
200. Chapter II of Regulation 1435/2003, Articles 17 to 35. The similarities can be noted between s. 1 ('General', Articles 17 to 18), s. 2 ('Formation by merger', Articles 19 to 34) and s. 3 ('Conversion of an existing cooperative into an SCE', Article 35) of this Chapter of Regulation 1435/2003 and s. I ('General', Articles 15 to 16), s. 2 ('Formation by merger', Articles 17 to 31) and s. 5 ('Conversion of an existing public limited-liability company into an SE', Article 37) of Title II of Regulation 2157/2001.
201. Article 2, second paragraph of Regulation 1435/2003 as compared with Article 2, fifth paragraph of Regulation 2157/2001.
202. Article 6 of Regulation 1435/2003 as compared with Article 7 of Regulation 2157/2001.
203. Article 7 of Regulation 1435/2003 as compared with Article 8 of Regulation 2157/2001.
204. Articles 3 to 6 and Article 7 of Directive 2003/72 as compared with Articles 3 to 6 and Article 7 of Directive 2001/86.

205. Chapter III of Regulation 1435/2003 (Articles 36 to 51), in particular s. I (two-tier system: Articles 37 to 41) and s. II (one-tier system: Articles 42 to 44), as compared with Title III of Regulation 2157/2001, in particular s. I (two-tier system: Articles 39 to 42) and s. II (one-tier system) in particular with s. I (two-tier system: Articles 39 to 42) and s. II (one-tier system: Articles 43 to 45).
206. Regulation 1435/2003, Preamble recital (18).
207. But cooperatives regulated by national laws may form an SCE by way of merger or conversion: s. 2 ('Formation by merger', Articles 19–34) and s. 3 ('Conversion of an existing cooperative into an SCE', Article 35) of ch. II of Regulation 1435/2003, see note 200.
208. Article 2, first paragraph of Regulation 1435/2003.
209. For example the provisions concerning the two-tier system and the one-tier system in the SCE regulate the calling of meetings of the management organ and of the supervisory organ (in Articles 38, 39 and 44 of Regulation 1435/2003) which are not dealt with by the corresponding provisions of Regulation 2157/2001, and indicate in greater detail the power of representation and liability of the SCE (Article 47 of Regulation 1435/2003, which finds no corresponding provision in Regulation 2157/2001).
210. See above 2.1 and 2.2.
211. Hopt, K.J. (1998), 'Europaisches Gesellschaftrecht – Krise und Neue Anlaufe', *Zeitschrift fur Wirtschaftsrecht*, 19, 99; Wenz, M. (2004), 'The European company (*societas Europaea*): legal concepts and tax issues', *European Taxation*, 1 (44), 4. In the academic literature, after the issue of the ECS in October 2001, see inter alia, also: Colombani, J.L. and M. Favero (2002), *Societas Europaea, la société Europeénne*, Paris, France: Jolis Editions; Teichmann C. (2003), 'The European company: a challenge to academics, legislators and practitioners', *German Law Journal*, 4, 311–318; www.germanlawjournal.com; Edwards, V. (2003), 'The European company: essential tool or eviscerated dream?', *Common Market Law Review*, (40), 443–450.
212. Wenz, note 211, p. 6.
213. Wenz, note 211, p. 7. Other German commentators agree that the lack of specific tax rules is to be welcomed: Schultz, A. and K. Eicker (2001), 'The European Company Statute: the German view', *Intertax*, 10 (29), 332–341, at 340.
214. See above 3.1.
215. See above 2.1.
216. See Communication, 'An internal market without tax obstacles: achievements, ongoing initiatives and remaining challenges' (COM (2003) 726 final), p. 6 with regard to the 'tax-engineering' strategies which may have the same detrimental effects for the achievement of the Lisbon objective.
217. Preamble, recitals (1) to (3).
218. In this regard, the text will argue, below 4.2.3 and 5.1, that this solution requires a more 'competitive' tax regime than each of the national taxation regimes applying to companies entirely governed by the laws of Member States, for the purpose of 'compensating' the limits of the ECS from the corporate law viewpoint. If, after 2009, amendments were adopted pursuant to a proposal from the Commission under Article 69 of the Regulation, the supranational solution as regards the tax regime would go in the same direction as these amendments in increasing the attractiveness of the SE in the business world and thus in allowing it to achieve its objectives.

PART II

The response to the challenge of legal competition: a supranational solution?

This part will propose, for the purpose of research and discussions at academic and decision-making level, the conditions allowing supranational instruments to become a solution capable of ensuring a legal competition between Member States compatible with the objectives of EC law in terms of proper functioning of the internal market.

4. Alternative routes towards the level playing field for companies in the European Community: suggestions

After evidencing that the tax Directives and the company law Directives have to a considerable extent followed a 'variable geometry' towards each others, and that the same requirements for compatibility with EC law apply to the legal competition among the Member States in both fields, this chapter will ultimately argue that, under certain conditions, supranational instruments may become effective routes, in contrast to the harmonization pursued up to the current time, towards a level playing field while ensuring a legal competition compatible with EC law.

4.1 EC CORPORATE TAX DIRECTIVES AND COMPANY LAW HARMONIZATION PROGRAMME: COHERENCE OR 'VARIABLE GEOMETRY'?

4.1.1 Need for Coherence between the Two Groups of EC Directives

The overviews of the implementation of the first two Tax Directives have indicated (in particular, as regards the Merger Directive) that some Member States have been delaying implementing its provisions granting tax relief for intra-EC mergers and divisions on the ground that no EC company law Directive dealing with such operations had been introduced: together with the regulation of intra-EC mergers under the ECS, the company law Directive 2005/56/EC on cross-border mergers of limited liability companies solves the problem with regard to mergers, but not with regard to divisions.[1] The granting of tax relief for a certain type of operation would be of little significance for the potentially interested companies if the operation in question were not allowed from the company law viewpoint: therefore, it becomes important to establish whether the tax Directives and the company law harmonization programme have been coherent with each other in contributing to the creation of a 'level playing field' for companies within the Community or whether they have followed a sort of 'variable geometry',[2] that is whether the tax and company law harmonization Directives have been introduced without taking into consideration each other's provisions. The need for consistency between the two groups of EC legislative measures, which at first sight might be considered as independent from each other, given their different legal bases and the different fields of law, emerges from an overall reading of the Treaty and of its goals in terms of market integration. Article 44, the legal base for the company law harmonization Directives, empowers the Council to facilitate freedom of establishment in other Member States, one of the essential freedoms which must exist in order for national markets to integrate in a common market, of which the provision of Article 94, the legal base of the tax Directives, aims at ensuring the (proper) functioning by enabling the Council to approximate those laws, regulations and administrative provisions which directly affect the establishment and functioning of such common market.

Consequently, in the case of a 'variable geometry' between these two groups of Directives, it is evident that the 'legal competition' among Member States, 'unintentionally' encouraged in the taxation field by the tax Directives as well as by the ECJ case law and, in the company law sector, by the limits of the harmonization programme has certainly not been discouraged by the overall EC intervention in companies' legislation. The answer depends on the extent to which (a) the two groups of EC measures apply to the same companies, and (b) as a result, whether the cross-border operations dealt with by the tax Directives, on the whole, have been in any way facilitated by the company law harmonization programme.

4.1.2 And the Resulting 'Variable Geometry'

The typologies of companies which have been covered by the tax Directives do not exactly coincide for each of the Member States, and they also include more legal forms of companies than those envisaged as beneficiaries of the company law harmonization programme. In the first respect, from the Annex of the original version of each of the tax Directives it can be immediately noted that, whereas for some countries the beneficiaries, in addition to companies having specific legal forms, have been identified by general definitions, such as 'industrial and commercial public establishments and undertakings'[3] or 'public and private entities carrying on industrial and commercial activities'[4] or 'commercial companies or civil law companies having a commercial form cooperatives and public undertakings',[5] for other countries they have only been identified by the legal forms,[6] whose range differs from one country to another. In the second respect, the companies covered by the company law harmonization Directives have only been indicated according to their legal forms, among which, on the whole, public limited companies are the main typology.[7] The list of beneficiaries of the three tax Directives thus ends up being broader than that of the beneficiaries of the company law harmonization directives. Accordingly, for some typologies of companies which fall within the range of beneficiaries of the tax Directives (or which may be included in this group by any amendments of the relevant tax laws of Member States)[8] but which are not listed amongst those falling within the scope of some company law Directives, the company law harmonization programme has facilitated neither the 'grouping together' envisaged by the Parent-Subsidiary Directive (90/435/EEC which, ultimately, is also the precondition for the status of 'associated company' under the Interest-Royalties Directive 2003/49/EC) nor the restructuring operations considered by the Merger Directive 90/434/EEC. Moreover, the 2004 amendments to the Parent-Subsidiary Directive, the 2005 amendments to the Merger Directive and the proposed amendments to the Interest-Royalties Directive,[9] by extending their coverage to new types of legal forms subject to corporation tax, have the effect of broadening the 'discrepancy' between the range of companies which ought to benefit from the tax Directives and the beneficiaries of the company law Directives. Nevertheless, even for those companies which have been included within the scope of the tax Directives and, at the same time, are listed amongst the types of companies subject to the company law harmonization Directives, it may well be questioned whether the company law harmonization programme as a whole has in any way either been a precondition for or facilitated the intra-EC operations for which the tax Directives have attempted to ensure tax neutrality. The answer seems to be largely negative. The company law Directives have certainly been a precondition neither for the creation of subsidiaries in other Member States nor for the restructuring operations, for at least two reasons. First, the setting up (or the acquisition) of subsidiaries by foreign companies – the requirement for the application of the Parent-Subsidiary Directive and of the Interest-Royalties Directive – is allowed by the laws of all Member States (as well as by the laws of extra-EC countries). Secondly, companies from any Member States interested in any restructuring operation envisaged by the Merger Directive with partners from another Member State know, after the *SEVIC Systems* ruling, that EC company law measures are not a precondition, and may argue that national rules governing the corresponding types of domestic operations should apply to operations involving companies from other EC countries too, in the light of the EC law principles of non-discrimination on ground of nationality.[10] On the other hand, whether the creation of subsidiaries and the restructuring operations have been facilitated by the company law Directives seems to be a more complex issue and the answer is certainly less immediate.

It may be assumed that this depends on the degree of approximation of national laws which such Directives have managed to achieve: the higher the similarity in all areas of company law (constitution, disclosure, annual accounts, restructuring operations, winding-up and so on), the greater the extent to which companies from a Member State can be encouraged in their decisions to exercise their freedom of establishment through the setting up of intra-EC subsidiaries (for which they may benefit from the Parent-Subsidiary Directive and from the Interest-Royalties Directive) and/or to consider restructuring operations (falling within the scope of the Merger Directive) with companies from other Member States (or, after setting up subsidiaries, within other Member States). As is recognized by the APCLCG, this assumption underlies Article 44 of the Treaty.[11] Nevertheless, from this perspective, it is inevitable to stress that, due to the many options left to Member States which have resulted in considerable differences between the 'harmonized' company laws,[12] the harmonization programme has not played a decisive role in creating the conditions for companies from one Member State to encounter similar company law provisions in any other Member State or, at least, has not done so in important areas. To the contrary, in the light of the scope of each of the adopted company law Directives, it would seem that the harmonization programme has been only partly effective in providing such a legal framework as to encourage the creation of subsidiaries and the intra-EC restructuring operations envisaged by the 1990 tax Directives. If this result may have been achieved by the first two company law Directives (the 'first generation Directives'), containing few options for Member States, and (although to a lesser extent due to the greater number of options left) by the Third and Sixth Directives providing for a basic procedure for internal mergers and divisions, the same does not apply to Directives concerning other areas, such as the Fourth and Seventh Directives on annual and consolidated accounts, which are certainly of primary importance for the possibility of understanding the financial situation of both potential intra-EC subsidiaries and companies from other Member States with whom to plan and implement restructuring operations, and of taking the related decisions.[13] In addition, the limitation of the scope of the Second, Third and Sixth company law Directives to public limited liability companies is not coherent with the realization that even private limited-liability companies, as beneficiaries of the two tax Directives, necessitate an intra-EC legal context so as not to discourage them from the 'grouping together' and the restructuring operations considered by the Merger and the Parent-Subsidiary Directives. Given the company law Directives issued to date and their overall features, it can thus be noted that such Directives may have on the one hand 'harmonized' more aspects than necessary to achieve coherence with the tax Directives but, on the other hand, have omitted some aspects which would be necessary for this purpose. The underlying reason may well lie in the circumstance that, as was argued in a different context of analysis of the company law programme, 'the failure of

European "representatives" to respond to their electors may have resulted in provisions which deal with irrelevant subjects and which ignore issues of real concern'.[14] Accordingly, if accepting that companies are encouraged to create or acquire subsidiaries in other Member States and to carry on restructuring operations involving companies from other EC countries by the approximation of national laws, it appears necessary to conclude that there has been to a considerable extent a 'variable geometry' between the two groups of Directives.

Alternatively, it might be supposed that, to the extent that companies' decisions to create subsidiaries or carry out restructuring operations are affected by legal provisions, the greater the difference between national company laws within the EC, the greater the incentive for companies to create subsidiaries in those Member States offering the most liberal company law rules or to plan restructuring operations leading to the creation or the acquisition of companies within such jurisdictions. In this latter case, paradoxically, it is the survival of differences in important aspects of national laws – or, in other words, the limit of the harmonization programme – which encourages companies to carry on the operations for which the Merger, the Parent-Subsidiary and the Interest-Royalties Directives have attempted to remove tax obstacles: as a result, it may be argued that the lack of any 'harmonizing' company law Directives would have offered an incentive to the operations at stake to an even greater extent. In fact, the general EC law principle of non-discrimination results in the application of the liberal rules of a state of destination to companies moving into that jurisdiction.[15] By moving from this second assumption, no coherence could be found between the three tax Directives and the company law harmonization programme, in the sense that the company law Directives could certainly not be considered as facilitating (and thus encouraging) the intra-EC operations envisaged by the tax Directives.

Given the objectives of the Treaty and the reasons why the two groups of Directives introduced in the fields of tax law and of company law may be seen as largely incoherent (or scarcely coherent) with each other, the conditions under which the 'variable geometry' could have been avoided (thus, under which tax Directives and company law Directives could have been able, to a much larger extent than they have actually done, to go in the same direction in creating a level playing field) may be easily deduced. Irrespective of the underlying assumptions about the incentive for companies to set up subsidiaries or to carry on the other operations envisaged by the tax Directives, two conditions could have been necessary and sufficient to achieve this outcome: (a) the inclusion, within the range of companies interested by the company law coordination measures, of all the categories of companies indicated by the second paragraph of Article 48 of the Treaty as entitled to freedom of establishment, which would have ensured the inclusion of all current and potential beneficiaries of the tax Directives;[16] (b) the approximation, by the company law harmonization measures, of all those aspects of national company laws (to be identified through an in-depth comparative study) which would be essential in order to create, for the possibility of setting up subsidiaries and of carrying on restructuring operations within the EC, conditions analogous to those of an internal market of an individual Member State. Had such conditions been met, the following results could have been achieved: (1) Member States would not have been able to fail to implement that part of the Merger Directive dealing with mergers and divisions on the ground that no company law Directive dealing with these operations has been introduced; (2) as a consequence, no margin would have been left for tax competition with regard to the range of the operations eligible for tax relief under the national laws implementing the tax Directives; (3) tax competition could also have been limited as regards the range of beneficiaries of the tax relief for restructuring operations which, by contrast, in some Member States is broader than in others;[17] (4) in turn, competition between national legislators would have been limited, in company law, to aspects other than those approximated by the EC law measures under consideration. The realization that the two groups of Directives have indeed to date followed, to a considerable extent, a 'variable geometry' from each other, indicates that the overall EC policy in the area of companies' related legislation has offered, though unintentionally, wide room for manoeuvre to the legal competition among the Member States on its whole, which may take place, in addition to the tax competition already encouraged by the tax Directives and by the case law on the freedom of establishment, and to the competition in company laws, through combinations of corporate taxation and company law competition strategies. It also contributes to making of crucial interest an attempt to provide an overall legal response to the issue of the compatibility of competition in corporate taxation, and in company laws, with EC law.

4.2 COMPETITION IN CORPORATE TAXATION WITHIN THE EC AND EC LAW

4.2.1 Competition in Corporate Taxation among the Member States in light of the Treaty

The issue whether the EC should rely on tax competition rather than on tax harmonization, dealt with by a considerable body of literature and discussed in seminars,[18] is still topical for at least two reasons. First, a conclusion that tax competition is compatible with EC law unless it uses special tax regimes could only reflect the current political conception of fair tax competition and the realization that, in the present state of ECJ case law on the exercise of the freedom of establishment and of other fundamental freedoms, the Member States' obligation to exercise their fiscal competence consistently with EC law has been identified solely in the prohibition of unjustified discriminations and restrictions.[19] Secondly, some arguments expressed in the literature, in support of tax competition based on general tax measures, rely on the fact that differences in the internal costs' situation in Member States, including those determined by tax rules, fall outside the scope of fundamental freedoms provided there are no discriminations nor restrictions,[20] or on the circumstance that the ECJ's rulings do not consider the protection of the tax base a valid justification for breach of the Treaty's provisions:[21] nevertheless, these arguments also lack an overall legal analysis based on the attempt at a comprehensive interpretation of the goals set out by the Treaty, in the light of the legal means offered by the Treaty itself and of other statements of general principles formulated by the case law of the ECJ.

According to another opinion, current thinking means that, whereas special tax measures must be assessed to evaluate their compatibility with the EC market in the light of the Code of Good Conduct against harmful tax competition, no assessment can be carried out on general tax measures.[22] This position seems to consider a statement in the 1998 Commission Notice on the application of state aid rules to measures relating to direct business taxation, whereby only special tax regimes, in addition to the scrutiny under the Code of Good Conduct, can be examined under Article 87 concerning state aids as fiscal support measures,[23] as evidence that the tax competition in special tax measures is refused whilst that in general tax measures is accepted. The question would thus be not whether market competition is distorted, but how it is distorted and this would depend on a choice of the Treaty's drafters, who 'only rejected fiscal support measures and did not object to general tax measures': therefore, the distortions and inequalities arising from general tax measures would be 'covered by the principle of fiscal sovereignty' of individual Member States.[24]

Nonetheless, in the 1998 Notice, the Commission itself stated that Article 87 cannot be seen as the only relevant provision. It admitted, in fact, that some general tax measures may impede the proper functioning of the internal market and that, in these cases, the Treaty on the one hand provides for the harmonization of national tax provisions on the basis of Article 94 and, on the other hand, makes possible the elimination of distortions on the basis of Articles 96 and 97,[25] whereas other literature considers that 'it is not very credible to adhere to national sovereignty in extremis in areas where the current situation affects the proper functioning of the EU Single Market'.[26] In effect, the drafting of the Treaty almost 50 years ago, at a time when international tax competition did not have the relevance which it has assumed over the last decades, justifies to an even greater extent an attempt to find, in the unchanged Treaty's provisions, the legal basis and the criteria to deal thoroughly with this phenomenon. Distortions caused by competition among the normal tax regimes can in fact compromise the ambitious 'Lisbon objective',[27] which the founders of the EEC did not set at the time but which must, by definition, be seen as compatible with the Treaty.[28] It was also admitted that Member States' freedom to distort competition by using structural elements in their tax systems has to be restricted in an economic and monetary union.[29]

A first group of provisions which suggest that the Commission's statements about general tax measures formulated in the 1998 Notice may also hold true for the tax competition which uses these measures are to be found in Articles 2, 3 let. (g) and (h), 4, 5, 94, 96, 97 and 293 of the Treaty. Although the Treaty contains no provisions dealing with corporate taxation, the objectives laid down in Article 2 in terms of economic development, to be achieved inter alia under Article 3 through the creation of a system of undistorted competition[30] and the 'approximation of the laws of Member States to the extent required for the functioning of the common market',[31] read together with the provision of Article 293 requiring Member States to enter negotiations, so far as necessary, to eliminate double taxation within the Community, offer two indications. The (proper) functioning of the common market, essential for the achievement of the goals stated in Article 2, is ensured to the extent to which, within this market, competition amongst companies is not distorted, and, in this regard, any distortion caused by taxation, such as, for example, double taxation (referred to in Article 293 in general terms, without distinction between direct and indirect taxation) ought to be eliminated. Consequently, Article 293 shows that the functioning of the common market under conditions of undistorted competition should be hindered neither by indirect nor by direct taxation rules, and the awareness of a link between the tax rules of Member States and the functioning of the common market, which is evidenced by Articles 90 to 93 only in the sector of indirect taxation, emerges also in the field of direct taxation. Moreover, the coordinated reading of this first group of provisions suggests that the elimination of double taxation was expressly indicated because it was perceived as a major factor of distortion, but by no means as the only element to be removed if causing distortions, in the field of direct taxation too. Although commentators and official reports only began addressing the direct link existing between company taxation and the common market in the early years of the EEC,[32] it may thus be deduced that the approximation of national laws, referred to in Article 3, was already conceived by the Treaty's drafters as the instrument, to be used with discretion by the EC institutions, to eliminate any obstacle to the proper functioning of the common market by removing inter alia any factor hindering undistorted competition which existed in all sectors of national laws, with no exceptions for corporate taxation: this marks the limits of the concepts of 'extent required' (in the wording of Article 3) and/or of 'so far as necessary' (in the wording of Article 293).

Therefore, the Treaty intends neither to commit the EC institutions to approximate national corporate tax laws nor completely accepting the effects of the exercise of national sovereignty in such sector. This is confirmed by Article 94 which, by endowing the Council with the authority to issue Directives for the approximation of laws, regulations or administrative provisions of the Member States which directly affect the establishment or functioning of the common market, draws no distinction between different sectors of law. Nor is such a distinction drawn by Articles 96 and 97, which enable the Council to take measures to eliminate distortions detrimental to the common market, on a proposal from the Commission and after a consultation procedure, when the Commission finds that a difference between national provisions is distorting the condition of competition, and that the resultant distortion needs to be eliminated. The Treaty thus simply charges the EC institutions with the legal obligation to assess whether and when national corporate tax regimes ought to be approximated, and offers them two criteria to be used in such assessment: the approximation is necessary if the differences between national company taxation rules directly affect the common market, and this occurs whenever such differences lead to (not negligible) distortions (Article 96) of market competition within the Community. Consequently, the subsidiarity principle (Article 5 of the Treaty) has little relevance because it applies in the sectors which do not fall within the exclusive competence of the Community, whereas Articles 3, 293, 94, 96 and 97, read together, show that the obligation to assess the need for approximation of national corporate tax regimes is exclusively placed on EC institutions and, solely to the extent to which any measures which may be necessary to eliminate distortions caused by different national corporate tax laws fail to be adopted by the Community ('so far as necessary'), Member States need to enter negotiations to conclude Conventions aimed at achieving the same goals (as may be argued from Article 293). This interpretation is not in conflict with the argument – one of the two behind the current conception of tax competition[33] – that the level of taxation, under the principle of subsidiarity, is a matter for Member States to decide, but rather completes it. In fact, whereas the principle of subsidiarity (and of national sovereignty) undoubtedly requires competence in the structuring of direct taxation regimes to remain vested with Member States, a different competence, that is that of assessing whether the exercise of Member States' sovereignty creates distortions in the functioning of the common market, is left to EC institutions.[34] From the opposite perspective, the combined reading of all these provisions shows that, in the Treaty, there is no assumption that the lack of harmonization in corporate tax regimes necessarily affects the common market by generating distortions in the competition among companies located in different Member States.

As a result, it may be deduced that the lack of harmonization, and with this the (higher or lower) degree of competition among Member States in corporate taxation regimes, is legally compatible with the Treaty provided it takes such forms as not to affect directly the proper functioning of the common market, that is such as not to distort the competition among companies within the Community. Indirectly, this (first) requirement appears to be confirmed by the wording of Article 87 itself and, in general, of a second group of provisions, Articles 81, 82, 90 and 93, which are included in Title VI, devoted to 'Common rules' on competition, on taxation and on the approximation of national laws, as the setting of common rules necessarily supposes common principles, and common goals, underlying such rules. These provisions reveal the underlying concern of the Treaty's drafters in all areas directly affecting (as corporate taxation can do) the market conditions within the EC for companies established in the various Member States. In this regard, it can easily be noted that Articles 81, 82 and 87, respectively dealing with restrictive agreements between companies, with the abuse of a dominant position and with state aids to enterprises, do not forbid these practices on their own, but only to the extent to which they prejudice the trade between Member States and/or damage competition or (in the case of state aids) threaten to damage competition: anyway, in all these cases, which have in common with competition in corporate taxation the potential to impair genuine market competition, the Treaty pays attention to their effects on the market. The same principle can be deduced from Articles 90 and 93 on indirect taxation, the first preventing a Member State from applying to products coming from other Member States internal taxes aimed at indirectly protecting other productions, the second requiring harmonization of indirect taxation if necessary for the establishment and functioning of the internal market: even these two provisions, in fact, show that the Treaty's drafters were concerned with the consequences of internal indirect taxes (Article 90) and of the lack of harmonization (Article 93) (or, in other words, of the (greater) competition among Member States) in this field.

A second requirement in order for competition among Member States in corporate taxation regimes to be compatible with the Treaty may be inferred from the third paragraph of Article 4, whereby the actions undertaken by the Member States and the Community, with a view to securing an economic policy geared to the achievement of the key EC objectives set out in Article 2, must respect essential principles such as, inter alia, sound monetary conditions and public finances. This means that competition in corporate taxation regimes should not, on its own, damage the public finances of Member States. Such further conditions appears to be directly confirmed by some provisions of Title VII, dealing with economic and monetary policy, in particular by the combined wording of Article 99 requiring Member States to consider their economic policies an issue of common interest and imposing a stricter coordination of economic policies and a durable convergence of their economic results, and of Article 104, clearly stating that Member States must avoid excessive public deficits. No contradiction can be found between this second requirement which can be deduced from the Treaty and the continuous rejection, in the ECJ case law, of the argument based on the loss of tax revenues which national authorities have often submitted for justifying the refusal to grant tax advantages:[35] the loss of tax revenues, which can be caused by the inability of a state to deny tax advantages, as well as by tax competition (leading Member States to attempt to protect revenues at the expense of each other), does not damage public finances to the extent that it is compensated by a limitation in public spending.[36]

Consequently, when it does not meet both of the two requirements, competition in company taxation among national legislators can be regarded as hindering the achievement of the goals set out in the Treaty and, for this reason, as legally incompatible with EC law. Lastly, this first conclusion does not appear to be affected, in the light of the suggested interpretation, by other key Treaty provisions, such as Article 10 imposing on Member States the obligations of Community loyalty and cooperation and Article 12 prohibiting any discrimination on grounds of nationality. Article 10 contains, in fact, a negative obligation to abstain from any measure which could jeopardize the objectives of the Treaty, but such obligation would be fulfilled if a Member State introduced in its corporate tax regime a measure which, even if designed to compete with other Member States' regimes, assumes such contents and forms as not to distort directly the competition between companies located in its territory and companies located in other Member States. In turn, the other negative obligation imposed by Article 12 is met by definition in the case of competition in company taxation among the Member States, to the extent to which the underlying objective implies, by its very nature, that a Member State, in introducing more favourable rules than other states, applies those rules to both its domestic companies and companies from other states. Ultimately, the interpretation whereby the Treaty does not regard competition in corporate taxation as automatically (in)compatible with the achievement of the objectives of the Community but offers the EC institutions two criteria – the two indicated conditions – to be used in this assessment, translates the general issue of the compatibility of competition among national corporate taxation regimes with the Treaty into the more specific question concerning the features which such competition should assume to fulfil the two requirements.

4.2.2 And in light of Secondary EC Legislation, Soft Law and ECJ Case Law

The analysis does not find further elements (others than those implicitly offered by Articles 3, 4, 293, 94, 96, 97, 81, 82, 87, 90 and 93) from the secondary EC legislation to date issued, that is from the Tax Directives (Chapter 1), aimed at approximating elements which can be considered as belonging to structural corporate tax regimes such as the treatment of dividend distributions, of restructuring operations or of interest-royalties payments. Consistently with the task left by the Treaty to EC institutions, to assess the need for approximation of national tax provisions, in their Preambles[37] these Directives reflect an assessment whereby differences between national tax provisions tend to produce distortions and to contrast with the need to have within the common market, for the operations envisaged, tax-neutral rules from the viewpoint of competition (among companies located in different Member States).[38] Moreover, by expressly emphasizing the importance of tax neutrality, this secondary legislation also confirms one of the two conditions for the compatibility of tax competition with EC law (this competition is, in fact, a source of those differences which tend to produce distortions).

'Soft law' instruments can also be read together with the Treaty.[39] Compared with the secondary legislation, a piece of 'soft law' such as the 1994 Commission Recommendation concerning the taxation of SMEs[40] seems to go further, by exemplifying a difference in businesses taxation which has been considered as distorting competition between enterprises and, thus, as incompatible with the common market. This Recommendation invited the Member States either to give sole proprietorships and partnerships the right to opt to pay corporation tax in respect of reinvested profits or to restrict the tax charge on these profits to a rate comparable to that of corporation tax, on the ground that the progressive structure of rates of personal income tax, applying to sole proprietorships and partnerships, 'hampers the development of the self-financing capacity of such enterprises' and 'consequently *restricts their investment capacity*',[41] which distorts competition between enterprises, depending on their legal forms, to the detriment of sole proprietorships and partnerships.[42] The Recommendation considered it necessary to eliminate this distortion by achieving 'a greater tax neutrality, at least as regards the implications which systems of taxation have for profits reinvested by enterprises and, hence *for their self-financing capacity*'.[43]

Accordingly, this Recommendation strengthens the argument which can already be drawn from the Treaty's provisions, that differences in enterprises' taxation regimes are acceptable to the extent that they do not distort competition between enterprises.[44] On the other hand, by providing an example of differences to be eliminated, it can be seen as offering the further indication according to which, whenever for just one or some of the categories of enterprises they affect an objective factor which is crucial for enterprises' possibility of facing market competition (such as their self-financing capacity), the differences in the taxation regimes are presumed to distort competition between enterprises and thus, in the Treaty's wording, to 'directly affect' the establishment and functioning of the common market. Given the general scope of the previously examined Treaty provisions,[45] this indication may also be regarded as offering a general criteria to analyse, on a case-by-case basis, when competition among the national corporate taxation regimes is to be seen as distorting market competition between companies located in different Member States, that is as lacking one of the two requirements suggested by the Treaty for its compatibility with the common market.

This interpretation can be reconciled with another important and more recent piece of 'soft law', the Code of Good Conduct on business taxation,[46] which applies to special tax regimes, that is to all company tax measures of special character which may only be introduced by Member States by way of derogation from all national tax regimes of general application and which are to be examined under specific and well-defined aspects.[47] Due to this limitation of its scope, the Code of Good Conduct is not in conflict with the suggested interpretation, which refers to normal company taxation regimes of general application to resident and non-resident companies. On the contrary, the criteria set out by the Code to assess special tax regimes is complementary to the above indicated criteria (directly emerging from the Treaty's provisions, implicitly confirmed by the Preambles to the tax Directives and further specified by the Commission Recommendation) to be used by the EC institutions for assessing the compatibility of measures introduced by Member States to compete with each other in their normal company taxation regimes. The Code of Good Conduct merely confirms, in fact, that a case-by-case approach is to be adopted, by using predefined criteria, to assess the compatibility of special tax regimes too. Nor is a different approach suggested by the 1997 Council Resolution[48] which, in addition to introducing the Code, noted that several of the tax schemes falling within the scope of the Code itself could also be reviewed in the framework of Articles 87 to 89 of the Treaty, that is of the Treaty's rules on state aids to enterprises. The recognition that these special tax regimes may often be regarded as a form of state aids implies in fact that the selective approach, based on an individual scrutiny, required by Articles 87 to 89 to assess the compatibility of state aids with the common market, necessarily must also apply to the tax regimes at issue. Ultimately, the Code of Good Conduct and the related Council Resolution evidence only one difference between the assessment of tax competition based on normal tax measures and that of tax competition based on special tax measures: the criteria to evaluate special tax regimes in the light of EC law and, as a result, to regard as 'harmful' the tax competition from which they may originate, are more specifically defined, and therefore of easier practical application, than the criteria to be used to evaluate the (effects of) differences between normal corporate tax regimes suggested by the above-mentioned Treaty provisions and, indirectly, further clarified by the Commission Recommendation. In turn, this difference may certainly be due to the non-binding nature of the Code of Good Conduct (as a 'soft law' instrument) and, with this, to the lack of an interest on the part of Member States to oppose the adoption of a Code (containing much more detailed provisions on corporate taxation than the Treaty) which they knew to be bound to have a very limited effect upon their domestic tax regimes.[49]

In addition, the Preamble to the Commission Recommendation, in stressing the disadvantage caused by the method of taxing sole proprietorships and partnerships, generally subject to personal income tax, states that such method 'hampers the development of the self-financing capacity of such enterprises' and, in an economic environment where access to external financing is becoming more difficult, consequently restricts their investment capacity.[50] This indicates that the evaluation as to whether or not the differences between the normal enterprises' taxation regimes (including those between the company taxation regimes)[51] have to be considered as affecting, for some of the categories of enterprises, an objective factor which is crucial for the possibility of facing market competition (and, thus, as distorting competition), is to be carried on in a relatively flexible manner, by considering the conditions of the economic environment in which companies competing within the Community, given their location in different Member States, find themselves to operate.[52] Conversely, the Code of Good Conduct contains an 'escape clause'[53] which applies to special tax measures intended to promote the economic development of certain regions and which requires, in this case, the evaluation of compatibility to consider whether the scheme is proportional to the objectives to be achieved: this clause suggests that, outside this specifically envisaged hypothesis, the evaluation of compatibility must be carried out in a strict manner, that is by following with no possibility of exceptions the rigorous criteria which the Code indicates. Nevertheless, as the Code deals with all special corporate tax regimes only, it offers no reason why its strict method toward the evaluation of compatibility should extend to normal corporate tax regimes too.[54] The comparison between the wording of the Commission Recommendation above quoted and of the Code of Good Conduct therefore seems to indicate that the same case-by-case approach for the evaluation of compatibility with EC law should be adopted: with flexibility, when assessing the competition based on general tax measures; in a rigorous manner, when assessing the competition based on special tax measures.

Conclusively, competition concentrating on companies' normal taxation regimes can be regarded as compatible with EC law provided it does not directly affect the functioning of the common market, that is it does not distort competition between companies within the Community, and it does not damage Member States' finances, conditions which have to be evaluated on a case-by-case base by the EC institutions. In turn, to meet the first of these two requirements, the tax competition in question must not affect – for just some of the categories of competing companies – one of the crucial factors, of an objective nature, at the root of their ability to face market competition, which has to be assessed in the light of the economic environment and of their current and potential market of reference,[55] in which their location leads them to operate. On the whole, these criteria appear also to be coherent with a general statement by the ECJ about the need for approximation of national laws (and, implicitly, about the need to limit differences between national laws, potentially originating from competition among national legislators), whereby, to give effect to the fundamental freedoms indicated in the Treaty, harmonization is 'necessary to deal with disparities between the laws of the Member States *in areas where such disparities are liable to create or maintain distorted conditions of competition*'.[56]

They can thus be used to formulate a concrete hypothesis of an EC law compatible competition among national company taxation regimes.

4.2.3 Features of a Tax Competition Compatible with EC Law: Hypothesis

The (legal) criteria for the assessment of the compatibility of competition among normal company taxation regimes with the goals of EC law, emerging from the suggested coordinated reading of the Treaty, of the secondary legislation and of the relevant soft law instruments, should enable the Commission, at the time when it may be induced to reconsider its current approach of tolerance towards this competition, to evaluate when the legitimacy of a measure introduced by a Member State in its normal corporate tax regime[57] with a view to making it more 'attractive' than the regimes of other EC partners (thus of general application to the category(ies) of enterprises taking one (or all) of the legal forms of companies within a given jurisdiction, and placing them, from the viewpoint of market competition, in a better position than the corresponding category(ies) of enterprises from other Member States) can be called into question in the light of EC law objectives.[58] These criteria[59] suggest that, in order to meet them and thus to pass what may be defined as a 'compatibility test', the measures introduced by a Member State to make its normal company taxation regime more 'competitive' than those of other Member States ought to have two basic features: (a) they should be introduced as a part of a transparent competition; (b) they must not lead to such a 'race to the bottom'[60] as to cause the limitation of the scope of the Code of Good Conduct to become useless.[61] The coordinated reading above referred to does indicate decisive arguments for these two features.

First, it must be recalled, in order to assess whether competition in corporate taxation directly affects the functioning of the common market, that measures such as a reduction of corporate tax rates or the introduction of more favourable rules for determining taxable profits are not the only elements – despite their importance – which influence the objective factors at the root of companies' ability to face market competition within the Community: availability of infrastructure, costs of public services, availability of skilled labour force, labour costs and national laws granting financial support for investments, are just some of the other objective elements affecting the economic environment in which companies operate. The greater the differences in these other elements from one state to another, the higher the difficulty in evaluating whether and to what extent measures intended to improve the attractiveness of the taxation regime may actually be, on their own, the decisive factor distorting competition among companies in the market (that is directly affecting the functioning of the market) or whether they can only have (because of their combination with the other elements) an indirect influence on companies' objective competitive position (in which case, by definition, no problem of compatibility with EC law would arise). Nevertheless, it appears unquestionable that, as EC policies in areas different from taxation (for example vocational training policies, regional development policies, state aids-related policies) which find their legal base in the Treaty[62] tend to make the other objective elements affecting competition among companies located in different Member States increasingly similar from one state to another (consistently with the goal, set by Article 2 of the Treaty, of a 'balanced' economic growth within the Community), the differences between company taxation regimes are bound to become, to a greater and greater extent, the decisive factor. This although (to borrow the words of the EC Commissioner for internal market and taxation at the time of the release of the 2001 Commission Report on *Companies Taxation in the Internal Market*) it may be said that the effects of competition in corporate tax regimes on market competition 'are not quantifiable at the present stage'.[63] Assuming the similarity of other objective factors, the greater the effect of a corporate tax measure of structural nature, introduced to compete with the taxation regimes of other Member States, in determining the competitive advantage of companies located in a given jurisdiction, the greater its direct influence on the functioning of the internal market. In fact, it can certainly be stressed that every company within the Community, in the present state of EC law, is in principle free to avail itself of the most favourable corporate taxation regime offered by a given Member State by establishing its fiscal residence in that state,[64] and it may be added that this appears to be even truer due to the developments of the ECJ case law on companies' right of primary establishment, that is to say the *Uberseering* ruling.[65] However, two points have to be considered. First, a massive 'migration' of companies towards the most favourable tax jurisdiction inevitably affects the objective competitive position of those competitors which, for whatever practical and/or legal reasons, may find the transfer to this jurisdiction less easy. In fact, even if *Lasteyrie du Saillant*[66] were definitively interpreted as meaning that the moving out of the central administration (and, with this, of the tax residence) were possible from all countries, national provisions different from exit taxes (at least in the current state of EC law) could continue to make the migration easier from some states than from others for the same categories of domestic companies. Secondly, such migration, to the extent to which it is deemed to result in an improvement of economic conditions and jobs creation in a Member State at the price of a worsening of these conditions in other states,[67] generates effects which would appear to be difficult to accept in the light of goals set by Article 2 of the Treaty (balanced and sustainable economic growth, increasing convergence of economic results in the Member States). In addition, a massive companies' relocation to the Member State which, for the time being, offers the most favourable corporate tax treatment, by causing revenue losses to other Member States because of the decrease in the number of taxpayers, may directly prejudice the economic policies of such states and prevent the achievement of the 'convergence' required by Articles 98 and 99 of the Treaty. Such an outcome may take place, it can be observed, unless and until the measures adopted by the first Member State, which have made it the most favourable location for tax purposes, are 'compensated' by competing measures introduced by the other states and capable of maintaining unaltered their domestic companies' competitive position while retaining them in these states.[68] This supposes, however, that companies are in a position easily and exactly to evaluate which corporate tax regime would turn out to be best, that is to assess whether or not it would be convenient to relocate to a different jurisdiction. The global assessment in question is more easily possible, without the risk of misleading conclusions, the greater extent to which the competing measures introduced by the various states lead to *transparent* tax competition, that is to a competition focusing on specific elements – tax rate, tax base – based on identical (or almost identical) definitions of the same underlying technical concepts (for example of deductible expenses, of relevant revenues, of dividends, of tax losses, of reserves and so on).[69] If this were not so, a comparison based only on tax rates and tax base could risk making a given corporate taxation system appear more favourable than another even though, in the light of the features of the business activity of the company, this might not hold true, and a decision grounded on such comparison might also lead to allocation inefficiencies from the economic viewpoint.[70] As mentioned above, exactly an altered tax competition has resulted from the implementation of the two 1990 tax Directives.[71] On the other hand, it can be argued that, to the extent that companies' taxation is not the only element affecting businesses' competitive positions and location decisions, the greater the degree of transparency in the tax competition at issue, the greater the possibility for companies planning their overall strategies to recognize the boundaries of such competition and to outweigh the influence of the other elements.

Nonetheless, if for these reasons transparency turns out to be a necessary feature for an EC law compatible competition among normal company taxation regimes, it cannot be regarded as sufficient. A transparent but limitless competition, generating a continuous 'race to the bottom' among national legislators in the introduction of structural measures aimed at making their company tax regimes more attractive than those of their EC partners, could hardly be seen as compatible with EC law objectives.[72] First, it would tend to approximate, in the medium or long run, the outcome of some features of normal tax regimes (in terms, for example, of reduced rate of taxation of general application or of exclusion of some items of income from the taxable base) to that of the special tax regimes: this would cause the Code of Good Conduct to have a contradictory effect on its original aim, and, in the wider international context, would conflict with the OECD's efforts to combat harmful tax competition based on special tax regimes.[73] Secondly, it could not, by definition, contribute to the harmonization of national company taxation regimes: the argument that competition may serve to produce 'spontaneous' harmonization cannot apply in the situation considered, in which each Member State continuously changes the key features of its tax regime to make it more attractive than the others. Thirdly, it would run the risk of causing an endless loss of revenue to all Member States, that is of causing excessive budget deficits, although to a different degree from one state to another depending on the possibility for the various national tax legislators to off-set the decrease of revenue from companies' direct taxation (which constitute, for all countries, one of the fundamental components of the overall tax system) with reduction in government spending and/or with increases of direct and/or indirect taxes in other sectors. In turn, this outcome may prejudice the capacity of individual states to achieve the economic convergence with each other required by the Treaty (which would create most problematic consequences, at both legal and political level, in the light of the economic parameters imposed by and after the adoption of the single currency). The suggestions which have been formulated since the 1992 Ruding Report for a minimum corporate tax rate at EC level clearly reflect a widespread awareness of the need to prevent an endless race to the bottom competition among the Member States in normal tax regimes, awareness which may well be strengthened by the potential effects of the latest ECJ rulings.[74] These proposals,[75] if reconsidered against the current situation, may however meet two objections. First, if aiming at establishing such minimum rate at a higher level than the national corporate tax rates which are already in force in one or more states, such proposals would certainly (continue) to be rejected by those Member States, which would consider it as damaging their interests (and would be particularly unwelcome by the companies which are already established in those states).[76] Secondly, the existence of a minimum corporate tax rate may not suffice, on its own, to prevent an endless tax competition which, if not on tax rates, may concentrate on the definitions of some elements of the taxable base, with the risk of actually becoming more difficult to perceive (and less transparent) than a competition concentrating on the tax rates too.

Accordingly, it can be argued that, to be compatible with EC law, the tax competition, in addition to being transparent, should also produce the result of making all the competing national company taxation regimes approximate to well-defined elements in terms of both the tax rate and the definition of the tax base. In other words, such competition should prove itself capable of spontaneously achieving an outcome which can hardly result from a legislative harmonization, and of doing so while avoiding the above described 'race to the bottom'. The most effective instrument leading to a competition with such features would probably be the tax regime, if structured in all its elements (tax rate, tax base, underlying technical concepts) of a supranational company law vehicle, that is an optional but self-sufficient supranational company taxation regime, introduced by an EC Regulation aiming to complement, from the tax law viewpoint, the company law features of a supranational scheme. Specifically, such tax regime ought to be more favourable than each of the national regimes, in order to compete successfully with them in businesses' choices, and should be accompanied by a binding measure calling for a scrutiny of those (normal) national tax regimes assuming more favourable features than this supranational regime, with a view to analysing their compatibility with EC law. Such a measure, which will have a realistic chance of being approved by the Council to the extent that all Member States will consider the need to avoid an endless 'race to the bottom' competition in the structural aspects of corporate taxation at issue to be in their national interest,[77] may also consist of an amendment to the Code of Good Conduct, if this latter were to become 'hard law'.[78] The tax regime of a supranational company law vehicle could become, in these conditions, the companies' taxation system towards which the different competing national regimes should tend, which would contribute to increase the transparency of the competition itself, to 'determine the general boundaries' of the race to the bottom in normal company taxation regimes (which is unintentionally encouraged by the ECJ's tax rulings) and, ultimately, to facilitate the achievement of a 'spontaneous' harmonization.[79]

4.3 INTRA-EC COMPETITION IN COMPANY LAWS AND EC LAW

After indicating the objectives of EC company law policy in the strengthening of shareholders' rights and of third party protection on the one hand, and in the efficiency and competitiveness of EC businesses on the other hand, the APCLCG laid down a plan for several legislative measures, one of which, a Fourteenth Directive on cross-border seat transfer, implicitly presupposes the survival of significant differences in the legal context from one Member State to another.[80] This feature of the company law environment within the Community makes the assessment of the need for any future harmonization Directive, and of merit under EC law of the inter-jurisdictional competition in company law, of utmost importance.

4.3.1 Most Immediate Implications raised by the ECJ Case Law for Future EC Company Law Developments: What Scope for the Draft Fourteenth Company Law Directive and Other Harmonizing Directives?

In this assessment, the case law of the ECJ (in particular, the *Uberseering*, *Inspire Art*, *Lasteyrie du Saillant* and *SEVIC Systems* rulings)[81] should be considered: since 2004, the Commission has expressed its intention to focus on the transfer of the registered office, rather than of the head office alone which is permitted by the ECJ case law.[82] Accordingly, the Fourteenth Directive would enable companies, without dissolution, to transfer their registered office, together with the head office, for the purpose of changing the applicable national law and thus their legal personality. To the extent that this type of transfer is regarded as a 'restructuring' operation, from the ECJ statement in *SEVIC Systems* that restructuring operations are modalities of exercising the freedom of establishment[83] it may be argued that the only purpose of this proposed Directive would be that of facilitating it. The operation would be facilitated by this Directive through a rigorous procedure, similar to those required by the Third and Sixth Company Law Directives for internal mergers and divisions[84] and to that imposed by the ECS for the transfer of the seat of an SE.[85] The procedure, which marks a compromise between the incorporation system (no dissolution of the transferring company) and the real seat criteria (compliance with the law of the host state), would be aimed at providing legal certainty, which should be the ultimate purpose of the proposed Directive for an operation considered, as a type of restructuring, an extraordinary event in the life of the company.[86]

Nevertheless, the fact that the transfer of the head office alone without the registered office and without the change of applicable law, on the basis of the ECJ case law,[87] could be regarded as an ordinary operation may well induce most businesses, in a cost-benefit analysis of the procedure laid down by the proposed Directive, to prefer the transfer of the head office alone. Specifically, whereas the Fourteenth Directive would allow the transfer of the registered office (change of applicable law) after the creation of the company in one jurisdiction by businesses who consider another jurisdiction most suited to their needs, entrepreneurs, when selecting the EC jurisdiction in which to create companies, can choose from the outset the jurisdiction offering the most 'liberal' company law for incorporation, and these companies could maintain the registered office there even if they prefer to have the formal or de facto head office (either the primary seat or a branch from which all activity is carried out) in another Member State. To the extent that this specific type of 'forum shopping' (originating a 'Delaware effect') which was at issue in the situations dealt with by the ECJ case law may be perceived as more straightforward and less costly and thus become more attractive in the business world than the rigorous procedure necessary to implement the alternative modality (transfer of the registered office), the proposed Fourteenth Directive would risk becoming obsolete before entering into force. In effect, from businesses' viewpoint, the key reason for transferring the registered office (change of applicable law) under this Directive after the creation of the company in one jurisdiction would be the legal certainty ensured by a procedure aimed at protecting the interests of creditors, employees and third parties.[88] Compliance with this procedure would allow them to eliminate the risk of falling within the 'certain circumstances' and the 'certain conditions' which otherwise, in the case of the transfer to a jurisdiction of the head office of a company created in another jurisdiction, may according to the ECJ justify a restriction on the freedom of primary establishment of the company.[89] Nevertheless, this 'advantage' is deemed to disappear to a large extent, since the ECJ case law tends to restrict these circumstances and conditions to situations of case-by-case abuse to be proved by Member States, with the result that businesses can be expected to be increasingly encouraged to resort to the modality of forum shopping which was already at issue in the situations that came before the ECJ.[90] It thus becomes evident, through the ECJ case law, that the proposed Fourteenth Directive may be rendered largely useless. According to an opinion expressed in the academic literature, regulatory competition within the EC is not certain to become as relevant as in the US, because the mobility of entrepreneurs within the EC only extends to incorporating companies, not to re-incorporating ones, and concerns only small-sized companies, privately held companies, whose founders wish to avoid a minimum capital, rather than large, publicly held listed companies to whom the EC company law harmonization has been primarily addressed.[91] Nevertheless, irrespective of the fact that, as a result of *SEVIC Systems*, re-incorporation should be considered already possible as a restructuring operation, and that the adoption of the draft Fourteenth Directive would facilitate it, this position seems not to consider two decisive aspects. First, the ECJ case law, even if, to date, it has concerned mainly (except for SEVIC) small-sized, privately held companies, clarifies the possibilities of exercise of the freedom of establishment, including transfer of the head office alone, which are available to companies of any size. Secondly, small-sized businesses represent the overwhelming majority of all EC businesses, and the need for protection of both members and third parties, which is highlighted by Article 44 and set out by the APCLCG as the first goal of EC company law policy, arises in respect of their activity too. Consequently, the fact that the greater the number of areas which remain outside the scope of the harmonization programme, the greater the extent to which the forum-shopping practices exemplified by the situations dealt with by the ECJ case law can be designed and implemented, requires the EC institutions to make a final choice on whether to continue to tolerate a 'Delaware effect' within the Community; if so, for which category of companies, in which areas and for which purposes.

4.3.2 Legal Grounds for (Greater or Lesser) Competition among National Company Laws

As the current business environment is very different from that which existed at the time when the (then) EEC was first established, the assessment of the merit of any future harmonizing Directive, irrespective of the area of company law, lies in a central issue: whether the same patterns, such as harmonization, can still be considered to be appropriate for achieving the same objectives set out by the Treaty in terms of free movement of companies, undistorted market competition and (proper) functioning of the internal market (Article 3 and Articles 94 to 96 of the Treaty). It has already been stressed that, in the Treaty, the provisions of Articles 43, 44 and 48 dealing with companies' freedom of establishment, the approximation of law provision of Article 94, the wording of Article 293, calling for Member States, 'so far as necessary', to enter negotiations aiming at concluding Conventions with a view to ensuring the mutual recognition of companies and the possibility of seat transfer from one state to another, and the provisions of Article 308, all offer legal bases to be used for achieving the identical and ultimate goal of turning different national markets into a properly functioning internal market, in which companies would not find barriers in establishing in other Member States and within which they should, without distortions, freely compete with each other (the so-called 'level playing field').[92]

Accordingly, the harmonization of national company laws is still the appropriate pattern, as it would have been at the time of establishment of the Community, where individual Member States use differences in their internal provisions to create or maintain barriers to the access into their jurisdictions of companies formed in other Member States. In this case, the need for approximation of national laws clearly emerges from the coordinated reading of Articles 43, 44, 48 and 94 EC, and the proper legal base can be found either in Article 44, second paragraph let. (g) (if the differences in question lie in the protection provisions prescribed for companies for the benefit of shareholders and third parties) or in Article 94 (in the event such differences exist in other areas of national laws). In this situation, which could perhaps be described in terms of 'race to the top' , Member States would 'compete' with each other in introducing stricter provisions applicable to both companies formed under their national law and companies formed under the law of other Member States, for the purpose of protecting creditors and stakeholders in general. Any individual Member State would thus respect the EC law principle of non-discrimination, in the sense that its rules would equally apply to domestic companies and to secondary establishments (subsidiaries or branches) of companies created in another Member State, but these rules may be such as to discourage companies formed in other states from creating secondary establishments in its territory, even where this may be appropriate on economic and market grounds. In a similar hypothesis of differences between national provisions creating distortions to the functioning of the market, there would be a legal ground for eliminating the distortions through harmonization Directives based on Article 44 (or, in other words, for 'minor competition' between national jurisdictions), and harmonization would still be (as it was in the intentions of the Treaty's drafters) the way of facilitating companies' free movement throughout the Community.

Nevertheless, in the current reality where numerous examples can be found of Member States introducing more favourable regulations than those of EC partners,[93] the merit of the 'race to the bottom' legal competition needs to be analysed. In this regard, in the academic literature there are those who take the position that the concept of competition is theoretically convincing and, in any case, express the view that it would be quite inappropriate to attempt a generalizing analysis embracing all areas, institutions and matters requiring regulation;[94] there are others who regard the abolition of the still existing differences in regulatory standards, even where these differences lead to a 'race to the bottom' in the competition among the national jurisdictions, as the true aim of the Treaty.[95] In turn, this latter position assumes that competition between the different jurisdictions of the Member States would always be harmful.[96] Undoubtedly, Articles 3 and 94 of the Treaty would offer legal grounds for limiting a 'race to the bottom' competition in the field of company law if this were harmful: nevertheless, if Articles 43, 44, 48 and 293 are read together, their wording does not appear to suggest that this kind of legal competition must always be regarded as harmful. The only objective these provisions aim to achieve (to contribute to the creation of a system of undistorted market competition within the EC) is a legal environment in which 'companies and firms' from each Member State[97] are entitled to be recognized in any other Member State and to establish there with no kind of barriers created by national law (outside the public policy exception laid down in Article 46 EC); they also expressly state that the 'instruments' indicated for this purpose – the coordination of national laws and the negotiations for concluding Conventions between Member States – are to be used 'to the necessary extent' (Article 44) and 'so far as necessary' (Article 293). It would seem to follow that, in the case of a 'race to the bottom' competition among national legislators, in which each Member State not only does not use its national provisions to raise barriers but, on the contrary, recognizes all business entities formed in other Member States and strives to attract them into its jurisdiction, no obstacle exists, by definition, to intra-EC companies' recognition and free movement and it is not necessary to use the instruments indicated by the Treaty to remove such obstacles. This reading, whereby in the event of a 'race to the bottom' competition in the field of company law there would be no need for (further) harmonization, would appear to be strengthened by the ECJ case law on the right of establishment. In other landmark cases before *Uberseering* and *Inspire Art*, such as the *Segers*[98] and the *Centros*[99] rulings, the ECJ, in dealing with situations where differences between national company laws of two Member States had been used for forum-shopping practices implemented through the resort to the right of establishment, has in fact never regarded these differences as incompatible with the Treaty.

It is, however, unquestionable that the differences in question, which did induce the involved entrepreneurs to choose the most favourable jurisdiction, can be expected to be the result of a 'race to the bottom' competition among national legislators, particularly in the areas which have not yet been affected by the company law harmonization programme. Consequently, there appears to exist no argument to affirm that the ECJ has rejected, in principle, the concept of a race to the bottom competition among Member States in the field of company law. The crucial question becomes whether or not it can be assumed to have unconditionally accepted this kind of competition among national jurisdictions or, in other words, to have recognized no legal ground for limiting it. Article 3 and Articles 94 to 96 of the Treaty, by drawing no distinction based on the sector of law where approximation of national provisions may be needed to eliminate (relevant) distortions, indeed suggest – as they do for the case of competition in the area of corporate taxation[100] – that even a race to the bottom competition in the area of company law is to be regarded as harmful when it causes distortions in market competition between companies formed in different Member States and, due to such distortions, when it impairs the proper functioning of the internal market.[101] In turn, all the above mentioned case law of the ECJ, even though it has accepted an exercise of the right of establishment aimed at choosing the most favourable jurisdictions for creating legal entities whose purpose was to carry on their business in other jurisdictions (as pseudo-foreign companies),[102] has consistently recognized that there may be 'suitable measures' for combating abuse,[103] that the Member States involved can cooperate towards this purpose[104] and that there may be circumstances (which certainly include cases when the abuse is proved) where restrictions on the freedom of establishment are justified.[105] Although the ECJ has not specified the suitable measures or in which way the Member States can cooperate to combat fraud, it is evident that these general statements can be easily reconciled with a coordinated reading of Articles 43, 44, 48 and 293 in the light of Articles 3 and 94 of the Treaty. In other words, both the relevant Treaty provisions and the case law of the ECJ on the right of establishment suggest that a race to the bottom competition among Member States in the field of company law can neither be regarded as necessarily harmful nor unconditionally accepted. Specifically, by jointly considering the Treaty's provisions and the case law, it may be deduced that the race to the bottom competition under consideration may generate distortions in the functioning of the EC market when it leads to abuses of the right of establishment, that is when it induces entrepreneurs to exercise this right for the *unique purpose* of circumventing national laws in order to prevent the protection of creditors, employees and third parties.[106] This appears to be confirmed by an important soft law instrument such as the APCLCG, which refers to the legal competition between the Member States. Specifically, in highlighting the importance of a sound framework of company law for fostering business efficiency and competitiveness and, for this purpose, the need for a proper balance between actions at EC level and actions at national level, the Commission stated that 'some competition between national rules may actually be healthy for the efficiency of the single market'.[107] Nevertheless, in emphasizing the primary objective of EC company law policy (the strengthening of shareholders' rights and third party protection), it acknowledged that this will be even more important in the future, in view of the increasing mobility of companies within the EU, and stated that the protection inter alia of third parties 'will be ensured by a limited number of measures aimed at combating fraud and abuse of legal forms'.[108] It follows that, implicitly, the Commission regarded the interjurisdictional competition in company laws as healthy for the efficiency of the single market when it does not induce businesses into an intra-EC mobility which could conceal fraud and abuse of (national) legal forms at the expense of third party protection.

In addition, because the general wording (and scope) of Articles 3 and 94 EC, when requiring the elimination of any distortions in the functioning of the market, makes it impossible to distinguish not only between the different sectors of national law, but also between the different areas of company law in which national diversities may induce abusive forum-shopping practices, this criteria to identify possible distortions turns out to apply to all areas of company legislation. The case law suggests that, in these circumstances, 'suitable' measures can be legitimately adopted to combat fraud: depending on the concrete situation, such measures can be either unilaterally adopted by the Member State in which a pseudo-foreign company exercises its freedom of establishment or by this state in cooperation with the Member State under whose law the company has been set up, and this may lead to forms of restriction of the right of establishment.[109] On the other hand, by virtue of Articles 94 to 96, measures aimed at eliminating the distortions through the approximation of national laws can be adopted by the Commission and the Council too. In this regard, the subsidiarity principle under Article 5 of the Treaty may be invoked to draw a general distinction between the cases in which the measures in question, globally considered, can be adopted by the Member States (through forms of restriction of the right of establishment) and the situations in which (in the form of approximation Directives) they can be adopted by the EC institutions: the sector of company law does not fall, in fact, within the exclusive competence of the Community, as is clearly shown by Article 44, second paragraph let. (g) ('coordinating ... to the necessary extent'). Accordingly, it can be deduced that, when the objective of combating abuses deriving from a race to the bottom competition in this sector can be sufficiently achieved by the Member State(s) concerned, by means of (legitimate) forms of restriction on the right of establishment, there is no legal ground for (further) EC Directives aimed at approximating national laws and limiting the competition at stake. On the contrary, such directives would become necessary when, due to the scale of the distortions to be combated, action by one or two Member States would not prove sufficient.

However, in the light of the incentive to the exercise of the right of establishment deriving from a race to the bottom competition in company law, if the ECJ case law and Articles 5 and 94 of the Treaty are considered together, it may be argued that both individual Member States and EC action should meet the 'proportionality test' under EC law. In fact, whereas the Member State in which a pseudo-foreign company, after having been formed in another Member State offering more liberal company law provisions, exercises all its business activity[110] for the sole purpose of circumventing provisions protecting creditors and third parties, may legitimately impose forms of restriction on the freedom of establishment in its jurisdiction, subject to the absence of less restrictive means to achieve the same purpose, the second paragraph of Article 5 seems to indicate that Community action should also meet the 'proportionality test' in any attempts to limit the legal competition in question through binding measures. This paragraph of Article 5 provides that Community action should not go beyond what is necessary for achieving the objectives of the Treaty: such objectives do require the Commission and the Council to eliminate distortions to the functioning of the market, but not to discourage the exercise of the right of establishment. It can therefore be argued that, provided no other measure, such as 'soft law' measures, can be implemented for limiting the race to the bottom competition among the national legislators without discouraging the exercise of the right of establishment, the issue of EC legislation aimed at limiting the competition by means of the approximation of national company laws does become necessary under Articles 5 and 94 of the Treaty. In other words, if the relevant Treaty Articles and ECJ case law are read together, legal ground for EC legislative measures aimed at limiting the race to the bottom competition among national company laws (that is for preventing a 'Delaware effect' in the exercise of the freedom of establishment) can be found only in the extent to which: (a) the resulting distortions cannot, by reason of their scale, be sufficiently combated by measures taken by Member States; and (b) the proper functioning of the market makes the restriction of margins for forum-shopping practices through 'hard law' the inevitable choice,[111] although this may discourage, to a certain extent, the freedom of establishment. Different questions are whether (further company law) Directives would be effective in achieving their purpose, which features they should assume to be such and when regulations based on Article 308 would be more appropriate than Directives.[112]

A second, and complementary, argument can be deduced from the Treaty. The coordinated reading of Articles 3 and 94 suggests that neither Member States' measures nor EC approximation Directives are required when the race to the bottom competition in the field of company law induces businesses to choose to locate from the outset in those jurisdictions in whose territory they would also be in a better position to carry on their activity for market-related reasons. Article 3, in requiring the establishment of a system of undistorted market competition, demands in fact that all companies be given the same possibility of competing in the EC market, and Article 43 clarifies that the freedom of establishment for EC nationals includes the right to set up and manage undertakings and companies within the meaning of Article 48 EC[113] in the Member State of their choice. Consequently, if the more favourable company law offered by a given Member State contributes to a decision to locate in that state, and to carry on business from there, which would on its own be appropriate on market grounds, no 'Delaware effect' takes place by definition. Neither should there be any risk of abuse against creditors established in other Member States having stricter regulatory standards, with whom the company in question may make deals. In fact, they would be in a better position (than in the case of business with pseudo-foreign companies) to understand, from the beginning of the relationship, that the company is regulated by provisions different from those with which they may be familiar (with regard for example to minimum capital requirements or to accounting documents disclosure), and to seek to protect their interests through other means, such as international sales contracts containing appropriate clauses as regards terms of payment and applicable law in the event of litigation.

To summarize, the analysis of the relevant Treaty provisions and of the ECJ's conclusions, taken together, suggests that whether or not a race to the bottom competition among national company laws is to be limited by EC measures ultimately depends on its effects and on their scale, provided, in the event of negative effect on the functioning of the market, that any such measure meets the proportionality test. This is in order to strike the necessary balance between the need to prevent distortions and the need not to discourage the exercise of a freedom – the freedom of establishment – guaranteed by the Treaty. The final realization seems therefore to be that: (a) there is no reason to continue to tolerate a 'Delaware effect' other than the legitimate concern to discourage, to an excessive extent, the free movement of businesses within the EC; (b) when the proportionality test suggests that this effect can be tolerated, it should be so both in all areas of company law and for all categories of 'companies and firms' intended as beneficiaries of the freedom of establishment under the second paragraph of Article 48, since all such companies and firms must be offered the same possibilities of facing competition within the internal market and the same treatment as competitors, which can be deduced not only from Article 3, but also from the wording of all other Treaty Articles dealing with economic issues (such as competition rules and state aids) referring to 'undertakings'[114] without distinction; (c) no problem arises when the race to the bottom competition in company law only contributes to choices of jurisdiction which would on their own be appropriate on purely market grounds (lack of a 'Delaware effect').

Nevertheless, if the coordinated reading of the Treaty and of the ECJ case law makes it possible to deduce the legal grounds for greater or minor competition among national company legislators and, in the case of a race to the bottom competition, the general criteria to be applied to identify those situations in which EC law would require this kind of competition to be limited, the practical application of such criteria would be unlikely to be easy. This suggests that, rather than testing when the existing legal competition may be accepted, tolerated or limited in the light of EC law objectives, the features of an 'optimal competition' would need to be identified and the more suitable instruments to achieve it would have to be introduced.

4.3.3 An Optimal Competition (under EC Law) among National Company Laws

The practical application of the criteria identified by the coordinated analysis of the Treaty and of the ECJ case law which should serve to distinguish the situations where the existing competition should be tolerated (because it does not meet the proportionality test), limited (because it meets the proportionality test) or accepted (because it does not generate on its own a 'Delaware effect'), may be difficult for at least two reasons.

First, given all the areas of company law which have not yet been covered by the harmonization Directives to date issued, it would be necessary to verify in which of these areas there are such differences between national provisions as to generate (and which actually generate) forum-shopping practices having the unique goal of abusing the right of establishment at the expense of creditors, employees and other stakeholders' protection. On the other hand, this analysis should be extended to each of the 'harmonized' areas in which noticeable differences have survived in national company law, to the extent that even these differences may cause distortions in the functioning of the market. The analysis should be carried out, area by area, by taking into consideration the effects of the ECJ case law which, as may occur in the case of the draft Fourteenth Directive,[115] might in the end deprive some of the proposed Directives of much of their practical importance without a rethinking of their scope and provisions, and it would be the first step towards the application of the proportionality test. Nonetheless, irrespective of the fact that the cases of abusive forum-shopping practices, and the differences between national legislation in any area of company law leaving scope for them, can only come before the ECJ at the initiative of an interested party, a thorough review of these differences and of their actual effects in terms of abuses of the right of establishment would require a Report by the Commission based on an in-depth survey to be carried out in the field. Such a survey would, however, hardly be feasible without some direct collection of responses from businesses, who, in turn, can certainly be expected to indicate reasons other than the circumvention of national laws at the expense of creditors, employees and third parties as behind any choice of jurisdiction, with the risk of leading to meaningless results.

Secondly, some current market trends and some likely legislative developments may make the task of distinguishing between abusive forum-shopping practices, and choices of the most favourable legislation which would also be appropriate on market grounds, increasingly difficult. On the one hand, in the modern, computerized economy, companies located in any of the Member States find the opportunity to reach new customers, who may be located in any different country, through technological means such as 'e-commerce', which did not exist when the drafters of the Treaty expected companies to be interested in moving throughout the Community for market-related reasons. This possibility of expanding in foreign markets without moving the central administration might induce a belief that, given a certain number of intra-EC seat transfers, the proportion of relocations consisting of abusive forum-shopping practices may be greater than in previous times. On the other hand, to the extent that likely legislative developments at the EC level may create new safeguards for creditors in addition to those strictly provided for by company law (such as the minimum capital requirements and disclosure obligations) as well as for employees and third parties, any planned forum-shopping practices for abusive purposes induced by a race to the bottom competition among the national company laws might be certain to become even less effective in achieving its goals. The legislative developments gradually leading to this outcome might be, with regard to creditors' protection, the approximation of accounting regulations[116] and of contract law with the envisaged and far-reaching project for a 'European Civil Code'[117] and, with regard to safeguarding employees and other stakeholders, the progress of the approximation of national provisions in fields such as labour law and financial markets regulation.[118]

These difficulties in the practical application of the criteria to verify when the existing competition between national company laws is to be tolerated, limited or accepted do not imply, however, that any possibility of competition among national jurisdictions should be banned. It has always been generally agreed that the concepts of 'coordination' or 'approximation' of national laws referred to in the Treaty's wording[119] are not synonymous with 'unification' of national laws (and that this difference applies in all fields of law).[120] The Treaty's drafters did not require the EC institutions to make national company laws of Member States identical, as such an objective would have been politically unattainable and not necessarily essential for the proper functioning of the market, and thus accepted that a certain degree of legal competition would remain. As already discussed,[121] the Treaty requires that this competition, exactly as in the case of competition in the field of companies taxation, neither distorts the market competition among companies nor contributes to distort it: in short, it should be 'neutral' from the viewpoint of market competition. To meet this condition (and to be, by definition, compatible with EC law) competition between the different national jurisdictions in company law should thus be such as: (a) to avoid all problems of comparability of national provisions deriving from the limits of the harmonization programme;[122] (b) not to induce businesses into purely abusive forum-shopping practices (which may also be at the root of locational inefficiencies),[123] while striking a balance between the protection of their interests for flexible regulation on the one hand and the safeguarding of creditors, employees and in general third parties on the other hand; (c) to reconcile the Member States' desire to preserve margins of autonomy in the light of the subsidiarity principle with the need to ensure that such autonomy is not exercised through the introduction of provisions leading to effects contrary to the Treaty's objective in terms of undistorted market competition; last, and as a result, (d) to ensure that the protection of creditors, employees and third parties tends to be equally effective throughout the Community.

With regard to each of these requirements of an 'optimal competition' (under EC law) among national company law legislators, the following arguments apply. First, as for condition (a), the literature has consistently stressed the disadvantages of a failure of harmonization, because of '*lack of transparency*, or *uncertainty about the legal situation* in other parts of the internal market and *about the delimitation between European and national law*',[124] and highlighted that 'these problems may lead to increased transaction costs, more litigation and a special need to protect shareholders'[125] and third parties. It has also widely demonstrated that these disadvantages and problems, particularly in terms of comparability of national provisions, which may offer different levels of protection, can also derive from the process of harmonization itself, when it leaves (as has occurred with the company law harmonization programme) noticeable differences between the 'harmonized' national provisions.[126] In this case, they exist not only in the areas left outside the harmonization programme, but also in the 'harmonized areas' of national company laws, and arise due to Member States' tendency to adapt the implementation of Directives to their existing internal systems and models of companies rather than to modify these latter. Lack of transparency, uncertainty and ultimately difficulties of comparability between (two or more) national provisions of different Member States would tend to disappear in the opposite situation. In a situation in which all national legislators had the objective to make their models of companies converge toward the same models of reference, governed by a self-sufficient set of provisions, and (spontaneously and) openly competed amongst them in doing so, the provisions regulating these models would offer an objective parameter to compare the national provisions. In turn, from the viewpoint of businesses, this kind of legal competition would provide the transparency needed easily to carry out a comparative evaluation of national provisions: given the market-oriented values underlying the Treaty, the provisions governing the common models of reference should in fact, by definition, be tailored to the needs of a favourable business environment, so that the greater the extent to which, in all aspects of the regulation, the provisions of a Member State tended clearly to approximate these 'target provisions' more than those of another Member State, the greater the capacity of the first state to become (for the time being) the 'optimal' jurisdiction. It would also, on its own, avoid any problem of recognition of the delimitation between European law and national law resulting from an ineffective approximation: all provisions would be part of national law. With regard to condition (b) which, as shown by the coordinated reading of Articles 3, 44, second paragraph let. (g) and 94 of the Treaty and the ECJ case law,[127] is also essential to ensure the absence of distortions, this kind of competition may be expected not to encourage businesses to move from one country to another for the sole purpose of circumventing national laws and preventing creditors' and third party protection. They would know, in fact, that the provisions of all Member States would tend towards the same models of companies and would thus have the same objectives in terms of protection of creditors and third parties. In other words, in this situation businesses (even if interested in forum shopping) would know that any difference between national provisions could be expected to be a *temporary* rather than a *definitive* one because, in converging towards common models, the competing national legislators would also inevitably tend to make the national provisions approximate to each other. For this reason, any such difference could not, from the viewpoint of businesses, be relied upon to plan and implement effective forum-shopping practices for abusive purposes (which, to achieve their goal, need legal certainty on the survival of at least some amongst the main differences between national laws). Condition (c) must be considered in the light of the coordinated reading of the above-mentioned Articles with Article 5 EC, which indicates the Treaty drafters' intention both to preserve Member States' margins of autonomy and to ensure that this autonomy not be exercised in such a manner as to jeopardize the objectives of the Treaty. However, this condition would be satisfied by definition in the context resulting from the envisaged type of legal competition, as Member States would see their autonomy preserved and, in exercising it, would create within the EC such a 'company law environment' as not to induce businesses into practices generating effects contrary to the Treaty's goals. In turn, condition (d), which is essential in order to guarantee the absence of distortions in the functioning of the market, directly emerges from the wording of Articles 3, 44, second paragraph let. (g) and 94, read together, and it is (although in other words) expressly indicated by Article 44, second paragraph let. (g) itself, calling for the Commission and the Council to coordinate the safeguards required for the protection of members 'and others' for the purpose of making them equivalent throughout the EC. The protection of 'others' referred to in this provision (which has been the legal base of the harmonization programme) includes, as clarified by the ECJ, that of creditors, of employees and any other third party,[128] so far as necessary (according to the wording of Article 44) to avoid distortions (to the proper functioning of the market) which can derive from the abusive forum-shopping practices generated by the co-existence within the Community of different levels of protection of their interests. Even this condition would, however, be fulfilled by definition in the event of a competition between national company law legislators with the indicated features: in tending towards common models for 'companies and firms' and in approximating national provisions to these models – and, as a result, to those of each other – national legislators would spontaneously tend to make the protection of creditors, employees and third parties equally effective throughout the EC. In other words, the same objectives which they would have in terms of protection of creditors and third parties would bring about national provisions with such similarity as to lead, from one Member State to another, to an equally effective protection.

Ultimately, the features of a competition among national jurisdictions in the field of company law which would be 'optimal' (under EC law) thus turn out to be complementary to each other. To sum up: this optimal competition would completely reverse the approach underlying the company law harmonization programme with a view to the same goals envisaged by the Treaty's authors. The (spontaneous) approximation of different national legislators towards common models (and provisions) of reference characterized by the same values and objectives would be its key mechanism, rather than the fitting of common pieces of EC legislation into different systems characterized, to a greater or lesser extent, by different values and objectives. Both opposite approaches may leave different national provisions, but the nature and the underlying meaning of these differences would be deeply distinct. Whereas the differences left by the harmonization programme (in both the not yet harmonized and the harmonized areas) are the expression of the deep-rooted divergences in the conception of company law as well as of the consequent desire of Member States to retain all possible margins of autonomy, and are likely for this reason to remain definitive, even in important aspects, and to induce businesses into abuses of the right of establishment, the differences resulting from an 'optimal' legal competition cannot but be the result of a different speed of progress of the approximation of all national legislators towards the same 'target provisions'. As such, these latter differences would be deemed to be only temporary (and/or to remain in marginal aspects): accordingly, they would be unlikely to generate an effect on businesses' strategies other than that of contributing to choices of jurisdictions which would on their own be appropriate on economic and market grounds.

4.4 SUPRANATIONAL INSTRUMENTS AS VEHICLES FOR A LEGAL COMPETITION COMPATIBLE WITH EC LAW?

4.4.1 General Requirements

The previous analysis gives rise to a specific question: for what reason would all national company law legislators spontaneously tend to approximate their internal provisions to common models and provisions of reference, if, as stressed by the literature,[129] there are in fact deep-rooted differences from one Member State to another about the conceptions of the role of company law itself? The following answer seems to be inevitable: to the extent to which any supranational option for a company law instrument introduced by the EC were preferred by businesses to all company law schemes governed by national laws, all national legislators wishing to compete with such supranational instruments would inevitably have to introduce into their systems provisions causing national company law schemes to approximate to these instruments. Assuming the existence of one or more supranational company law schemes either having such features as to be more attractive than each of the corresponding types of national law schemes, or offering new and more attractive structures than those available at the national levels,[130] national legislators would have two alternative choices: either to leave their company law provisions unchanged or to attempt to 'compete' with these supranational company law vehicles. In the first case, the achievement of the level playing field throughout the Community would directly result from the choice of the supranational vehicles, rather than of the national ones, on the part of all businesses. In the second hypothesis, the competition among national legislators would automatically meet the requirements to be compatible with EC law, because the supranational instruments would become (each for its specific type of company or, in the hypothesis of new business structures not yet introduced at national level, each for the type of economic entity which it would be designed to suit) the common models of reference, governed by the same provisions of reference, towards which all competing national laws would tend; as a result, it would make the achievement of the level playing field possible to a greater extent than the harmonization programme has actually done.

Consequently, the requirement which any supranational instruments introduced by the Community should meet to be successful in the business world – to offer a clear and valid alternative to the corresponding national law schemes, thus to offer better solutions than these latter to all issues concerning the setting up, the operation and the dissolution of the business enterprise[131] – is also the same condition which they should fulfil to become the vehicle for an EC law compatible legal competition. This condition, in turn, requires that the provisions governing each of these instruments: (a) cover all aspects of the regulation, including, for the categories of companies on which the harmonization efforts of the EC have been concentrating, those aspects which have remained outside the scope of the harmonization programme; (b) are recognized as the regulatory standards below which the 'enabling' role of the law relating to the business enterprise would no longer be ensured; and, as a result, (c) are also considered to be the dispositions that admit of no exception, in order to safeguard the interests of both members and all other parties (creditors, employees and any other) involved in the life of enterprises. Requirements (b) and (c) are complementary to each other: if an enabling philosophy whereby the role of company law is that of providing a legal framework in order for business ventures to exist and perform (that is in order to facilitate rather than to regulate businesses' operations) is essential for any supranational vehicle intended to compete successfully with all business forms offered by those Member States traditionally adopting such a philosophy of company law,[132] this role could hardly be played if third parties dealing with the business enterprise or involved in its life considered their interests not to be protected and were, for this reason, discouraged from doing business with or working for the enterprise itself. In other words, to become the vehicles for an EC law compatible competition among national legislators and thus to be more attractive for businesses than each of the national types,[133] the supranational instruments would need to be governed by provisions: (a) avoiding any resort to the different national company and tax laws, so as to create a truly uniform body of European law; (b) designing such structures as to offer businesses the flexibility they need to a greater extent than national company law structures can; (c) reconciling this flexibility with the same degree of protection for all (groups of) members and third party interests. The uniformity would not be contrary to the flexibility: the uniform EC law governing any supranational instrument should in fact offer flexibility through its own provisions, by making possible various alternatives (to be chosen *by businesses*) resulting in the same quality of protection for (members and) all third party interests. Moreover, in the light of the second paragraph of Article 48 of the Treaty, stressing the objective of its drafters to ensure the free movement within the Community for all kinds of 'companies and firms' having a profit-making purpose, a variety of supranational instruments should be introduced, each designed to suit the needs of businesses belonging to a particular economic category.

Although the introduction of supranational instruments having these features can realistically meet difficulties at a political level, any intended 'supranational' vehicle whose overall regulation lacks these features (such as, from the company law viewpoint, the SE up to this point in time[134] and, to a minor extent, the SCE)[135] would be unlikely to be regarded by businesses as a true and convenient alternative to the structures which are provided by national laws which, given the case law of the ECJ, already enable them to operate and to circulate within the EC.[136] As a result, it would risk not managing to contribute to the achievement of the legal objective – the creation of a level playing field for all categories of enterprises, in conditions of undistorted market competition – envisaged by the Treaty's authors.

This argument also applies, in addition to the SE and the SCE, to the creation, envisaged in the APCLCG, of a European form of private limited company (European private company, EPC)[137] and to any other supranational vehicle that could be envisaged.

4.4.2 Basic Features of 'Optimal' Regulations of Supranational Instruments and Minimum Requirement of 'Acceptable' Regulations

The coordinated reading of the relevant Treaty Articles has suggested that the race to the bottom competition among national legislators in the field of both companies' taxation and company law should meet the same conditions to be compatible with EC law, in terms of transparency and protection of the interests of all stakeholders participating in the life of the business enterprises (from the taxation authorities of the Member States to creditors, employees and third parties in general). In turn, these conditions would be fulfilled if the legal competition in both fields tended to approximate internal provisions to supranational company law and tax law provisions governing EC law instruments.

For this purpose, the 'optimal' regulations of these supranational instruments, which would enable them to become the vehicle for a legal competition compatible with EC law, should have the same basic features, that is they should at least:

1. From the company law viewpoint:
    a. make the creation of each of these instruments possible to both founders from different Member States and founders from a single Member State, as well as to founders from third countries wishing to invest in any Member State, and include in the range of possible founders natural persons, legal persons[138] and, in general, all kinds of 'companies and firms' falling within the definition of the second paragraph of Article 48 of the Treaty;
    b. as a result, make each of these vehicles available in all forms (not just in the four forms of a holding company, a subsidiary, a merged company or a converted company contemplated by the current ECS)

and allow at any time the transformation from any of the legal schemes governed by national laws to any of these supranational vehicles (and vice versa);

c. allow, on the one hand, the intra-EC transfer of both the registered and the head office at any time during the life of the business, and, on the other hand, both the location from the outset and the subsequent transfer of the head office in a Member State different from that of the registered office (thus, adopt the incorporation system),[139] while making these choices subject to no more than publicity requirements;[140]

d. in the events of transfer of the registered and head office to another Member State, and of subsequent migration of the head office of businesses taking limited-liability legal forms, ensure the protection of creditors not through complicated procedures,[141] but by means of simple and effective alternatives, which could consist of an agreement, enforceable in the state of departure as well as in that of destination, setting out the means and time schedule of debt settlement between the enterprise wishing to make the transfer and its creditors, or, in the absence of such an agreement, of a provision contemplating the application of the contract law of the state of departure for the protection of creditors existing at the time of the transfer (at least until the formation of a European contract law);

e. allow the possibility of the head office being either situated from the outset, or later transferred, outside the EC, in third countries following the incorporation system[142] and, from there, retransferred within the Community;

f. in the cases of location from the outset of the head office in a state different from that of the registered office with business operations carried out in both states, and of location of the head office outside the Community, allow businesses and third parties to agree the application to their relationships, in addition to the already developed international contract law,[143] of agreement-based provisions (supplemented by the choice of the competent court) or, as an alternative, of the contract law of the State of location of creditors (again, with regard to creditors established in different Member States, at least until the development of a uniform contract law at EC level);

g. allow the resort, by businesses choosing these supranational vehicles, to the widest possible range of management styles and structures and, in general, of internal organization rules, to suit their different individual needs;

h. offer the same flexibility with regard to the rules governing the powers of the representatives of the 'company or firm' towards third parties, subject, in the case of limited-liability forms, only to the requirement that such rules be clearly made known to third parties;

i. permit the easy transformation from one legal form to another, that is as between legal forms offering limited liability, as between forms with unlimited liability and from a form belonging to one category to one belonging to another;[144]

j. allow businesses taking any of these supranational forms to acquire, and to set up throughout the EC, agencies, branches and subsidiaries under their own legal form, under the legal forms of the other supranational vehicles and, if they wish, under the legal forms provided by the laws of Member States;

k. permit the creation of agencies, branches and subsidiaries (and their acquisition), with the same range of possibilities with regard to the legal forms, in third countries;

l. allow, with a less rigid procedure than that required by the Third and the Sixth Company Law Directives for domestic mergers and divisions,[145] intra-EC mergers, divisions, transfer of assets and exchanges of shares involving both businesses having the same legal form and businesses having different legal forms;

m. offer easy solutions for the winding-up of businesses, with simple and inexpensive procedures in case of insolvency.[146]

2. From the tax law viewpoint:

a. ensure the 'tax neutrality' of the location in a Member State rather than in another[147] which, in turn, would be possible by means of an EC tax regime for each of these instruments, the revenue from which could be assigned partly to the EC and partly to the Member States in which any business taking one of the supranational legal forms has the registered office, the head office or any secondary establishment;

b. as a consequence, guarantee the tax neutrality of all operations of 'grouping together' and restructuring (which, for companies from different Member States, has not been fully achieved by the two 1990 tax Directives)[148] involving businesses having the legal form of any of these supranational vehicles throughout the EC, as well as the absence of transfer pricing problems and of double taxation on the intra-EC payments of interest and royalties (which Directive 2003/49/EC is unlikely to be able to achieve fully for associated companies from different Member States),[149] by means of self-sufficient and unambiguous provisions;

c. offer a definition of taxable income without the limitations on the deductibility of certain business expenses which can generally be found in Member States' tax regimes,[150] but with the most favourable amongst the various 'participation exemptions' contemplated by national legislations for received dividends and capital gains;[151]

d. allow, in the determination of this taxable income, the setting of losses incurred in any Member State against the profits obtained in any other[152] and permit the carrying back and forward of losses with no time limits;[153]
e. apply tax rates which, through either a fixed rate or different rates for different brackets of income, result in a lower effective tax charge than that deriving from the most favourable tax regime amongst those imposed by Member States.

These basic features, common to the regulations of all supranational instruments, ought to be specified and supplemented, for each supranational vehicle, by the features of its own particular regulation, which should bring together the most favourable aspects of all the different national regulations evidenced by an in-depth comparative study of the company law and tax law provisions of each Member State.[154] It is evident that regulations of EC law supranational vehicles having such features would be the 'optimal' ones, because they would be able to ensure their success in the business world and, with this, the full achievement of the level playing field within the Community under conditions of market competition not distorted by differences between the legal provisions of Member States. Businesses from any Member State would in fact prefer these vehicles to the national ones, as they would find that in no aspect of the overall regulation were the solutions offered by the supranational instruments less favourable than those offered by the schemes governed by national laws, whereas, in one or more aspects, they would be more favourable than these latter. As a result, the place of establishment within the EC could only be chosen on economic and market grounds.

It may be noted, however, that, with regard to company law aspects, the possibility of allowing businesses choosing each of these EC legal forms to have their head office and to create agencies, branches or subsidiaries outside the Community could require, in the light of the subsidiarity principle, a unique and bilateral Convention between the EC and third countries, which some Member States wishing to retain the widest margins of freedom in their relationships with non-EC member countries may consider not to be in their interest. Moreover, it may be objected that the actual introduction of supranational vehicles having such features is not (yet) politically feasible,[155] despite the awareness of the need for 'genuine supranational legal quality'.[156]

Nevertheless, the same final outcome would be likely to be ensured by a 'second best' – but probably more realistic – solution: the creation of 'supranational' vehicles which, although in some respects may not be governed by genuinely European sources and/or be less favourable than national ones, do offer more favourable solutions than the national schemes in other more important aspects of their overall regulation. In other words, businesses, who weigh the advantages and disadvantages of the legal forms available before choosing amongst them or changing from one legal form to another, can still be reasonably expected to opt for the intended supranational vehicles if their overall regulations, on balance, can be regarded as more favourable than the national ones. This requirement, which would make the vehicles in question still 'acceptable' as instruments for the achievement of the level playing field, would be met if the aspects which find a less favourable or stricter regulation than that provided for by national provisions are, from the viewpoint of enterprises, more than compensated by the aspects which find a more favourable regulation. In so far as their overall (company law and corporate tax law) regulations are not yet completed or are still in the proposals phase, the possibility of meeting from the outset such condition seems still open for the SE as regards tax treatment, for the SCE and, to a greater extent, for the proposed EPC.

The hypothesis of supranational vehicles more attractive, at least on balance, than company forms governed by national law would also be consistent with the two goals indicated by the Commission in the APCLCG[157] and would help their achievement. This hypothesis, by contributing to eliminate the scope for business practices that can compromise third party protection and the necessary degree of confidence in business relationships and, at the same time, by offering businesses more attractive instruments than the national ones, could help, on the one hand, the protection of members and third parties and, on the other hand, the efficiency and competitiveness of businesses, and would thus deserve to be analysed as a strategy that could be complementary to the measures foreseen in the APCLCG.

Last, the implementation of key medium and long-term measures indicated in the APCLCG could contribute to make this 'supranational solution' more important. In fact, although the Commission stressed the need for a distinction between categories of companies and the desirability of a more stringent framework for listed companies or companies which have publicly raised capital, in particular in the area of disclosure, and for a more flexible framework for SMEs,[158] it indicated measures which, once implemented, would increase the scope for differences between national provisions (and thus for the resulting interjurisdictional competition) with regard to all categories of companies irrespective of their size. Amongst these kind of measures there would be, by 2008, not only a Directive extending to all listed companies under national forms the choice between a dualistic or a monistic board structure that is currently available to the SE, but also the simplification of the Third and Sixth Company Law Directives, and, from 2009 onwards, the simplification of the Second Company Law Directive subject to the result of a feasibility study.[159] The envisaged amendments to these Directives, which concern public limited companies, would allow Member States if they so wish to relax some procedural requirements prescribed by the current versions in respect of such companies. This would be consistent with the general statement by the Commission, in the APCLCG, that flexibility should be available to companies as much as possible[160] but it could create or increase, for larger businesses too, the scope for designing and implementing forum-shopping strategies by availing themselves of the possibilities clarified by the ECJ case law (dissociation between the states of location of the registered office and of the head office; carrying out of all business activity through a branch in a Member State different from that of incorporation) in which smaller businesses were involved.

Consequently, to the extent to which the possible introduction of such measures may increase the legal competition in respect of larger companies too and thus generate new risks for the protection of the interests of an even wider public of stakeholders, a 'supranational solution' which could manage to deprive all businesses of the scope for practices which risk threatening the protection of these interests, and which thus could further contribute to the proper functioning of the single market, may become increasingly important.

NOTES

1. See above 1.1 and 3.1 and 3.2.8.
2. The term 'variable geometry' was first used in the area of EC institutional law, after the 1992 Maastricht Treaty, to indicate the recognition of the possibility of some Member States not moving toward the same objectives as the others (at Maastricht, two countries, United Kingdom and Denmark, were allowed to opt out of the third stage of Economic and Monetary Union). It would seem that this term may well be 'borrowed' from this area of EC law and used to indicate a situation where two groups of EC provisions which, in the light of the goals stated in the Treaty, ought to pursue the same objective, have been introduced as if they were completely independent from each other.
3. In the case of France. For the Directives, with the Annex, see OJEC L225 [1990].
4. In the case of Italy.
5. In the case of Portugal for the Parent-Subsidiary Directive 90/435/EEC.
6. In the cases of Denmark, Germany, Greece, Luxembourg, the Netherlands and, essentially, Ireland and the United Kingdom. The range of companies listed in the Annex of the first two 1990 Directives exactly coincides with that listed in the Annex of the Interest-Royalties Directive 2003/49/EC (except that this latter also expressly includes companies established in Austria, Finland and Sweden).
7. See above 2.1 and 3.1.
8. Because companies, to fall within the scope of the tax Directives, must have one of the legal forms listed in the Annex and must be corporate taxpayers without the possibility of an option or of being exempt, any amendment of the relevant tax laws of Member States which imposed the indicated corporate income taxes, with no possibility of options, on companies having the required legal form would broaden the range of beneficiaries of the tax Directives.
9. See above 1.1 on the Parent-Subsidiary Directive (1.1.2 and 1.1.3) and on the Merger Directive (1.1.4, 1.1.5 and 1.1.6); 1.2. on the Interest-Royalties Directive; in particular, 1.1.1

(amendments to the Parent-Subsidiary Directive), 1.1.5 (amendments to the Merger Directive) and 1.2 (proposed amendments to the Interest-Royalties Directive).

10. And, in general, of the tax rulings of the ECJ: see above 2.5 and 1.4.3.
11. Communication, 'Modernising company law and enhancing corporate governance in the European Union: a plan to move forward' (COM (2003) 284 final), p. 6, and the wording of Article 44, first paragraph and second paragraph, let. (g), taken together.
12. See above 3.1.
13. From this viewpoint, the Fourth and Seventh Directives, with the excessive number of options left both to Member States and to companies with regard to annual and consolidated financial statements, have not facilitated the comparability of these financial reports, at least not for non-publicly traded companies that remain outside the extension of the IAS principles from 2005 (see above 3.1). For the list of company law Directives introduced to date, see above 2.1.
14. Villiers, C. (1998), *European Company Law: Towards Democracy*, Aldershot: Ashgate/Dartmouth, UK, p. 179. It seems, in fact, that the important observation quoted in the text can be generalized.
15. Given the ECJ case law on the free movement of companies (see above 1.4 and Chapter 2).
16. The wide definition of Article 48, second paragraph EC includes all profit-making entities.
17. Owing to the different conditions to be met by involved companies: see above 1.1.7.
18. Inter alia: Beveridge F. and C.A. Riley (1996), 'The tax goals of the EC' in Geraint G. Howells (eds), *European Business Law*, Aldershot: Ashgate/Dartmouth, UK, ch. 6, pp. 137–168, Schon, W. (2000), 'Tax competition in Europe: the legal perspective', *EC Tax Review*, 2, 90–105; Morton, P. (2005), 'Report on the Joint CFE/CSE Seminar "Tax competition versus tax harmonization"', *European Taxation*, 1 (45), 25–26.
19. See above 1.5 and 1.6 on the current Commission's orientations and 1.4 on the developments of the case law.
20. Schon, note 18, p. 98.
21. Morton, note 18, p. 26.
22. Vanistendael, F. (2000), 'Fiscal support measures and harmful tax competition', *EC Tax Review*, 3, 152–161, at 159.
23. Commission Notice on the application of the state aid rules to measures relating to direct business taxation, OJEC C384/3 [1998], Introduction, 4, Point B), 17, Point C), 30 ('1998 Notice').
24. See Vanistendael, note 22, p. 160.
25. See 1998 Notice, note 23, Point A), 'Community powers of action', n. 6. See also 1.6 and 4.1. These statements, if read together with the current orientations (above 1.5 and 1.6), seem to confirm that the current approach means that the tax competition at issue is tolerated rather than (unconditionally) accepted.
26. Ruding, O. (2005), 'The past and the future of EU corporate tax', Editorial, *EC Tax Review*, 1, 3.
27. As recognized, ultimately, by Communication COM (2003) 726 final: see above 1.1.8.
28. See W. Schon, in 'Tax competition in Europe, General Report' to the 2002 Lausanne Conference, at p. 4, where he also recognizes that the emergence of tax competition poses new questions to the EC legal order, and Schon, W. (2002), 'Tax competition in Europe: the national perspective', *European Taxation*, 12 (42), 491, where he highlights difficulty in reaching consensus upon a borderline between fair and unfair competition.
29. Vaninstendael, F. (2000), 'No European taxation without European representation', *EC Tax Review*, 3, 143.
30. Article 3, first paragraph, let. (g), EC.
31. Article 3, first paragraph, let. (h), EC.
32. Report of the Fiscal and Financial Committee, 1962 (the 'Neumark Report').
33. See above 1.5 and 1.6.
34. In the light of Member States' competence in structuring the tax systems under the principle of subsidiarity, an assessment of the need for approximation of the national tax laws resulting from the exercise of that competence was carried out by the Commission, when it

considered a 'minimum harmonization' as necessary, in its 1990 Guidelines on Company Taxation and, in 2003, when proposing the amendments to the tax Directives (see above 1.1.8). As regards *Member States' competence to structure direct taxation systems*, see Case C-336/96, *Gilly* [1998] ECR I-2823, where the ECJ found that the Member States, due to the fiscal sovereignty principle and in the absence of harmonization, were free to adopt any tax system and in particular to set the associated tax base and rates. The distinction between these two levels of competence also emerges, indirectly, from some ECJ judgments about the application of the subsidiarity principle to the internal market in a sector different from taxation. In these cases, exemplified by Cases C-377/98 and C-491/01 below where Member States challenged Directives based on Articles 94 and 95 on grounds, inter alia, of breach of the subsidiarity principle, the ECJ found that compliance with this principle was necessarily implicit in specific statements in the Preamble to the contested Directive, whereby in the absence of action at EC level the development of the laws and practices of the different Member States impedes the proper functioning of the internal market (see Case C-377/98, *Netherlands v. Parliament and Council* [2001] ECR I-7079, paras 30 to 33), and that the subsidiarity and proportionality principles were complied with by a stated objective of eliminating barriers, resulting from differences still existing in the relevant sector between Member States' laws, regulations and administrative provisions, which could not be eliminated by action taken by individual Member States (see Case C-491/01, *British American Tobacco* [2002] ECR I-11453, paras 124 and 180 to 185). As the objectives stated by any EC measure in terms of removal of impediments and/or of barriers to the proper functioning of the internal market that are created by differences between national provisions necessarily reflect an assessment by the EC institutions, *a priori*, about the effects of the exercise of Member States' legislative competence in the area involved, these ECJ rulings on the application of the subsidiarity principle in the internal market confirm the exclusive competence of the Community in making this assessment (which assessment is reflected in the stated goals of an EC measure). This competence leads, with reference to company taxation, to the line of argument developed in this paragraph.

35. See above 1.4.1.
36. Which Member States must in fact inevitably adjust to their revenue trends, to comply with the parameter laid down since the establishment of Economic and Monetary Union.
37. As they do: see above 1.1.1 (on the two 1990 Directives) and 1.2 (on the Interest-Royalties Directive).
38. Although their provisions were drafted according to a more limited concept of tax neutrality than the concept which would have been necessary to guarantee the achievement of the goals stated in their Preambles: see above 1.1.8.
39. See Vanistendael, note 22, p. 160, where he writes that 'the Code of Good Conduct allows fiscal support measures [of special character] to be identified and differentiated from general fiscal support measures', which would be coherent with the fact that 'Article 87 [of the EC Treaty, on state aids to enterprises] only prohibits support measures that have adverse effects on free and fair [market] competition'. Although they are non-binding measures, soft law instruments necessarily have to be supposed to be coherent with the achievement of the goals set out in the Treaty, and to represent interpretations of the principles which can be inferred from the Treaty. Moreover, soft law provisions may be converted, by the ECJ's judgments, into 'hard law' (see above 1.5).
40. Commission Recommendation 94/390 of 25 May 1994, OJEC L177/1 [1994].
41. Ibid. Preamble, recital (6) (emphasis added).
42. Ibid. Preamble, recital (7).
43. Ibid. Preamble, recital (7) (emphasis added).
44. The quoted sentences of the Preamble to the Commission Recommendation refer to 'enterprises' and to the disadvantage in which sole proprietorships and partnerships find themselves in comparison with enterprises having the legal forms of companies. Nevertheless, if the Treaty's provisions referred to in the text, the tax Directives' Preambles and the Recommendation's Preamble are read together, there are no arguments to deny that the concern expressed in this Preamble about the need to avoid distortions to competition

between those enterprises taking the legal forms of sole proprietorships and of partnerships and those having the legal forms of companies applies to the competition among companies too.

45. Calling for the creation of a system of undistorted competition which, clearly, refers to the need to avoid distortion to the competition between enterprises taking different legal forms as well as between enterprises having the legal forms of companies located in different Member States.
46. Already mentioned above 1.5 and 4.2.1.
47. The Code specifies that these special tax regimes must be examined taking into consideration, inter alia, whether (a) tax benefits are reserved for non-residents; (b) tax incentives are granted in a manner which isolates the beneficiaries from the national economy; (c) tax abatements are given despite the fact that no real economic or business activity is taking place; (d) the basis of profit determination for companies in a multilateral group departs from internationally accepted rules, in particular from the rules approved by the OECD; and (e) tax benefits lack transparency (as would happen, for instance, if the incentive is afforded by relaxing the application of legal norms by administration without making it public) (Point B of the Code of Good Conduct, No. 1 to 5).
48. Resolution of 1 December 1997 on the Code of Good Conduct, OJEC C002 [1998] (see above 1.5).
49. In this sense, see also Martin Jiménez, Alfonso J. (1999), *Towards Corporate Tax Harmonisation in the European Community: an Institutional and Procedural Analysis*, London: Kluwer Law International, p. 321.
50. See note 42.
51. See note 44.
52. If accepting (note 44) that the concern expressed in the Recommendation's Preamble about the intra-EC competition between enterprises taking the forms of proprietorships or partnerships and companies, applies *mutatis mutandis* to the competition between companies located in different Member States, the need to consider the conditions of the economic environment, clearly emerging from the wording of this Preamble, also refers to the competition between companies located in different Member States. These companies may find themselves competing with each other with different general economic conditions in their states, which may either reduce or amplify the effect of differences in the normal taxation regimes.
53. See Point G(2) of the Code of Good Conduct.
54. Regimes to which the criteria identified by the Code could not apply by definition: see note 48. In addition, ECOFIN's Code of Good Conduct should be viewed against the backdrop of the increasing intolerance towards preferential tax regimes at a more global level and as a complementary measure to the OECD recommendations intended to oppose 'tax havens' (Nias, P. and N. Purcell (1999), 'Harmonization moves closer by stages', *International Tax Review*, July/August, p. 11).
55. Which, in the light of economic reality, can reasonably be supposed to interact, as a both cause and effect, with the economic environment.
56. Case C-300/89, *Commission v. Council* (*Titanium Dioxide*) [1991] ECR I-2867, para. 15 (emphasis added).
57. Such as an amendment in the determination of the taxable profit or a reduction in the tax rate of the ordinary corporate income tax.
58. Given that this competition can be seen, to date, as not *accepted on legal grounds* but, simply, *tolerated* by the Commission: see above note 25 and 1.6. On the other hand, Vanistendael, note 22, who interprets the current Commission position as an unconditional acceptance, from the legal viewpoint, of the competition among the normal corporate tax regimes and argues that the Treaty was not intended to deal with this type of tax competition (see above 4.2.1), agrees (p. 159) that market competition within the EC may be distorted by both special tax measures and general tax measures and concludes, at p. 161, that 'there is a need … to introduce a number of general tax regulations that may help to determine the general boundaries of tax competition among Member States'.
59. Which should also allow Member States to appreciate exactly the margin of freedom which

EC law leaves them to use their normal company taxation regimes for competing with each other.

60. The term 'race to the bottom' is used here to indicate a situation where Member States compete with each other by continuously introducing more favourable rules (reduction of tax rates, exclusion of some types of income from the taxable base).
61. See also Meussen, G. (2002), 'The EU-fight against harmful tax competition: future developments', *EC Tax Review*, 3, 157–159, at 158 who highlights that 'researchers of the CPB Netherlands' Bureau for Economic Policy Analysis ... state that if governments no longer have the freedom to introduce special tax regimes to attract mobile capital, they might enter into a reduction of general corporate tax rates. For this reason, the Code of Good Conduct ... may lead to a situation where revenues on company taxation may in the end turn out to be lower than would have been the case without the Code'.
62. For example, Title VI, ch. 2 ('Aids granted by states', Article 87 *et seq.*); Title VIII ('Employment', Article 125 *et seq.*); Title XI ('Social policy, education, vocational training and youth', Article 136 *et seq.*); Title XVII ('Economic and social cohesion', Article 158 *et seq.*); Title XVIII ('Research and technological development', Article 163 *et seq.*).
63. See above 1.5 and 1.6.
64. The tax residence, which according to the OECD Model is determined by the place of effective management, can reasonably be assumed to coincide with the central administration, that is with the head office. Vaninstendael, note 22, p. 158, uses this realization (with regard to the migration to Ireland of businesses from other Member States) to argue that, as long as every company within the EC can avail itself of the most favourable tax regime, competition among Member States, in trying to attract companies, does not distort the free and fair competition within the common market.
65. See above 2.2.
66. Where the ECJ removed barriers created by the state of origin under the form of exit taxes: see above 2.4.
67. Which, in turn, is bound to result in a worsening of the economic environment for those who, for reasons other than the tax treatment, wish to set up companies in any of these states.
68. Competing measures may consist of tax rate reductions and/or of tax base restrictions. The losses of revenue to Member States deriving from these competing measures in the field of companies' taxation might be compensated, up to a certain point, by increases of taxes in other sectors (indirect taxes); in any case, even a transparent competition in corporate taxation should find necessary limits (see below).
69. Which has not been the case, at least in part, for the tax competition resulting from the implementation of the 1990 tax Directives: see above 1.1.6.
70. Suppose that Member State A has a lower corporate tax rate than Member State B and that the tax base is given in both countries (as is the normal case), by the difference between revenues of the company and business expenses: an assessment whereby a location in Member State A is more favourable than one in Member State B may turn out to be not necessarily correct if, in Member State B, the items deductible as business expenses are more widely defined than in Member State A and/or the time limit within which losses may be carried forward is more extended than in Member State A.
71. See above 1.1.6.
72. Although the current reality has not reached this situation, the doubt might arise as to whether the various examples of favourable rules (in the determination of the taxable base or in terms of reduction of the tax rate) which Member States have been introducing over the last few years (see Appendix I) may indicate the risk of a move in this direction.
73. Meussen, note 61, p. 158. On the OECD's opposition to harmful tax competition, see inter alia: OECD (1998), *Harmful Tax Competition: an Emerging Global Issue*, Paris: OECD.
74. See *Report of the Committee of Independent Experts on Company Taxation* (Ruding Report), 1992, p. 202 and Meussen, note 61. As regards the potential effects of the latest ECJ rulings to strengthen tax competition, see above 1.6 and Chapter 2.
75. Contrasting with the current Commission and European Parliament approaches: see above 1.5 and 1.6.

76. Ireland, with its 12.5 per cent corporate tax rate, seems to be a significant example of a Member State which may be assumed to have an interest to oppose such proposals.
77. The entry into the Community of countries like Estonia and Cyprus (the first of which does not tax undistributed profits, whereas the second applies from 2002 a 10 per cent corporate tax rate) was seen as an element in the perception of this interest: see Meussen, note 61, p. 159.
78. The turning of the Code of Conduct into 'hard law' is suggested by Meussen, note 61, p. 159.
79. In other words, due to the continuous rejection in the ECJ case law of justifications based on the risk of revenue losses and to the increasing rejection of all other justifications (see above 1.4.1 and 1.4.3), Member States are being encouraged to protect their revenues in the alternative way of competing with each other to attract new companies (see above 1.3.3, 1.4.3 and 1.6), which causes each state to try to protect its tax revenues at the expense of other states, who will therefore lose tax revenues. This risks causing excessive deficits and, since the concern to protect revenues, as indicated by the agreement on the Code of Conduct, is common to all states, a supranational solution can create boundaries to the tax competition among normal tax regimes, in order to prevent it from generating results comparable to those of the tax competition between special tax regimes. The expression 'to determine the general boundaries' to the tax competition, used by Vanistendael, note 22, appears to be particularly appropriate. The analysis in this subparagraph may also offer further arguments to assess, in the light of the fundamental freedoms, the current approach against a strictly legal viewpoint: Cerioni, L. (2005), 'Harmful tax competition revisited: why not a purely legal perspective under EC law?', *European Taxation*, 7 (45), 267–281, at 275–277.
80. See COM (2003) 284 final, note 11, pp. 9 and 20 and above, 3.1.
81. On the *Uberseering, Inspire Art, Lasteyrie du Saillant and SEVIC Systems* ruling, see Chapter 2.
82. See the consultation document published by the Commission in 2004; Kieninger, E.M. (2005), 'The legal framework of regulatory competition based on corporate mobility: EU and US compared – Part II/II', *German Law Journal*, 4 (6), www.germanlawjournal.com/, 1 April; The Law Societies Joint Brussels Office, The Brussels Office Law Reform Update Series: Company Law and Financial Services, March 2006, at 10. By considering the transfer of the head office as already allowed by ECJ case law, the Commission has implicitly accepted the interpretation of the *Lasteyrie du Saillant* ruling according to which the real seat criteria must in principle be given up by the states of origin: see above 2.4.
83. See above 2.5.
84. Directive 78/855/EEC on mergers of public limited-liability companies, OJEC L295/36 [1978], Articles 3 to 9; Directive 82/891/EEC on divisions of public limited-liability companies, OJEC L378 [1982], Article 3 *et seq.*
85. See Articles 3 to 10 of the draft Directive (draft XV/D2/6002/97-EN-REV2), Article 8 of Regulation 2157/2001 on the ECS (complemented by Directive 2001/86/EC on employee involvement in the European company), and the analogous provisions concerning the SCE: see above 3.2.4 and 3.3.
86. In this subparagraph, the terms 'proposed Directive' and 'draft Directive' are used interchangeably, although the idea is still in the draft stage and is being discussed before the presentation of an official proposal from the Commission.
87. See above 2.1 and 2.2.
88. See Commission Press Release IP/04/270, 'Company law: Commission consults on the cross-border transfer of companies' registered offices', 26 February 2004, and CCBE (Councils of the Bars and Law Societies of the European Union) response to the European Commission consultation on the cross-border transfer of the registered office of companies, 15 April 2004, available at www.ccbe.org
89. As stated in the *Uberseering* ruling: see above 2.2.
90. That is the creation of a company in the jurisdiction offering the most liberal rules and the exercise of all activity of this company, if they so wish, in another country (see above 2.2 and 2.3). German lawyers (law firm Dolce & Lauda, Frankfurt, letter to clients, 2004) indeed note that, after *Uberseering*, this phenomenon has been gaining pace and an increasing number of 'Ltd' incorporated in the United Kingdom have been operating in Germany, to

such an extent that, to make the 'GmbH' form capable of competing with the 'Ltd' form, the GmbH minimum capital was reduced from 25 000 to 10 000 Euros as of 1 January 2006.

91. Kieninger, note 82.
92. See inter alia Stein, E. (1971), *Harmonisation of European Company Laws: National Reform and Transnational Coordination*, The Bobbs-Merril Company Inc., ch. 2, pp. 24–57; Fitchew, G. (1992), 'The European dimension in company law?', *Company Lawyer*, 1 (13), comment; Timmermans, C. (1991), 'Methods and tools for integration: a report', in Richard M. Buxbaum, Gérard Herting, Alain Hirsch and Klaus J. Hopt (eds), *European Business Law: Legal and Economic Analysis on Integration and Harmonisation*, based on a conference held in 1988 in Lugano, Switzerland, Berlin: de Gruyter, pp. 129–148; Wolff, G. (1993), 'The Commission's programme for company law harmonisation: the winding road to a uniform European company law?', in M. Andenas and S. Kenynon-Slade (eds), *EC Financial Market Regulation and Company Law*, London: Sweet & Maxwell, pp. 19–29; more recently, Ebert, S. (2003), 'The European company in the level playing field of the Community', *European Business Law Review*, 2 (14), 183–192, at 184. In the text, 'companies' is used as synonymous with 'companies and firms' referred to in the second paragraph of Article 48 of the Treaty. Moreover, any reference to Article 94 is intended as indicating the Treaty's Articles 94 to 96.
93. See Appendix I.
94. Hopt, K.J. (1999), 'Company law in the European Union: harmonisation and/or subsidiarity?', *International and Comparative Corporate Law Journal*, 1 (1), 42–61, at 50–51. This view also seems to emerge from Charny, D. (1994), 'Competition among jurisdictions in formulating corporate law rules: an American perspective on the "race to the bottom" in the European Communities', in Wheeler, S. (ed.), *A Reader on the Law of the Business Enterprise*, Oxford Readings on Socio-Legal Studies, Oxford, UK: Oxford University Press, pp. 365–391, and from Moch, S. (2002), 'Harmonization, regulation and legislative competition in European corporate law', *German Law Journal*, 12 (3), www.germanlawjournal.com/, 1 December.
95. Ebert, note 92, p. 184. This competition, as already indicated (see above 2.1 to 2.3), is encouraged by the latest ECJ company law rulings and may be further strengthened by *Lasteyrie du Saillant*.
96. Ebert, note 92, p. 184, who clearly affirms: 'The true aim of the EC Treaty is, however, to abolish (still existing) differences in regulatory standards between the Member States and to harmonise the laws. In order to counter harmful competition between the different jurisdictions of the Member States and thus distortion of competition not covered by the EC Treaty ("race to the bottom"), the laws within the Community are to be harmonised'.
97. As defined by Article 48, second paragraph EC.
98. Case 79/85, *Segers* [1986] ECR 2375 (see above 2.2 and 2.3).
99. Case C-212/97, *Centros* [1999] ECR I-1459 (see above 2.2 and 2.3).
100. See above 4.2.1.
101. In addition it can again be noted that a distinction based on the sector of law causing distortions is not drawn by the ECJ general statement quoted above 4.2.2.
102. A situation which, although under different forms of exercise of the right of establishment, was common to *Segers, Centros* and *Inspire Art*.
103. In the *Segers* and *Inspire Art* rulings (see above 2.2).
104. In the *Centros* ruling (see above 2.1 and 2.2).
105. This may be deduced by reading *Uberseering*, where the 'certain circumstances' were admitted as a ground for restriction on the freedom of establishment, jointly with the *Inspire Art* ruling, where the ECJ stated that abuse is to be proved on a case-by-case basis (see above 2.2 and 2.3).
106. In other words, the ECJ having accepted that abusive forum-shopping practices create a distortion in the functioning of the EC market (see above 2.3), the same must also hold true for the race to the bottom competition in company law which encourages these practices.
107. COM (2003) 284 final, note 80, p. 9.
108. COM (2003) 284 final, note 80, pp. 8 and 9.

109. This can be deduced from *Segers* and *Inspire Art*, note 105, from *Centros*, note 104 and from *Uberseering*, note 105.
110. Under the form of either a secondary establishment constituting the de facto real seat or the transfer of the real seat.
111. In this regard, no reason suggests that the argument put forward by the EC Commissioner on Internal Market and Taxation, shortly after the 2001 Commission Report on Companies' Taxation, whereby Community action in the field would not be needed so long as welfare losses due to locational inefficiencies caused by differences in tax rates are not quantifiable (see above 1.5 and 1.6), should not apply, *mutatis mutandis*, to the not yet harmonized sectors of company law too. In other words, when the dimension of distortions generated by abusive forum-shopping practices induced by a race to the bottom competition in company laws become quantifiable at Community level, there is certainly a legal ground for limiting such competition.
112. The response to these questions, which would be likely to stimulate discussions such as those which have been taking place in the academic literature as regards the features of the company law harmonization programme (see above 3.1), goes outside the scope of the present work, which will propose a kind of solution different from further measures approximating national laws.
113. Article 43, second paragraph EC.
114. Articles 81 to 86; 87 to 89.
115. See above 4.3.1.
116. Particularly in the case of publicly traded companies (see above 3.1).
117. Which may be the final outcome of an ongoing process of discussion and consultation, launched by the Commission's Communications in the area of contract law: Communication on European contract law (COM (2001) 398 final) and in particular 'A more coherent European contract law: an action plan' (COM (2003) 68 final), pp. 7–45, which sets out the options for a systematic approach after various EC Directives, already issued, applying to particular commercial situations.
118. Which can be regarded as interdependent with company law: Hopt, note 94, p. 60.
119. Article 44, second paragraph, let. (g), Article 94.
120. Wolff, note 92, p. 19, stresses that: 'The purpose of harmonisation is not … the reduction of the choices open to companies … in many cases different standards might be equivalent and do not necessarily imply any difference in quality'.
121. See above 4.3.2.
122. See above 3.1 and below in the text.
123. Which, with regard to tax forum shopping, have been recognized as the origin of 'welfare losses' (See above 1.5 and 1.6) and which can also be seen as such as regards forum-shopping practices originated by different national company laws (see above 4.3.2, note 113).
124. Hopt, note 94, p. 51, emphasis added. Wolff, note 92, also underlines that the purpose of harmonization is 'increasing transparency, reducing the cost of cross-border transactions, removing obstacles to establishment, and equalising conditions of competition'.
125. Hopt, note 94, p. 51.
126. Villiers, C. (1996), 'Harmonisation of company laws in Europe, with an introduction to some comparative issues', in Geraint G. Howell (ed.), *European Business Law*, Aldershot: Ashgate/Dartmouth, UK, pp. 169–195, demonstrates this result of the harmonization programme through a comparative overview of the implementation of Directives in the United Kingdom and Spain. The same analysis is carried out in Villiers, C. (1998), '*European Company Law: Towards Democracy?*', Aldershot: Ashgate/Dartmouth, UK, pp. 161–176.
127. See above 4.3.2.
128. See Case C-97/96, *Daihatsu Deutschland* [1997] ECR I-6834, paras 18 to 20 of the ruling where the ECJ, in clarifying the direct effect of a provision of the First Company Law Directive, had occasion to interpret the term 'others' in Article 44, second paragraph, let. (g).
129. Dine, J. (1991–1994), *EC Company Law*, London: Chancery Law Publishing, loose-leaf,

ch. 1; Du Plessis J.J. and J. Dine (1997), 'The fate of the draft of the Fifth Directive on Company Law: accomodation instead of harmonisation', *Journal of Business Law*, 25–29; Villiers (1998), note 126, pp. 171–173.

130. Villiers, C. (2001), 'Reorganisation of European Company structures in the twenty-first century', *International and Comparative Corporate Law Journal*, 2 (3), vii–x, highlights the need to make available 'a *greater variety of legal entities* designed to suit the different types of economic entity' (emphasis added).
131. As already indicated with regard to the SE: see above 3.2.14.
132. Such as the United Kingdom and Ireland.
133. In other words, 'to make European registration equivalent to registration in Delaware': Dine, J. (1989), 'The harmonisation of company law in the European Community', *Yearbook of European Law* (9), 93–120, at 119.
134. See above 3.2.14.
135. See above 3.3.
136. Particularly in the light of the *Centros*, the *Uberseering*, the *Inspire Art* and the *Lasteyrie du Saillant* rulings (see above 2.2 and 2.3, 4.3.1 and 4.3.2).
137. See COM (2003) 284 final, p. 21. On the proposed EPC, see below 5.2.
138. Since the creation on behalf of both natural and legal persons is already possible for company law schemes governed by national provisions. In the text, the reference to 'company law' is intended as reference to the law governing all forms of business organizations, thus both companies as technically defined and partnerships.
139. To be in line with the legal systems of Member States already adopting it and with the latest developments of ECJ case law on the right of primary establishment (see above 2.2 and 2.3).
140. To be competitive, from the viewpoint of businesses, with the provisions of those Member States adopting the incorporation theory and, at the same time, to offer creditors adequate knowledge of the dissociation between the state of the registered and that of the head office.
141. Such as that imposed by the current ECS for the seat transfer (see above 3.2.4).
142. Since this possibility is already admitted by the legal systems of some Member States for companies incorporated under their national laws (and the possible existence of companies regulated by national laws and having the head office outside the EC is recognized by the ECS itself: see above 3.2.2).
143. Such as the UN Conventions concerning the international sale of goods.
144. These two possibilities – flexibility as regards the rules for representation toward third parties, and for easy transformation – would make such aspects of the regulation more attractive than the national regimes since, in each of them, national regulations contain quite strict provisions.
145. Which set out strict requirements: Third Company Law Directive 78/855/EEC, OJEC L295 [1978], Articles 3 to 9; Sixth Company Law Directive 82/891/EEC, OJEC L378 [1982], Article 3 *et seq*.
146. Such area has remained outside the company law harmonization programme.
147. Intended as irrelevance of the location within the EC (and thus intended according to the broadest concept of tax neutrality, which was not followed by the drafters of the tax Directives: see above 1.1.1, 1.1.8 and 1.2).
148. See above 1.1.7.
149. See above. 1.2.
150. Which would make the determination of the taxable income more favourable and less difficult than that which is necessary in almost all Member States for businesses choosing the national company law forms.
151. The 'participation exemption' is the exclusion from the taxable base of dividends and often of capital gains accruing on the sale of securities, one of the most typical forms of tax benefits which several Member States (most important examples are offered by the Netherlands, Sweden and Denmark), under conditions different from each other, have been introducing to make their jurisdictions attractive, in particular for holding companies.
152. A result which, only in part, has been achieved by the ECJ case law on company taxation: see above 1.4.2.c, the *Marks & Spencer* case.

153. As the carrying back and/or forward of losses is already allowed by some national legislations (see Appendix I).
154. For example, a European public limited-liability company should have had the lowest amongst the minimum capital requirements prescribed by national laws, which does not occur for the ECS (which establishes a minimum capital requirement of 120 000 Euros whereas, for example, a German AG only needs a minimum capital of 50 000 Euros and a Belgian SA of 61 500 Euros).
155. As some Member States may oppose it in the EC Council, believing in this way to protect their national interests (such as revenue interests, which in reality, in the medium and longer run, realistically would be protected by the introduction of a supranational tax regime, for each envisaged supranational vehicle, more favourable than the national ones: see above 4.2.3).
156. Ebert, note 92, p. 192.
157. See COM (2003) 284 final, note 11, pp. 8–9.
158. See ibid. p. 8.
159. See ibid. pp. 24–25.
160. Ibid. p. 9.

5. Hypothesis for (truly) supranational developments

The arguments developed in the previous chapter ultimately rely upon an interpretation of EC law's ultimate objectives and upon three basic assumptions. According to the reasoning followed: (a) the Treaty aims at creating a system of undistorted market competition among all business enterprises operating within the Community market, to ensure the proper functioning of the internal market; (b) equal possibilities of free movement from one Member State to another for all EC enterprises are an essential component of this undistorted market competition; (c) differences between the national laws of Member States may cause distortions when they either create obstacles to such free movement or induce businesses into 'forum-shopping' practices damaging stakeholders; (d) to eliminate these distortions (which might derive from the legal competition between Member States) the EC institutions, in accordance with the subsidiarity principle, are empowered to harmonize national laws; but (e) legal competition among national jurisdictions of Member States is, by definition, compatible with EC law objectives – and may be a valid alternative to harmonization – when it does not distort market competition among enterprises.

The assumptions made are that (a) businesses tend to exploit differences between national company law and taxation regimes to move from one state to another without economic or market-related reasons, to increase their profitability at the expense of third parties;[1] and (b) they would be attracted by supranational schemes offering (at least, on balance) more favourable alternatives than the national ones in these two crucial sectors. If these assumptions are accepted, the interpretation adopted makes it possible to argue that supranational instruments meeting the requirements set out in Chapter 4[2] would become the solution which, by definition, would make legal competition compatible with the Treaty and ensure a Community-wide level playing field, with conditions of market competition not distorted by the differences between the national legal provisions. Such a solution would also provide a legally unquestionable response to the issue left open by the legislative developments at EC level in the field of companies' taxation (Chapter 1)[3] and would mark the overcoming of the limits of EC legislation in the field of company law (Chapter 3).[4]

However, at academic and political level, lively debates are currently taking place on the merits of legal competition versus harmonization in the achievement of a level playing field for business enterprises within the EC. In the area of company law (or, more precisely, of the law governing the creation, operation and dissolution of business enterprises) new ideas are being elaborated by the academic literature, whereas in the area of companies' taxation the debate has mostly been stirred by the perspectives introduced by the Commission's two-track strategy aimed at introducing the CCBT as a long-term solution. Tested against the approach emerging from the current debates at academic and political level, the interpretation adopted, the assumption made and the conclusion reached make it possible to better specify the ultimate solution proposed in Chapter 4 for the issue of legal competition in the two fields at stake while formulating some hypotheses for further research and discussions.

5.1 HYPOTHESIS FOR THE TAXATION REGIME OF THE SE

5.1.1 Other 'Comprehensive Approaches' to EC Company Taxation

The 'partly supranational' solution represented by a CCBT, currently regarded as the best option, is not the only long-term comprehensive approach to EU company taxation, which could eventually minimize, or remove altogether, the obstacles in a more unified manner.[5] Three other approaches to the tax treatment of multinational groups of companies have been indicated by the academic literature and discussed in the Commission's Report on *Company Taxation in the Internal Market*: Home State Taxation (HST), European Union Company Income Tax (EUCIT) and Single Compulsory Harmonized Tax Base (HTB).[6] All of them share with the CCBT the features given by the determination of the tax base according to a single set of rules and the sharing of this tax base, under an allocation mechanism, amongst the Member States involved. The difference between the CCBT and the last two solutions, the EUCIT and the HTB, lies in the circumstance that none of these latter is limited to the determination of an optional tax base. The EUCIT would lead to a genuine, either optional or compulsory, EU tax, with not only a common consolidated tax base but also a single EU tax rate, and would require the accruing of its revenues primarily to EU budget to fund the Community's institutions and activities with any excess allocated between Member States. The objection against EUCIT is that it would not reflect the actual political situation in the EC and would represent 'a major step towards the creation of a federal Europe'.[7] An HTB approach would imply the substitution of all the existing national corporate tax systems by a single one, to be applied across the EC to all enterprises with no possibility for them to opt out: this is clearly not a realistic proposition. In turn, the HST would be limited to the determination of the tax base (like the CCBT), but would be based on the mutual recognition of the different tax regimes existing in the Member States: the parent company and all its subsidiaries within the Community would compute the overall taxable base according to the rules of the Member State of location of the parent company (the 'Home State'). The HST is seen as a possible intermediate stage towards an optional common tax base,[8] that is towards the CCBT. In the Commission's and the European Parliament's view, the SE legal form would be the natural candidate for the CCBT[9] and the Commission considered 'piloting' the CCBT just for companies opting for the SE form.[10] Last, there seems to be agreement that the solution chosen for the SE should also apply to the SCE:[11] the arguments hereinafter presented for the taxation regime of the SE can therefore also be applied to the SCE.

5.1.2 And the Limits of the CCBT Solution

Although there is no doubt that a CCBT approach would lead to the definitive overcoming of obstacles to intra-EC activities such as the lack of cross-border loss compensation, the risk of economic double taxation of dividends or transfer pricing problems, two major issues need to be addressed in relation to the SE: (1) whether or under which conditions the CCBT approach would really be suitable to make the SE a valid alternative to company forms governed by national laws;[12] (2) whether it would be able to ensure, as a supranational tax regime for the SE would do,[13] that competition in companies' taxation becomes compatible with EC law.

In relation to point (1), an immediate observation can be formulated: since the CCBT would be open to *all* companies having branches and subsidiaries throughout the EC, even if choosing to incorporate under national company law forms, it would not be, on its own, a distinctive feature of the SE format. Furthermore, it would be useless for those companies potentially interested in the SE form but not having a multinational character: for example, a joint subsidiary (which is one of the ways of forming an SE)[14] which is set up in Member State A between a company A located in the same Member State A and a company B located in Member State B, and which does not have secondary establishments in other Member States, would be unable to benefit from the CCBT. This could be accepted only if the SE is conceived only as an additional company law instrument which is added to the company law schemes governed by national legislations, but not if the SE is seen as *the* instrument which should give a decisive contribution to the level playing field within the EC and which, for this reason, would need to be preferred, by all businesses involved in cross-border restructuring and reorganization operations, to national company law forms.[15] To play this role, which it has failed to do up to the present time, the SE would need to benefit from a more competitive tax regime than those applicable to each of the national forms of companies: this supranational tax regime would reasonably be able to compensate the limits of this form from the company law viewpoint.[16] Thus, assuming that the CCBT approach will, in the medium-long run, be introduced, a considerable problem would arise. If a certain common consolidated tax base will be made available to all multinational companies operating throughout the EC under national company law forms, a different and more favourable common consolidated tax base would in fact need to be envisaged for those multinational businesses considering the choice of the SE instrument. This would be the condition in order for the CCBT approach to manage to make the SE a valid alternative to national company forms, and would make it necessary, as a further problem, to identify the elements in which the common consolidated tax base available to SEs ought to be more favourable than that open to multinationals incorporating under other national company law forms. In its 2006 Communication,[17] the Commission acknowledges that, despite the setting up of a Working Group (CCBTWG) in late 2004, the effort it has been undertaking since then to define various technical aspects of the design of this tax base, and the support expressed by the European Parliament and the European Economic and Social Committee (EESC)[18] some Member States are still reluctant. If difficulties are arising in designing one unanimously accepted common consolidated base, those difficulties are likely to become (much) greater in designing two common consolidated bases, one for multinational companies opting for national company law forms, the other for multinational companies considering the SE format. On the other hand, the Commission's idea of piloting the CCBT approach with the SE, so that multinational businesses choosing the SE form would be the first ones to which a common EU tax base would be made available, after gaining initially considerable support, was recognized as deserving further analysis, in particular with regard to the existence of a possible discrimination towards those companies which cannot transform themselves into an SE and to competition issues, but was subsequently discouraged by an independent study contracted out by the Commission.[19]

Irrespective of these issues, linked to the initial application of the CCBT as a pilot scheme for the SE, the first observation above formulated remains valid: the SE would be only the first, but not the only, legal form to which this regime would be applicable and, if EC measures are to be introduced for the benefit also of companies remaining within national tax law rules to overcome the issue of cross-border loss compensation or transfer pricing problems,[20] the CCBT will again have to be competitive in comparison with national tax bases to be chosen by the eligible companies. Of course, if the CCBT approach is unlikely to make the SE a valid alternative to company forms governed by national law, this holds even truer for the solution followed up to date: the technical adaptations of the current body of EU company taxation law.[21] This solution finds its examples in the amendments of the Parent-Subsidiary Directive and of the Merger Directive, and in those proposed to the Interest-Royalties Directive,[22] which extend the scope of the tax Directives to the SE and, in the case of the revised Merger Directive, contain rules for the transfer of the registered office of the SE to another Member State.[23] As the Commission acknowledged, this solution may only be sufficient not to 'hinder or put at an undue disadvantage this new legal form'[24] (which, by definition, is insufficient to make it more 'competitive' than national company forms).

In relation to point (2), it was argued that, without an EC tax solution, the 'SEs may be tempted to change their nationality in order to take advantage of the most favourable company tax burden. This would induce unhealthy and harmful tax competition between Member States'.[25]

This conclusion may apply in the event of adoption not only of an HST but also of a CCBT approach, which would not be an entirely EU solution (as the EUCIT): in the case of companies adopting the CCBT, the application of the different national tax rates to an identical (EC) tax base would certainly result in a transparent tax competition (that is, in a tax competition fulfilling one of the requirements for its compatibility with EC law) which, however, would make the calculation of the differences between the company tax burden in the various Member States, and the identification of the most favourable one, even easier than it may be in the current context. Consequently, it would end up simplifying the task for international tax planners and, ultimately, it could still induce SEs into forum-shopping practices among the different tax jurisdictions.[26] The outcome would thus be the possible location of one or more units (parent company, subsidiary(ies), branch(es)) in a Member State rather than in another on tax grounds but without economic and market-related reasons, that is, exactly those 'locational inefficiencies' which were regarded as a source of distortion, although at present not quantifiable.[27] In this regard, the realization that 'at this point in time, there seems to be little empirical evidence of a "race-to-the bottom"'[28] (which can be called into question), may justify, from a political viewpoint, a position which considers tax competition as fair if based on tax rates and takes substantial note, amongst the Treaty's provisions, only of the principle of subsidiarity, concluding that the CCBT would be the preferable model. However, it cannot suffice to state, from the perspective of a legal analysis, that the CCBT would be the optimal solution. The implicit recognition that empirical evidence may change in the (nearer or farther) future (for example, due to the progressive enlargement of the EU involving new Member States in tax competition) and the need for a coordinated reading of the subsidiarity principle with the Treaty's other provisions, such as the obligation on Member States not to act in such a manner as to jeopardize the attainment of the EC's objectives, or the aim of undistorted (market) competition,[29] indicate that a CCBT approach cannot substitute for a genuine supranational solution. In other words, whereas an entirely supranational but optional solution for the taxation regime of the SE (which it is assumed businesses would consider on balance to be more attractive than each national regime) would manage to reconcile the subsidiarity principle with the goal of undistorted market competition and with the Member States' obligation not to jeopardize the achievement of Community objectives, the CCBT could not manage to achieve this outcome. The above arguments which suggest the limits of the CCBT seem to be ignored by the political positions advocating this regime.

From a legal viewpoint, the hypothesis for the taxation regime of the SE ought thus to be formulated in the context of a purely optional EUCIT regime: the objection that this kind of solution would not reflect the actual political situation in the EC and would represent 'a major step towards the creation of a federal Europe'[30] would certainly hold true for a compulsory EUCIT regime (which is just one of the two alternatives mentioned in the Commission's Report), but it may be questioned whether it is still necessarily true for an optional regime. This regime would require Member States to relinquish neither their power to establish the taxable base nor that to set their own tax rates; it would just allocate 'the taxing power and the revenues to each level of responsibility, that is, the European Union and the Member States'.[31] It would thus, exactly as an optional CCBT (which is regarded as the preferable model), preserve Member States' autonomy and would be coherent with an institutional framework which is not a fully-fledged federal one: ultimately, without modifying this framework, the optional EUCIT solution would merely allow the EC budget to have one more financial resource.[32] On the other hand, the scarce appeal of the SE instrument without an appropriate tax regime[33] confirms that this instrument would become attractive with an EUCIT solution offering, on balance, a more favourable tax regime than each of the national ones. Consequently, a workable hypothesis for the taxation regime of the SE should be formulated: (a) on the elements of this tax regime which would make it more competitive than the national ones; (b) on the administration of this system.

5.1.3 Some Hypotheses for an Optional and 'Competitive' EUCIT Solution

The design of an optional EUCIT tax regime for the SE, aimed at making this instrument attractive, would most probably not be more technically difficult than that of a CCBT having the same purpose. There would either be two elements – the tax base and the tax rate – or a combination of both, on which this regime could be shaped, rather than just one element as in the case of the CCBT, so that there would be more room for manoeuvre than in the case of a common EU consolidated tax base. With the assumptions made, the EUCIT tax regime could consist at least of: (a) a tax base simply having the features which are more common to all national tax bases, coupled with a proportional tax rate equal to the most favourable rate within the EC; (b) a tax base determined according to more favourable rules than those provided for by national corporate tax laws, accompanied by a proportional tax rate simply reflecting the average of tax rates within the EC; (c) a combination between a tax base and a tax rate governed by rules which, taken together, offer companies more choices, and thus more flexibility, than that allowed by national tax regimes. For example, that combination could be designed between a tax base offering more options with regard to the deduction of certain items of business expenses, coupled with a tax rate which, at the choice of companies, could either be proportional or progressive for certain brackets of income: businesses would thus find the advantage of a tax regime leading to a fiscal charge which could be better suited to their economic cycle. Such an EUCIT tax regime, which, by definition, would definitively remove all tax obstacles (cross-border loss compensation, transfer pricing and so on) to cross-border activity, should be made available to all SEs, irrespective of whether they have subsidiaries or branches throughout the EC or not.

It might be objected that a similar regime would lead to unpredictable losses in the tax revenues of Member States and that it would thus be impossible to administer, so that it would not be a realistic objective. Nonetheless, from the technical and legal viewpoint, such an objection does not seem to be well-grounded. First, losses in the tax revenues of Member States are in any case, to a greater or lesser extent, bound to be generated by what is regarded as fair tax competition:[34] the losses generated over time by such tax competition are difficult if not impossible to predict, whereas, as argued in the previous chapter,[35] a competition between the national regimes and a supranational (EUCIT) regime would generate, for the individual Member States, revenue losses which in the end are more predictable to the extent that the supranational tax regime becomes that towards which the competing national ones should spontaneously tend to approximate. This major predictability would be of help for the individual Member States in designing their overall fiscal policies. Secondly, the EUCIT solution suggested would not technically be impossible to administer. Businesses choosing the SE format and this EUCIT tax regime could be required to declare their choice at the outset, upon registration of the SE, and this choice would need to remain legally binding at least for a given number of years (such as four to six years) in order, on the one hand, to allow the EC and the individual Member States to stabilize the effects on their budgets and, on the other hand, to offer businesses incorporated under the ECS a medium-term period to observe the evolution in national tax regimes. At the end of that period, they could thus either confirm the choice for the EUCIT if this remains more convenient than the national regimes or opt out if, in the meantime, the competing national tax regimes have approximated to the supranational one to such an extent as to offer the same advantages. The collection of the corporation tax established under the EUCIT regime, to be made according to uniform procedures, could be left to Member States' tax authorities; the revenues should thus need to be allocated in part to the EC budget and in part to the Member States' budgets (according to a proportion to be agreed), in a similar way as currently happens for revenues from VAT. It would certainly be necessary, for the allocation of revenues from the taxation of SEs operating in several Member States, to devise an apportionment formula, which, however, could be the same which would be used to solve the allocation problem in the case of a CCBT solution (some formulae are currently under discussion).

Another objection could be that an EUCIT solution open to SEs only would imply a discrimination against those 'companies which factually or legally cannot easily transform themselves into an SE':[36] this issue was already raised as regards the idea of 'piloting' the CCBT solution with the SE. It might therefore be argued that, if a temporary application of a CCBT solution solely to the SE would entail a discrimination, this would hold even truer for a definitive application of an EUCIT solution to the SE only. Nevertheless, the concept of discrimination referred to in a similar argument ought to be clarified. If 'discrimination' is intended as different treatment of comparable (or identical) situations, it must be noted that all companies having the legal forms listed in Regulation 2157/2001 (and thus which are, from the legal viewpoint, in a comparable situation) can set up an SE, either by way of transformation or through one of the other routes to the creation of the SE. No discrimination would thus exist by definition, and an optional EUCIT for SEs may be conceived as supplementing the SE legal format, which is optional in itself and every company which fulfils the legal requirements regarding its form is free to decide whether or not to adopt. Since the companies which cannot transform themselves into an SE would thus be – legally – exactly those businesses having legal forms not indicated by the Regulation, the problem would be how to avoid a difference of treatment (rather than a 'discrimination' in the technical sense) between businesses which would have an EUCIT tax solution available and businesses which would not. The solution could be found in the design of other supranational regimes of taxation, suited to the features of the businesses having legal forms not indicated in the SE Regulation and offering them the same comparative advantages, in relation to their national regimes of taxation, which are offered by the EUCIT solution to businesses eligible to choose the SE format. On the other hand, new supranational instruments, with their taxation regimes, may also offer a convenient solution to those businesses which, de facto, for practical reasons (such as the costs of creating an SE), cannot opt for the SE: this may hold particularly true for SMEs. In fact, in a feasibility study to assess the need for introduction of the European Private Company, concluded in 2005 and carried out on the part of the Commission amongst more than 2000 SMEs in the 25 Member States (the '2005 study'), more than 80 per cent of the participating SMEs declared that they would not adopt the SE statute.[37]

5.2 HYPOTHESIS ON THE CURRENT PROPOSAL ON THE EPC

5.2.1 Amendments to the Company Law Aspects

The current project on the European Private Company (EPC), contained in a draft Regulation, aims to create an entity largely contractual, which should ensure the benefits of flexibility and of adaptability of form and which should assume a 'routine character' amongst SMEs,[38] helping them to approach the EC market and to carry on businesses throughout the EC. For these purposes, it leaves total freedom as far as the creation routes are concerned (the EPC could be set up by both individuals and companies, through direct registration or through merger, transformation of an existing national company or as a joint subsidiary, and would not be restricted to nationals of Member States) and as regards internal organization and operation, consistently with the adequate protection of shareholders and third parties. On the other hand, it refers to national legislations in areas such as insolvency and employees' representation, it adopts the real seat criteria and, to prevent a light or frivolous use of this instrument and to give it economic credibility, sets a minimum capital requirement. The 2005 study describes the current EPC version as more liberal than the company forms of Member States following the more stringent regulatory approach (Germany, France, Spain, Italy, Austria, Belgium, Greece, Portugal) but still too inflexible in comparison with the vehicles offered by the most liberal national systems (United Kingdom, Ireland, Cyprus, some new East European Member States which have based their company law reforms on Anglo-Saxon models) and thus finds that a considerable part of European SMEs may be reluctant to adopt it. Nevertheless, it recognizes that a vehicle offering both a 'European label' and a flexibility such as that of the British 'private limited' would be very appealing.[39]

Consequently, and in view of the features which supranational company law vehicles should have to become the instrument for a legal competition compatible with EC law, some amendments could be made to the current company law version of the EPC project to turn it into the general, routine choice of SMEs. First, the concern to avoid companies choosing the EPC format for the sole purpose of escaping national laws – which has led to the proposed minimum capital requirement of 25 000 Euros, to be fully paid up on subscription – would need to be reconciled with the case law of the ECJ, which has consistently accepted that the choice of the most 'liberal' provisions on company formation and capital requirement, amongst those of different national company laws, is not sufficient to demonstrate an abuse of the right of establishment, which abuse must be proved on a case-by-case basis.[40] In other words, if within this limit a pure forum-shopping phenomenon between national company law forms is to be accepted under EC law, it becomes difficult to argue that it should not be accepted, with the same limit, between the national company law forms and an intended supranational form such as the EPC. If the EPC were definitively introduced with more stringent requirements than those of some national company law forms, the marketing advantages and the recognition of its legal status in all Member States could not suffice to induce businesses to opt for this form: the recognition of the legal status is, in fact, generally assured, following the latest ECJ case law, to national company law forms too.

The economic credibility that the EPC needs could perhaps be ensured not only by a fixed minimum capital, but also by a more flexible requirement. One suggestion on formation of the company could be that of allowing a choice between a fixed minimum capital and the provision by the shareholders, as a consideration for acquiring their shares, of such an amount of financial resources as is consistent with the needs of the planned operations of the company during an initial period (such as three years) to be detailed in a financial plan to be filed together with the application for registration and made available to the public.[41] Even an initial minimum capital paid on registration would not constitute a proper guarantee, for it may be paid out 'on a totally risky venture and be completely lost',[42] whereas the shareholders would probably have an interest to maintain an amount of financial resources regarded as consistent with the needs of planned operations resulting from a financial plan available to the public (that is to maintain an amount of resources regarded as such by those potentially interested in entering into a business relationship with the company) in order for the company to be trusted by the public. On the other hand, the proposed adoption of the real seat criteria would, exactly as in the case of the SE, put the EPC at a disadvantage in comparison with companies governed by national laws of countries following the incorporation theory, and does not seem to take into consideration the latest developments of the ECJ case law on the freedom of movement of national law companies. In this respect, the proposal, if not amended in order to allow the location of the registered office and of the head office in different Member States, would thus be obsolete even before its possible adoption.

Moreover, the choice to rely on national law rules concerning employees' representation (that is, on the rules determined by the law applicable to the registered office of the EPC) may result in a lack of flexibility for those who might be interested in creating this type of company but might prefer different arrangements for employees' representation than those provided for by national laws: paradoxically, the EPC would risk being in this aspect less flexible than the SE, given that the Employee Involvement Directive 2001/86/EC supplementing the SE Regulation leaves space for negotiations-based solutions. Consequently, a third amendment which would be appropriate for the EPC would be that of limiting the reference to national law provisions regulating employee participation or other forms of involvement to the cases in which either no different agreement is reached between the management or administrative organs of the company and the employees, or they expressly agree to apply them. This solution should be envisaged for those companies which, according to the different national laws, reach the threshold, in terms of number of employees, making employee participation compulsory, to offer these EPCs more adaptability than that available to companies formed under national laws.

5.2.2 Taxation Regime for the Proposed EPC

The 2005 study, in dealing with the tax treatment of the EPC, excludes the idea of tax incentives and formulates two alternatives. A first possibility would leave the tax regime to national laws while extending to the EPC the existing tax EC Directives; a second would consist of a new EC tax regime specifically designed for the EPC as a European statute for SMEs which would replace, for this category, the national regimes. The justifications would be, basically, the equal treatment principle for the former hypothesis, and the necessity of compensating the higher incidence of tax obstacles for SMEs than for larger companies in the internal market (and thus of eliminating the structural disadvantages otherwise faced by SMEs) for the latter hypothesis.[43]

From the viewpoint of the requirements for supranational vehicles to become more attractive than national ones, the solution of leaving the tax aspects to be regulated by national law might only be considered acceptable if the company law aspects were sufficient (with some amendments to the proposal) to make this instrument more attractive than the national private limited company forms. In that case, the idea supported by the Commission of testing the HST solution as a pilot scheme for SMEs (which latter are identified on the basis of turnover, total balance sheet and number of employees)[44] could be translated into practice, first, with those SMEs choosing the EPC form, which will be more likely than those choosing national company law forms to carry on cross-border business throughout the Community and thus to encounter the tax problems which the HST approach (as well as the other comprehensive approaches) aims to solve.

The hypothesis of a supranational tax regime (EUCIT) for the EPC as well, introduced as a normal tax regime, would in any case be the best solution to overcome on a permanent basis the otherwise higher tax disadvantages faced by SMEs in the internal market in comparison with larger companies, as indicated in the 2005 study, but it would become necessary if the proposal would definitively result in an instrument which, from the company law viewpoint, does not manage on balance to be more attractive than the national ones. In this case, the task of making the EPC of general appeal to SMEs would be left to the EUCIT. There could be two possibilities for this supranational tax regime, which should have the same features indicated for the tax regime of the SE. For the largest businesses, amongst all those choosing the EPC, in terms of turnover, total balance sheet and number of employees, a EUCIT identical to that applicable to the SE could be made available. For other, smaller businesses (which may be identified, for example, as those having all or two of the above indicated parameters below certain thresholds) a EUCIT with the same features but with more favourable provisions (such as the deduction of certain expenses, or the creation of tax-free reserves for investments, or as to the tax rate) than those applicable to the SE, could be envisaged. Such an hypothesis would be consistent with the need to encourage the strengthening of the competitive position of SMEs.

5.3 EUROPEAN FORMS OF PARTNERSHIPS AND THEIR TAXATION REGIMES

In a context in which the majority of businesses within the EC are SMEs, the need for flexibility and adaptability typical of medium-sized and small enterprises is not, in the eyes of many, satisfied by the traditional company forms. The limited liability deriving from the corporate form, with the often related minimum capital requirements and protection rules, as well as with the accounting and disclosure obligations, is not always perceived as an advantage in comparison with unincorporated entities,[45] and these latter are still widely used especially by small businesses. Even such small businesses increasingly tend, however, to internationalize their activities within the EC: the recent project for a European contract law derives, ultimately, from the recognition of the increasing importance of intra-EC commerce for businesses of all sizes. It could thus make sense to start formulating a hypothesis for EC law forms of partnerships. These forms could meet the needs of those SMEs or micro-enterprises who carry on businesses in more than one Member State and would be interested to have an European label, but may not necessarily be attracted by the corporate form. They could represent a synthesis of the most attractive features of flexibility and adaptability of general partnerships and limited partnerships to be found in national legislations, which may be elaborated based on a comparative study of national laws concerning partnership forms. Their distinctive advantages would be (a) the recognition of their existence, thus of their legal capacity – in the sense of capacity to enjoy rights and to be subject to obligations, to sue and to be sued – in all Member States; (b) the possibility of free movement from one state to another (with the maintaining of their legal European identity) when members might consider this appropriate; (c) as a result, the familiarity to small businesses and micro-enterprises throughout the EC. It was pointed out[46] that there would be problems in identifying the date on which entities similar to these ones come into existence, as well as lack of transparency and representation problems. It would seem, however, that no more than two simple requirements could be considered: the drafting of a written contract and some form of publicity (its deposit either in a register held by a national administration of the state of creation or in a European register) could serve to establish the date of creation; the indication of the registration number with the name of the entity and with a proper abbreviation showing its European character may enable third parties to obtain from the competent authority copies of the contract. Representation may be conferred by the relevant EC legislation on all partners – or on all general partners, in the case of a European limited partnership – dealing with third parties, unless otherwise stated in the contract. Creditors from all Member States would be able, in any case, to rely on the unlimited liability of all partners or of all general partners.

Although the creation of similar entities would raise other issues and the issues mentioned would deserve deeper analysis, these entities would fully enable small and micro-enterprises, which would otherwise choose partnership forms governed by national laws, to enjoy the freedom of establishment under Articles 43 and 48 of the Treaty, and would offer them likely commercial advantages as compared with the use of partnership forms governed by national laws which may not be familiar to their business counterparts in other Member States. The advantages from the perspective of business law could render unnecessary a specific tax regime (which, by contrast, is necessary for those instruments which would not manage to be sufficiently attractive from the company law viewpoint), so that Member States could regard these European forms of partnerships as fiscally transparent for tax purposes, and could simply tax their resident partners on the share of profits deriving from their interests in such entities as laid down in the foundation contract. Nevertheless, it would be preferable to complement these European forms of partnerships with an option for the EUCIT regime applied for the EPC. This would avoid placing the businesses choosing these forms (which may be the smaller ones) at a competitive disadvantage in comparison with those choosing the EPC form, and would further increase their attractiveness.

NOTES

1. The choice of jurisdictions characterized by minimal regulation may be regarded as a global tendency, not only within the EC: it has been stated that: 'Over-regulation can also scare away badly needed foreign capital. According to a recent survey of corporate bosses conducted by AT Kearney, 72% of those polled thought that government regulation was the biggest risk in making new investments abroad' ('Learning to live with uncertainty', *The Economist*, 24–30 January 2004, p. 22).
2. See above 4.4.
3. See above 1.6.
4. See above 3.4.
5. Commission Report on *Company Taxation in the Internal Market* (SEC (2001) 1681), p. 14.
6. Ibid. p. 373.
7. Ibid. p. 377.
8. Speech by B. Della Vedova at the first EU Company Tax Conference in April 2002 quoting the Resolution of the European Parliament passed on 14 March 2004 after the European Parliament Report of 22 February 2002 (AS-0048/2002) (Motion for a Resolution on the Commission Communication to the Council, the European Parliament and the Economic and Social Committee on tax policy in the European Union: priorities for the years ahead (COM/2001 260-C5-0597/2001-2001/2248 (COS))).
9. Kok, C. (2001), 'EC update', *European Taxation*, 12 (41), 43; presentation by Stella Raventos Calvo, 'A common consolidated EU tax base for the Societas Europaea' at the second EU Company Tax Conference, Progress and New Challenges, 5–6 December 2003.
10. Idea presented at the first EU Company Tax Conference in April 2002; also Commission Communication, 'An internal market without company tax obstacles, achievements, ongoing initiatives and remaining challenges' (COM (2003) 726 final), p. 24.
11. In fact, both the SE and the SCE are included within the new range of companies falling within the ambit of the amended Parent-Subsidiary Directive and Merger Directive, and are subject to the same tax treatment regarding the transfer of the registered office: see above 1.1.2 and 1.1.5.
12. As it needs to be: see above 3.2.14.
13. See above 4.2.3.
14. See above 3.2.1.
15. As emerges from its Preamble: see above 3.2.14 and 3.4.
16. In its current version: see above 3.2.14.
17. Communication, 'Implementing the Community Lisbon Program: progress to date and next steps towards a Common Consolidated Corporate Tax Base (CCCBT)' (COM (2006) 157 final), pp. 8–9.
18. Ibid. p. 3.
19. COM (2003) 726 final, note 10, p. 25, and Deloitte EU Tax Group (2004), *Study on Analysis of Potential Competition and Discrimination Issues relating to a Pilot Project for an EU Tax Consolidation Scheme for the European Company Statute (Societas Europaea)* (TAXUD/2003/DE/305), London, UK: Deloitte & Touche LLP, 18 August 2004, pp. 2–3.

20. As it is necessary to do: see COM (2003) 726 final, note 10, pp. 9–10. As regards the issue of cross-border loss compensation and the steps undertaken in dealing with transfer pricing, see above 1.4.2.c and 1.5.
21. First indicated in COM (2003) 726 final, note 10, p. 25.
22. See above 1.1.2 and 1.1.5, and 1.2.
23. See above 1.1.5.
24. COM (2003) 726 final, note 10, p. 25.
25. Plasschaert, S.R.F. (2002), 'Further thoughts on the European Union Company Income Tax and its first cousins', *European Taxation*, 7–8 (42), 341.
26. As may well occur for other multinational businesses subject to the CCBT: see above 1.6. See also Helminen, M. (2004), 'The tax treatment of the running of an SE', *European Taxation*, 1 (44), 28–34, at 29, who predicted that the differences between national tax laws make 'country-shopping just as interesting for SEs as for any other European company' and that 'the introduction of the SE legal form will no doubt increase tax competition among the Member States'.
27. See above 1.5 and 1.6.
28. In this regard, see the 2001 Commission Report, note 5, p. 22. It seems, however, difficult not to consider as good evidence of a 'race to the bottom', again at a global level, the circumstance that 'Governments around the world are scrabbling for scarce corporate taxes' and 'OECD countries cut corporate tax rates by nearly seven percentage-points between 1996 and 2003. Some have cut aggressively' (see 'A taxing battle', *The Economist*, 31 January–6 February 2004, pp. 59–60). Within the EC, 'Ireland slashed corporate tax rates by some 23 percentage points over the same time period, and attracted much foreign investment as a result – to the fury of fellow EU members' (example cited in the same article). Consequently, it is the *pace* of the race to the bottom which can perhaps be questioned, rather than *evidence* of the phenomenon.
29. See the analysis above 4.2.
30. 2001 Commission Report, note 5, p. 377.
31. Plasschaert, S.R.F. (2002), 'Comprehensive approaches to EU company taxation: to which companies should they apply?', *European Taxation*, 1 (42), 10.
32. To be allocated in part to it and in part to Member States. This solution would thus repeat a choice which, in the field of indirect taxation, was already made long ago with the introduction of VAT.
33. Which was predicted by Communication (COM (2003) 726 final), note 10, p. 24, and by Plasschaert, note 31, p. 14. The need for a 'tax leg' was also stressed by Lannoo, K. and M. Levin, *An EU Company without an EU Tax? A Corporate Tax Action Plan for Advancing the Lisbon Process*, CEPS Research Report, Brussels, April 2002.
34. As to competition based on tax rates and other structural aspects of corporate taxation: see above 1.5 and 1.6.
35. See above 4.2.
36. COM (2003) 726 final, note 10, p. 25.
37. See Final Report, *Etude de faisabilité d' un statut européen de la PME*, July 2005, p. 15.
38. See Drury, R. (2001), 'A European private company?', *International and Comparative Corporate Law Journal*, 2 (3), 231–250, at 237; Draft Regulation Comments, available together with the draft Regulation at Paris Chamber of Commerce, www.ccip.fr/English/Studies,Reports,Proposals/Dossier, Article 1, third paragraph.
39. See Final Report, note 37, p. 20 and pp. 53–61.
40. ECJ findings in the *Segers, Centros and Inspire Art* rulings: see above 2.3 and 4.3.2.
41. This solution would be in part 'borrowed' from Belgian company law, which requires both a minimum share capital and the filing of a financial plan for the first years of operation, but it would be more flexible than that by leaving a choice between one of the two requirements.
42. Drury, note 38, p. 246.
43. See Final Report, note 37, pp. 94–105.
44. See Communication, 'Tackling the corporation tax obstacles of small and medium-sized enterprises in the internal market: outline of a possible Home State Taxation pilot scheme' (COM (2005) 702 final), p. 8. As to the three criteria used to identify the concept of SMEs,

see Recommendation 1996/280/EC and Recommendation 2003/361/EC, OJEC L124 of 20 May 2003.

45. Freedman, J. (1994), 'Small businesses and the corporate form: burden or privilege?', *Modern Law Review*, 4 (57), 555–584; Hicks, A. (1997), 'Legislating for the needs of small business', in Barry A.K. Rider and Mads Andenas (eds), *Developments in European Company Law*, vol. 2, London, The Hague, Boston: Kluwer Law International, pp. 35–96, at pp. 52–53.
46. Rammeloo, S. (2002), 'Partnership law in the twenty-first century: "Europeization" versus "Law Competition"?', *Maastrict Journal of European and Comparative Law*, 1 (9), Editorial.

6. Conclusions

The 'supranational solution' to the legal competition in corporate taxation and company laws might meet some criticism. Nevertheless, in the light of the arguments already developed and in the context of the EC legal order, this criticism may be answered by arguments underlining the reasons for taking such a supranational solution into consideration as a possible pattern for future developments in the two areas of EC company law and EC company taxation, in further academic research and in discussions at the level of political decision-makers.

6.1 AN INSTITUTIONAL VIEW FROM THE PERSPECTIVE OF MEMBER STATES: ANY PROBLEM FOR THE 'SUPRANATIONAL SOLUTION' TO THE LEGAL COMPETITION IN CORPORATE TAXATION AND COMPANY LAWS?

It was submitted, before the entry into force of the ECS, that different tax treatments between the SE and national public limited companies would lead to distortions and discriminations, not least from the perspective of EC and national constitutional laws,[1] and an independent study contracted out by the Commission on potential competition and discrimination issues relating to a pilot HST or CCBT scheme[2] targeted on the SE adopted this line of reasoning. According to this study, which described pilot HST or CCBT schemes as 'special tax regimes', tax savings brought about by any of these schemes to the benefit of the SE would risk creating an advantage within the meaning of the EC state aid rules, which aid could not be justified if it resulted in an infringement of the principles of equal treatment and/or non-discrimination, and there would be such infringement to the extent that these special tax regimes were not available to entities comparable to the SE including domestically operating companies.[3] In turn, the SE form would be comparable to company forms entirely governed by national forms, on this opinion, because it is largely based on the concept of public limited companies as known in the legal systems of Member States, and because, under Article 10 of the SE Regulation, subject to the Regulation the SE is treated in each

Member State 'as if it were a public limited-liability company formed in accordance with' national law.[4] On this reasoning, the SE could only be treated for tax purposes as a public limited-liability company formed in the Member State of location, so that a different tax treatment would conflict with Member States' tax and constitutional law and, in cross-border situations, with the principle of non-discrimination stated by Article 6 of the Treaty.[5] Such arguments might also be used, following the same line of reasoning, to criticize the hypothesis of an optional EUCIT complementing the SE and other European legal forms, that is to identify, in this hypothesis, a discrimination prohibited under EC law and under Member States' law between companies under the SE form or new EC legal forms and companies which intentionally decide to keep their national legal forms.

Nevertheless, this possible criticism of the supranational solution suggested in this work oversimplifies the key aspect: the supposed comparability between the SE legal vehicle and the national forms of (public) limited companies and, if generalized, between new European legal forms and national legal forms. Apart from the fact that, since its inception, the idea of a European public limited-liability company could not but be inspired by the universally known concept of public limited-liability company, Article 10 of the SE Regulation needs to be read only as an expression of a legislative assessment whereby there are areas where the functioning of the SE does not need uniform Community rules,[6] but not as a statement that the SE form is equivalent and thus comparable to national company forms: the choice of Article 308 EC as a legal base, and its stated purposes,[7] make the SE form not comparable to national company law forms because, ultimately, it was intended to contribute to the completion and to the proper functioning of the EC internal market, unlike the national company law forms. Accordingly, the principle of non-discrimination on grounds of nationality under Article 6 of the Treaty, which certainly prohibits discrimination between national company law forms (none of which has particular objectives regarding the proper functioning of the single market), could not automatically be extended to a company form such as the SE which, because of its very purposes, cannot be placed on the same footing as a national one. In other words, the significant role of national laws in governing the functioning of the SE, due to a legislative technique which has resulted in a 'limited supranationality' from the company law perspective, constitutes a limitation (that is, an inconsistency with the objectives) and thus cannot justify 'abjuring' the objectives themselves. This holds even more true as the Commission can, after 2009, propose improvements to make these features more consistent with the objectives.[8] If these objectives are attributed the necessary importance, the obligation on Member States to ensure that the provisions applicable to SEs do not result in discrimination caused by unjustified different treatment of SEs compared with public limited-liability companies[9] can thus be read as preventing provisions placing the SE at a disadvantage (which would, by definition, defeat the purposes of the SE), but not as a prohibition of a better treatment aimed at encouraging the use of SEs when this can offer a contribution to the completion and to the better functioning of the internal market which cannot be offered by national forms. In practice, the use by multinational businesses of the ECS which, despite the room for divergent national rules, leads to the application of more common provisions than those which have resulted from the 'harmonization' of national company laws, would reduce the margins that the use of (complex constellations of) company law forms entirely governed by national laws allows to those abusive forum-shopping practices (circumventions of national laws at the expense of third party protection) which, in the ECJ case law, have been regarded as distortions.[10] This type of distortion, which may well result from the legal competition and exist even when it is not brought to the attention of the EC legislator or of the ECJ, can (like other types of distortions) hinder the Treaty's socio-economic goals stated in Articles 2 and 3, so that a solution creating, *a priori*, the conditions for these distortions to disappear (or at least to be minimized) would offer a distinctive contribution to the Treaty's goals.[11] The greater the extent to which the SE form (through a complementary EUCIT and, after 2009, through possible improvements of its company law features as well) can manage to widen its 'audience', and new European legal forms characterized by greater flexibility, by the same attractive tax treatment and tailored to a much wider business public, manage to become the normal choices in the business world, the greater their contribution to the proper functioning of the internal market and to the Lisbon objective which presupposes this proper functioning. In other words, the idea (put forward long before the ECJ's rulings evidencing the kind of distortions caused by abusive forum-shopping) to make 'European registration equivalent to registration in Delaware',[12] thus to allow the European vehicles to be the normal choices in the business world, would be particularly significant in eliminating those distortions: it would be implemented by the suggested supranational solution to the legal competition in both the corporate taxation aspects and the company law aspects.

On this premise, that element of possible criticism which could be based on EC state aids rules (which, in particular, could argue that, if pilot HST or CCBT schemes addressed to the SE resulted in a state aid, this would also apply to a greater extent for an optional EUCIT regime addressed specifically to the SE and new European legal forms) also meets a decisive objection. The Commission in its 1998 Notice on the application of state aids rules to measures relating to direct business taxation, where it summarized the ECJ case law in the area of state aids, indicated the cumulative conditions necessary for a tax measure to fall within the meaning of state aid under

Article 87 EC: an economic advantage, introduced by an exception or a deviation from a normal tax regime, relieving recipients from charges normally borne by their budgets; an advantage attributable to the state or to any other body on which the state exercises a dominant influence – which is not the case for EC measures leaving no discretion to Member States – and leading to a loss of tax revenues; the effect on competition and on intra-EC trade; the non-inherence of the measure in the tax system and, above all, the selective effect of benefiting certain undertakings only.[13] These conditions show that essential requirements of a tax form of state aid would not exist in the case of the envisaged supranational solution to legal competition. The EUCIT would be a normal tax regime, although optional, for the purpose of respecting the current institutional framework which is not a fully federal one, and would only be attributable to the EC institutions. Unlike the HST, it would necessarily need to derive from a decision at EC level, such as a Regulation, which would leave no discretion to Member States but only to businesses. Unlike the CCBT, it would result in one more financial resource for the EC (even if this could then redistribute part of its revenues to Member States). Moreover, the 'supranational tax regime' would not be introduced as an exception or a deviation, but as the company tax regime which should be the normal model of reference for all national company tax regimes, and, as a complement to supranational company law vehicles which, particularly in the case of the EPC and of other possible forms, would need to become the normal choices for all groups of businesses according to the envisaged solution, it would ultimately be available not to a specific group of undertakings, but to the general business sector within the EC. Even the element of a tax advantage that would not normally be available, and the selective effect (both essential in the definition of (fiscal) state aid) would thus be lacking.

Ultimately, the assessment of the 'supranational solution' in the context of EC law and thus, of essential Treaty provisions such as the non-discrimination/equal treatment principle and the state aids rules, does not show any obstacles to this hypothesis. The lack of legal obstacles should not be surprising, however far-reaching the supranational solution considered might appear: Articles 81 and 87 EC indicate that even practices or measures that would in principle be prohibited can be accepted when leading to counterbalancing socio-economic benefits[14] which help to achieve the EC law objectives stated in Article 2 of the Treaty. To the extent that no legal impediment to the 'supranational solution' to the interjurisdictional competition in company law and company tax law can be found in the EC legal order and that, on the contrary, this solution can indeed help to achieve the ultimate EC law socio-economic objectives in terms of proper functioning of the internal market but it could not adequately be achieved by reason of its scale and effects by Member States,[15] the supremacy of EC law indicates that no obstacles based on their internal legal systems could be raised from the viewpoint of Member States, which bear the obligation not to hinder the achievement of EC law objectives.

Moreover, this 'supranational' approach to the issue of legal competition would help the 'Lisbon strategy', which needs to be seen as consistent with EC law objectives, in its original (2000) and its revised (2005) versions. The original version, to make the EU the world's most competitive economy, contemplated a wide economic, social and environmental agenda, whilst the revised version focuses on growth and employment.[16] However, when proposing the revised version, the Commission emphasized, inter alia, a line of action coherent also with the original version: to make Europe a more attractive place to invest and work and, for this purpose, to extend and deepen the single market, to foster (undistorted) competition and to improve European and national regulation.[17] In the Commission's view, the introduction of the CCBT is necessary to extend and to deepen the single market, for it will remove the obstacles and compliance costs to cross-border business activity created by 25 different tax bases.[18] However, these benefits would risk being defeated if the tax competition based on tax rates, which the CCBT could further encourage, together with competition in company laws, resulted in an increase of business practices detrimental to the functioning of the market and in a 'segmentation' within Europe between (groups of) jurisdictions (some of which may permanently become more attractive places to invest at the expense of others) rather than in all Europe becoming a more attractive place to invest. A solution to the legal competition based on European models introduced as being more attractive than all national ones and geared to businesses of all sizes would thus promote the Lisbon strategy, as it would enhance the benefits of the more 'extended and deepened' internal market while minimizing the risks of distortions that the legal competition would otherwise increase in parallel with this 'extension and deepening'. Specifically, it would, on the one hand, improve both the European tax law and company law regulations and the national ones (due to their convergence towards the European ones); on the other hand, it would lower business costs associated with the existence of different competing jurisdictions,[19] effectively remove legal barriers hindering in particular SMEs' access to the single market[20] and better foster an EU-wide market competition undistorted by different competing national regulations.

6.2 FINAL REMARKS

The present work has attempted to demonstrate that, in the light of the objectives of the Treaty, of the developments in the fields of EC tax law and company law and of some reasonable assumptions about businesses' internationalization strategies, there would be legal grounds for a 'supranational' solution as a winding road to achieve a level playing field in conditions of market competition undistorted by corporate taxation or company law provisions. Although the current debates do not seem to contemplate such a far-reaching goal, the aspects which do not appear to have drawn attention confirm that this solution could prevent the effects of legal competition in these two sectors from compromising the achievement of the Treaty's goals and of the 'Lisbon objective' and could be an alternative to further attempts at harmonization.

Nevertheless, the different question whether the evolution of EC legislation in these two sectors will actually be such as to create supranational vehicles having the indicated features will most probably find a response based on political, rather than on purely legal, considerations. Given the decision-making process at EC level, which prevents any measures from being adopted without the agreement of Member States – and, in the field of direct taxation, of all Member States – a solution such as that envisaged in this work would only have the chance to be accepted at a time when all Member States found it to be in their interest. This translates the problem into a specific question: is there any Member State who, in the medium to long term, would have something to lose from a 'supranational solution' to legal competition? The answer can reasonably be assumed to be in the negative: a legal solution which, like that envisaged, would effectively contribute to the achievement of the objectives of the Treaty, while maintaining Member States' tax sovereignty and making the effects of the legal competition in company law and corporate taxation more predictable than they may currently be, could also generate a political advantage for all Member States and for the Community as a whole in the ongoing historical phase. Moreover, from the specific viewpoint of Member States, which over the last two decades have been (and would otherwise continue to be) increasingly exposed to revenue losses by businesses' expansion strategies and by the gradual erosion of their tax autonomy resulting from the ECJ's rulings, this solution may well become the most 'pragmatic' way of effectively protecting, in the medium to long run, their own financial interests.

NOTES

1. Wenz, M. (2004), 'The European company (*Societas Europaea*): legal concept and tax issues', *European Taxation*, 44 (1), 7.
2. Deloitte EU Tax Group (2004), *Study on Analysis of Potential Competition and Discrimination Issues relating to a Pilot Project for an EU Tax Consolidation Scheme for the European Company Statute (Societas Europaea)* (TAXUD/2003/DE/305), London, UK: Deloitte & Touche LLP, 18 August 2004 ('2004 study').

3. The 2004 study, note 84, pp. 2–3. Commission officials stated, however, that the 2004 study represents only the views of its authors and not those of the Commission, which will consider the issue of competition and non-discrimination relating to a pilot project again when the technical work by the CCBTWG has made substantial progress.
4. The 2004 study, pp. 2 and 51–54.
5. On this view, see also Gonzalez Sanchez, E. and J.F. Fluxà (2006), 'Problems and options in calculating the tax base of companies in the European Union under Home State Taxation', *European Taxation*, 5 (46), 197–207, at 201–203.
6. Regulation 2167/2001, Preamble, recital (9).
7. Ibid. Preamble, recitals (3), (4), (6) and (7); see also retro, Chapter 3, par. 3.2, 3.2.1.
8. See above 3.2.
9. Regulation 2176/2001, Preamble, recital, (5).
10. See above 2.3 and 4.3.2.
11. Which would be stated with even greater emphasis in Articles I-2 and I-3 of the new 'Treaty establishing the Constitution for Europe' ('European Constitution') in terms, inter alia, of a market competition 'free and undistorted', if this Treaty ever enters into force after the stalemate caused by its rejection in popular referenda during 2005.
12. Dine, J. (1989), 'The harmonisation of company law in the European Community', *Yearbook of European Law*, (9), 93–120, at 119. Gammie, M. (2004), 'EU taxation and the *Societas Europaea*: harmless creature or Trojan horse?', *European Taxation*, 1 (44), 35–45, at 38, asked: 'why should those who choose to establish and operate through an SE benefit from special tax provisions as compared to those that choose to incorporate under national law but operate throughout the Union?'. The more competitive EUCIT regime envisaged in the text, without being a 'special' one in the technical sense (thus, in the sense of the Code of Good Conduct discussed above 1.5 and 4.2.2), would be the complementary tax assistance towards this purpose.
13. Commission Notice on the application of the state aid rules to measures relating to direct business taxation, OJEC C384/3 [1998].
14. See Article 81, third paragraph and Article 87, second and third paragraphs.
15. And would thus require EC action by virtue of the subsidiarity principle, which action could assume Article 308 of the Treaty as a legal base.
16. See Lisbon European Council, Presidency Conclusions, 23–24 March 2000, on the original version; 'Working together for growth and jobs: a new start for the Lisbon Strategy' (COM (2005) 24), on the revised version.
17. COM (2005) 24, note 98, pp. 16–20.
18. Ibid. p. 17; 'The contribution of taxation and customs policies to the Lisbon Strategy' (COM (2005) 532 final), p. 5; 'Implementing the Community Lisbon Program: progress to date and next step towards a Common Consolidated Corporate Tax Base (CCCTB)' (COM (2006) 157 final), pp. 3 and 8.
19. Both compliance costs and consultancy costs of in-depth comparisons between the company law and tax law regulations in different countries.
20. Within which SMEs constitute 99 per cent of business and two-thirds of employment: COM (2005) 24, note 98, p.16.

Appendices

Appendix I Examples of the 'race to the bottom' legal competition among Member States in corporate taxation and company laws[1]

COMPETITION IN STRUCTURAL ASPECTS OF CORPORATE TAXATION

In the 15 Member States until 1 May 2004

1998: Denmark abolishes withholding tax for all outbound dividends distributions irrespective of the state of residence of the recipient of dividends and of DTC and introduces a capital gains tax exemption regime for profits arising out of the sale of shares in Danish holding companies or of the liquidation of Danish holding companies.

1999–2003: Ireland allows the carry forward of losses without time limits, reduces corporate income tax for trading income from 28% to 24% as of 1 January 2000, and subsequently reduces corporate income tax for all business to 12.5% as of 1 January 2003.

2001: Germany reduces corporation tax to 25% on both distributed and undistributed profits; until 31 December 2000, the corporation tax rate was set at 40% for undistributed profits and 30% for distributed profits.

2003: Sweden, which allows the carry forward of losses without time limits, introduces, as of 1 July, a tax reform which offers fundamental tax advantages in the determination of the taxable base of corporation tax: participation exemption regime, which excludes from taxation all inbound dividends and capital gains; total deductibility of interests, with no thin capitalization rules.

2003: Spain introduces, with effect from 1 January 2004, new rules which extend the scope of its participation exemption regime and exclude from thin capitalization rules financing from parties resident in an EC Member State.

2004: Austria declares the intention to reduce corporate tax rate from 34% to 25% as of 1 January 2005, and to introduce an attractive system of group taxation which, inter alia, would provide cross-border group relief for losses of foreign-based subsidiaries which have not been deducted abroad for tax purposes.

2004: Ireland introduces a new attractive corporate tax regime for holding companies which owns at least 5% of capital of intra-EC and foreign subsidiaries, which regime allows the 'pooling' of the economic results of shareholdings in different subsidiaries, through the off-setting of losses incurred through the participation in some subsidiaries against dividends distributed by other subsidiaries at world-wide level.

2005: the Netherlands decides to reduce corporate tax rates, as from 1 January 2007, from 27% to 20% on the first 41 000 Euros of profits, and from 31.5% to 26.9% on the remaining profit, and to introduce, for the benefit of owners of small and medium-sized enterprises, an exemption of at least 5% of their profits.

2005: Germany, which had already reduced corporation tax rate to 25%, declares the intention to further reduce corporate tax rate to 19% as of 1 January 2006.

In the New Member States which Entered the EC on 1 May 2004

2000: Estonia approves a tax regime which does not tax undistributed profits.

2002: Cyprus introduces a 10% tax rate, which was deemed to give it the lowest rate in the EC.

2005: Poland reduces its corporate tax rate, which was set at 27%, to 19%.

COMPETITION IN COMPANY LAWS

1994: France introduces the 'simplified joint-stock company' (SAS) as a new form of corporate entity allowing more flexibility than the joint-stock company (SA) and the private limited company (SARL) schemes: members are left the complete freedom to regulate in their statutes issues relating to the management and administration of the company.

1999: France amends the 1994 Law on the SAS, by making its formation much less restrictive: the previous requirement that the members should be two or more companies each having a minimum fully paid capital is abolished and the formation of the SAS is open to any two natural or legal persons, as well as to single persons.

2000: the United Kingdom introduces, with effect from 6 April 2001, a new type of legal entity, the Limited Liability Partnership (LLP), which is intended to offer the internal flexibility of partnerships together with the benefit of limited liability for all its members.

2003: Italy introduces, with effect from 1 January 2004, a landmark company law reform, which, inter alia, abolishes judicial control on the formation of private limited companies and considerably increases the margin of contractual freedom in drafting the memorandum and articles of association of private limited companies.

2003: Denmark introduces the possibility of 'electronic meetings' of boards of directors and of shareholders, which enables directors and shareholders of Danish companies not to have a physical presence in the country and to express their vote through e-mail.

2003: France introduces a new form of SARL (private limited company), which can be founded without a minimum capital (nominal minimum capital 1 Euro), and makes it possible to create this form of company within 24 hours, to apply for registration electronically and to seek assistance from a specialized body (*Centre des Formalités des Entreprises* [Centre for Companies' Incorporation Formalities]).

2005: Germany reduces the minimum capital requirement for the private limited company form (GmbH) from 25 000 Euros to 10 000 Euros as of 1 January 2006.

NOTE

1. Sources: National investment promotion agencies; Investment Guides to individual countries; Wooldridge, F. (2001), 'Some new types of company and partnership in France and Germany', *International and Comparative Corporate Law Journal*, 3 (2), 211–229.

Appendix II Functioning of the pilot HST and CCBT schemes

A group of companies has the following structure:

- parent company (PA), located in Member State A;
- subsidiary (DB), located in Member State B;
- subsidiary (DC), located in Member State C;
- sub-subsidiary (DDC), located in Member State C.

HST

1. PA establishes the taxable profit of PA, DB, DC and DDC, in the tax year x, according to the tax legislation of Member State A.
2. The tax base is apportioned among Member States A (for PA), B (for DB) and C (for DC and DDC) according to an apportionment formula, for example, the proportions of payroll and/or turnover in each jurisdiction.
3. PA files a group comprehensive tax return in Member State A and (on the basis of Member State A's tax rate) pays tax.
4. DB files self-assessment (on the basis of Member State B's tax rate) and pays its individual tax liability in Member State B.
5. DC and DDC file self-assessment and pay (on the basis of Member State C's tax rate) their individual tax liability in Member State C.

CCBT

1. A common consolidated base taxation is introduced by way of an EC Regulation, which sets all the rules for determining the taxable base of businesses operating throughout the Community territory by means of subsidiaries and branches and for consolidating intra-group profits and losses.
2. PA opts for the determination of the group taxable base according to the EC rules; in the tax year x, PA makes a profit, DB incurs a loss, DC makes a profit and DDC incurs a loss, where both the profits of PA

and DC and the losses of DB and DDC are calculated according to the EC rules.

3. The profits of PA and DC and the losses of DB and DDC are summed up together by PA (tax consolidation), which therefore calculates the tax base of the entire group.
4. The tax base of the group is apportioned amongst Member States A, B and C according to an apportionment formula, for example, the proportions of payroll and/or turnover in each jurisdiction.
5. PA files a group comprehensive tax return in Member State A and pays its tax liability.
6. DB files self-assessment and pays its individual tax liability in Member State B, based on Member State B's corporate tax rate.
7. DC and DDC file self-assessment and pay their individual tax liability in Member State C, based on Member State C's corporate tax rate.

Appendix III EC corporate tax law implementation in Member States

IMPLEMENTATION OF THE PARENT-SUBSIDIARY DIRECTIVE[1]

In the Older 15 Member States

State	*Austria*	*Belgium*	*Denmark*	*Finland*	*France*	*Germany*	*Greece*	*Ireland*
Holding required	10% of capital	5% of capital or minimum acquisition cost	25% of capital	25% of capital or 10% of voting rights	5% of capital or minimum acquisition cost	none	none	5% of capital
Regime applied	exemp.	exemp. for 95% of dividend	exemp.	exemp.	exemp. for 95% of dividend	exemp. for 95% of dividend	tax credit	tax credit
Minimum holding period	12 months	none	1 year	none	none	none	none	none
Charges relating to participation	not deduct.	not deduct. up to 5% of gross dividend	deduct.	not deduct.	not deduct. up to 5% of gross dividend	not deduct.	deduct.	deduct.

Additional requirements:								
level of taxation in subsidiary's state of residence	Yes[(a)]	Yes[(b)]	Yes[(c)]					
DTC with the subsidiary's state of residence				Yes		Yes		

State	*Italy*	*Luxembourg*	*The Netherlands*	*Portugal*	*Spain*	*Sweden*	*UK*
Holding required	none	10% of capital or minimum acquisition cost	5% of capital	25% of capital	5% of capital or minimum acquisition costs	none	10% of voting rights
Regime applied	exemp. for 95% of dividends	exemp.	exemp.	exemp.	exemp.	exemp.	tax credit

Continued overleaf

In the Older 15 Member States – *continued*

State	*Italy*	*Luxembourg*	*The Netherlands*	*Portugal*	*Spain*	*Sweden*	*UK*
Minimum holding period	none	none	none	2 years	1 year	none	none
Charges relating to participation	Not deduct. up to 5% of gross dividends	Not deduct. up to 5% of gross dividends	Not deduct.	Not deduct. up to 5% of gross dividends	deduct.	deduct.	deduct.
Additional requirements:							
level of taxation in subsidiary's state of residence		Yes[d]			Yes[e]	Yes[f]	
DTC with subsidiary's state of residence							

In the New Member States[2]

State	*Cyprus*	*Czech Republic*	*Malta*
Holding required	1% of capital	none	10% of voting rights
Regime applied	exempt	tax credit	tax credit
Minimum holding period	none	none	none
Charges relating to participation	deduct.		deduct.
Additional requirements:			
level of taxation in subsidiary's state of residence	Yes[(g)]		
DTC with subsidiary's state of residence			

1 Implementation of the Directive concerning inbound dividends. exemp. = exemption; deduct. = deductible.
2 Information available to the author at May 2006.

(a) The subsidiary must be subject to a tax rate or tax base comparable with the Austrian tax.
(b) The subsidiary must be subject to a corporate income tax comparable with the Belgian tax or, for financing companies, to a tax regime not significantly deviating from the general regime applicable in the state of residence.
(c) The subsidiary must be subject to tax to an extent not substantially lower than Danish tax.
(d) The subsidiary must be fully subject to a tax comparable to Luxembourg taxation.
(e) The subsidiary must be subject to a tax comparable to Spanish tax with no possibility of being exempt.
(f) The subsidiary must be subject to an income tax comparable to Swedish tax (such requirement is deemed to be met if the subsidiary is resident in a state with which Sweden has concluded a DTC, provided that the income mainly derives from sources situated in Sweden or in the subsidiary's state of residence and the subsidiary does not benefit from preferential tax regimes).
(g) Either the subsidiary is subject to a foreign corporate tax rate not substantially lower than the tax rate applicable in Cyprus or less than 50% of the paying companies' activities result, directly or indirectly, in investment income.

IMPLEMENTATION OF THE MERGER DIRECTIVE[3]

State	*Austria*	*Belgium*(n)	*Denmark*	*Finland*	*France*	*Germany*(n)	*Greece*	*Ireland*
Mergers and divisions								
Roll-over relief for assets and liabilities transferred	Yes	No	Yes, but with prior approval from tax authorities	Yes	Yes, but with prior approval from tax authorities	No	Yes	Yes
Carry over of tax-exempt provisions or reserves	Yes	No	n.a.	Yes	Yes, but with prior approval from tax authorities	No	Yes	n.a.
Take-over of losses not exhausted for tax purposes	Yes(b)	No(a)	No	Yes(b)	Yes, but with prior approval not required for internal operations	No(a)	No(a)	Yes(c)
Roll-over relief for shares received	Yes	No	Yes	Yes	Yes, but with prior approval from tax authorities	No	Yes, but a 5% transfer tax is levied	Yes

Tranfers of assets								
Roll-over relief for assets and liabilities transferred	Yes	Yes	Yes, but with prior approval from tax authorities	Yes	Yes, but with prior approval from tax authorities	Yes	Yes	Yes
Carry over of tax-exempt provisions or reserves	Yes	No	n.a.	Yes	Yes, but with prior approval from tax authorities	No	Yes	n.a
Take-over of losses not exhausted for tax purposes	Yes[b]	No	No	No	Yes, but with prior approval from tax authorities	No	No[a]	Yes
Exchanges of shares								
Roll-over relief for shares received	Yes	No	Yes, but with prior approval of tax authorities	Yes, but the benefit is with-drawn if the taxpayer	Yes, but shares must be held for at least five years[d] and	Yes, but shares must be held for at least seven years[d] and	Yes, but a 5% transfer tax is levied	Yes

Continued overleaf

State	*Austria*	*Belgium*[n]	*Denmark*	*Finland*	*France*	*Germany*[n]	*Greece*	*Ireland*
Exchanges of shares – *continued*								
				becomes non-resident within three years	prior approval necessary	only if tax value for shares exchanged is also rolled over		

State	*Italy*	*Luxembourg*	*The Netherlands*	*Portugal*	*Spain*	*Sweden*	*UK*[n]
Mergers and Divisions							
Roll-over relief for assets and liabilities	Yes	Yes	Yes	Yes	Yes	Yes	No
Carry over of tax-exempt provisions or reserves	Yes	Yes	Yes	Yes	n.a.	Yes	n.a.
Take-over of losses not	Yes	No	Yes[b]	Yes, with prior	Yes, but it is unclear	Yes	Yes[c]

exhausted for tax purposes				approval of the tax authorities which is also needed for internal operations	whether prior approval of the tax authorities is required. It is not for internal operations		
Roll-over relief for shares received	Yes	Yes	Yes, with prior approval of the tax authorities in the case of merger by acquisition	Yes	Yes	Yes	Yes[(e)]
Transfers of assets							
Rollover relief for assets and liabilities transferred	Yes	Yes	Yes	Yes	Yes	Yes, but upon request and for certain assets	Yes

Continued overleaf

State	*Italy*	*Luxembourg*	*The Netherlands*	*Portugal*	*Spain*	*Sweden*	*UK*[(n)]
Transfers of assets – *continued*							
Carry over of tax-exempt provisions or reserves	Yes	No	n.a.	Yes	No	Yes, but upon request	n.a.
Take-over of losses not exhausted for tax purposes	Unclear	No	No	Yes, but with prior approval from tax authorities	No	No	Yes
Exchanges of shares							
Roll-over relief for shares received	Yes	Yes	Yes, but shares must be held for at least three years[(d)]	Yes	Yes	Yes	Yes

3 Information not yet available to the author at May 2006 on the implementation of the Merger Directive in the 10 new Member States. Sources: for the Parent-Subsidiary Directive: IBFD (1995), *Survey on the Implementation of the EC Corporate Tax Directives*, Amsterdam: IBFD Publications; National Reports at the International Congress 'Gruppi di societa' ed imposizione sui redditi: l'attuazione della direttiva CEE 90/435'; Faculty of Law, University of Bologna, September 2000; Overview by Maisto, G. (2002), 'Shaping EU company tax policy: amending the Tax Directives', *European Taxation*, 42 (8), 276–308, at 294–296; for the Merger Directive: IBFD (1995), *Survey on the Implementation of the EC Corporate Tax Directives*; National

Reports at the International Congresses 'Le imposte sui redditi e le riorganizzazioni societarie nell'esperienza Europea: l'attuazione della Direttiva 434/90', Faculty of Law, University of Bologna, September 1999; IBFD (2003), Survey on the Societas Europeae.

(a) Take-over of losses would be allowed in case of merger between domestic companies.
(b) Under certain conditions which are also applicable to internal operations.
(c) Under conditions and with restrictions which are also applicable to internal operations.
(d) Restrictions set on anti-abuse grounds.
(e) If share exchange qualifies as re-organization.
(n) The part of the Directive dealing with mergers and divisions is not implemented.

IMPLEMENTATION OF THE INTEREST-ROYALTIES DIRECTIVE[4]

State	*Austria*	*Belgium*	*Denmark*	*Finland*	*France*	*Germany*
Holding required	25% of direct capital	25% of direct or indirect capital	25% of direct capital	25% of direct capital	25% of direct capital	25% of direct capital
Minimum holding period	1 year, refund claimable if minimum holding period met after payment	1 year, if one year not yet met, provisional retention of withholding tax	1 year	none	2 years, exempt if committed to meet minimum holding period	none

Continued overleaf

Implementation of the Interest-Royalties Directive – *continued*

State	*Austria*	*Belgium*	*Denmark*	*Finland*	*France*	*Germany*
Option to exclude the cases of special relationship	Yes	No	No	No	Yes	Yes
Options to exclude certain payments from the exemption	Yes	No	No	No	Yes	Yes
Option to require certification of conditions/ advance clearance	Yes (certification only)	Yes	Yes (certification only)	No	Yes (certification only)	Yes
Anti-abuse clause[(a)]	Yes	General	General	General	Yes	Yes

State	*Ireland*	*Italy*	*Luxembourg/ Netherlands*[b]	*Spain*	*Sweden*	*UK*
Holding required	25% of voting rights	25% of direct voting rights	none	25% of direct capital	25% of direct capital	25% of direct capital or voting rights
Minimum holding period	2 years	1 year, if one year not yet met, provisional retention of withholding tax	none	1 year, refund claimable if minimum holding period met after payment	none	none
Option to exclude the cases of special relationship	Yes	Yes	No	No	Yes	Yes
Options to exclude certain payments from the exemption	Yes	Yes	No[b]	No	No	Yes

Continued overleaf

Implementation of the Interest-Royalties Directive – *continued*

State	*Ireland*	*Italy*	*Luxembourg/ Netherlands*[b]	*Spain*	*Sweden*	*UK*
Option to require certification of conditions/ advance decision	Yes (certification only)	Yes (certification only)	No	No	No	Yes
Anti-abuse Clause[a]	Yes	Yes	general	general	Yes for royalties	Yes

State	*Cyprus/ Malta/Hungary*[c]	*Czech Republic*	*Estonia*	*Slovakia*	*Slovenia*
Holding required	none	25% of either capital or voting rights	25% direct of capital	25% direct of capital	25% direct of capital
Minimum holding period	none	24 months	none	24 months	24 months
Option to exclude the cases of special relationship	No	Yes	Yes	Yes	Yes

Options to exclude certain payments from the exemption	No[c]	Yes	No	No	Yes
Option to require certification of conditions/ advance decision	No	Yes	No	No	Yes (decision only)
Anti-abuse clause[a]	general	general	general	general	general

4 Five Member States (Greece, Latvia, Lithuania, Poland and Portugal) benefit from a transitional regime and are thus not considered in this overview. Yes = option implemented. No = option not implemented. Source: KPMG, *International Treasury Tax Notes*, March 2004, pp. 11–13; IBFD (2006), *Survey on the Implementation of the Interest-Royalties Directive*, Amsterdam: IBFD, information as of 19 December 2005.

(a) Anti-abuse clause: Yes = specific provisions implementing the clause; General = no specific provision, but general application of domestic anti-abuse rules.

(b) Luxembourg and the Netherlands do not generally levy withholding taxes on both interest and royalty payments to non-residents, but the Netherlands can exclude certain payments from this exemption. Both countries apply general domestic anti-abuse rules.

(c) Cyprus, Malta and Hungary do not generally levy withholding taxes on both interest and royalty payments to non-residents; but Hungary can exclude certain payments from this exemption. All three countries apply general domestic anti-abuse rules.

Appendix IV Key cases of relevance to company direct taxation

28 January 1986	270/83 Commission v. France (Avoir fiscal) [1986] ECR 273
27 September 1988	81/87 Daily Mail (UK) [1988] ECR 5505
8 May 1990	175/88 Biehl l (L) [1990] ECR I-1779
28 January 1992	C-204/90 Bachmann (B) [1992] ECR I-249
26 January 1993	C-112/91 Werner (D) [1993] ECR I-429
13 July1993	C-330/91 Commerzbank (UK) [1993] ECR I-4017
12 April 1994	C-1/93 Halliburton (NL) [1994] ECR I-1137
14 February 1995	C-279/93 Schumacker (D) [1995] ECR I-225, 249
26 October 1995	C-151/94 Commission v. Luxembourg (Biehl II) (L) [1995] ECR I-3699
11 August 1995	C-80/94 Wielockx (NL) [1995] ECR I-2508
14 November 1995	C-484/93 Svensson and Gustavsson (L) [1995] ECR I-3955, 3971
27 June 1996	C-107/94 Asscher (NL) [1996] ECR I-3089, 3113, opinion Advocate General Léger I-3091
15 May 1997	C-250/95 FUTURA and Singer (L) [1997] ECR I-2471
17 July 1997	C-28/95 Leur-Bloem (NL) [1997] ECR I-4161
19 February 1998	C-8/97 Commission v. Greece [1998] ECR I-823 (non-transposition of Directive 90/434)
12 May 1998	C-336/96 Gilly (F) [1998] ECR I-2823, PR 33/98
16 July 1998	C-264/96 ICI (UK) [1998] ECR I-4711, opinion Advocate General Tesauro I-4698
9 March 1999	C-212/97 Centros (DK) [1999] ECR I-1459, opinion Advocate General La Pergola I-1461
29 April 1999	C-311/97 Royal Bank of Scotland (EL) [1999] ECR I-2651, opinion Advocate General Alber I-2652, PR 26/99
21 September 1999	C-307/97 Saint-Gobain (D) [1999] ECR I-6161, opinion Advocate General Mischo I-6163
28 October 1999	C-55/98 Bent Vestergaard (DK) [1999] ECR I-7641, opinion Advocate General Saggio I-7643

18 November 1999	C-200/98 X AB and Y AB v. Riksskatteverk (S) (payment to subsidiary), rapp. Edwards [1999] ECR I-8261, opinion Advocate General Saggio I-8264
15 February 2000	C-34/98 Commission v. France (CRDS) [2000] ECR I-995, opinion Advocate General La Pergola I-997
15 February 2000	C-169/98 Commission v. France (CSG) [2000] ECR I-1049, opinion Advocate General La Pergola I-1051, PR 9/2000
13 April 2000	C-251/98 Baars (NL) [2000] ECR I-2787, rapp. Wathelet, opinion Advocate General Alber I-2789
13 April 2000	C-420/98 W.N. v. Staatssecretaris van Financien (NL) [2000], ECR I-2847, opinion Advocate General Alber I-2850
6 June 2000	C-35/98 B.G.M. Verkooijen (NL) [2000] ECR I-4071, rapp. Wathelet, opinion Advocate General La Pergola I-4073, PR 42/2000
8 June 2000	C-375/98 EPSON Europe BV (P) [2000] ECR I-4243, opinion Advocate General Cosmas I-4245
14 December 2000	C-141/99 AMID (B) [2000] ECR I-11619, opinion Advocate General Alber I-11621
8 March 2001	Joined cases C-397/98 Metallgesellschaft Ltd v. Commissioners of Inland Revenue (UK) and C-410/98 Hoechst v. Inland Revenue Commissioners (UK) [2001] ECR I-1727, rapp. Wathelet, opinion Advocate General Fennelly I-1730
4 October 2001	C-294/99 Athinaiki Zythopoiia v. Greek State (EL) [2001] ECR I-6797, rapp. Wathelet, opinion Advocate General Alber I-6799
15 January 2002	C-43/00 Andersen and Jensen ApS (DK) (Directive 90/434); [2002] ECR I-394, opinion Advocate General Tizzano
12 September 2002	C-431/01 Mertens (B) (cross-border loss/profit situation, Articles 39 and 43 EC) [2002] ECR I-7073
5 November 2002	C-208/00 Überseering BV v. Nordic Construction Comp. Baumanagement GmbH (NCC) (D) (seat of company, Articles 43, 48 EC) [2002] ECR I-9919, 9943
21 November 2002	C-436/00 X and Y v. Riksskatteverket (S) (deferral of capital gains tax, share transfer to S-sub of B-company) [2002] ECR I-10829, opinion of Advocate General Mischo I-10832
12 December 2002	C-324/00 Lankhorst-Hohorst v. FA Steinfurt (D)

	('thin capitalization'), [2002] ECR I-11779, opinion Advocate General Mischo I-11781
18 September 2003	C-168/01 Bosal Holding BV (NL) (Articles 43, 48, 56 EC, deductibility of participation costs in foreign subsidiary) [2003] ECR I-9401, rapp. Edwards, opinion Advocate General Alber, PR 74/2003
25 September 2003	C-58/01 Océ Van der Grinten NV v. Inland Revenue Commissioners (UK) (Directive 90/435, DTA UK-NL withholding tax) [2003] ECR I-9809, opinion Advocate General Tizzano
30 September 2003	C-167/01 Kamer van Koophandel en Fabrieken voor Amsterdam v. Inspire Art Ltd (NL) (establishment, recognition of companies created abroad) [2003] ECR I-10155, opinion Advocate General Alber
4 March 2004	C-334/02 Commission v. France (non-availability of reduced final tax rate for foreign insurance proceeds) [2004] ECR I-2229, opinion Advocate General Ruiz-Jarabo I-2231
11 March 2004	C-9/02 de Lasteyrie du Saillant (F) (exit tax, Article 167bis CGI) [2004] ECR I-2409, opinion Advocate General Mischo I-2411, PR 13/2004
8 June 2004	C-268/03 De Baeck v. Belgium (B) (discriminatory treatment of sale of substantial participation to foreign company) [2004] ECR I-5961
1 July 2004	Joined cases C-361/02 and C-362/02 Tsapalos v. Diamantakis (EL) (retroactive application of Directive 76/308) [2004] ECR I-6405, opinion Advocate General Kokott I-6407
1 July 2004	C-169/03 Wallentin v. Riksskatteverket (S) (special income tax for foreign residents under Law 1991:586, request from Regeringsrätten, Article 39 EC) [2004] ECR I-6443, opinion Advocate General Léger I-6445
15 July 2004	C-501/00 Spain v. Commission (corporation tax relief for steel industry in Basque provinces) [2004] ECR I-6717
15 July 2004	C-315/02 Lenz v. Landesfinanzdirektion Tirol (A) (final taxation of income from abroad; issue identical to C-516/99) [2004] ECR I-7063, opinion Advocate General Tizzano I-7066, for CH dividends see C-157/05
7 September 2004	C-319/02 Manninen (FIN) (corporate tax imputation on income tax on dividends from S, Articles 56, 58

	EC) [2004] ECR I-7477, opinion Advocate General Kokott I-7480
13 December 2005	C-446/03 Marks & Spencer plc v. David Halsey (HM Inspector of Taxes) (UK) (cross-border compensation of losses) OJEC C304/18 [2003], opinion Advocate General Poiares Maduro, 7 April 2005, PR 29/05, PR 107/05
13 December 2005	C-411/03 SEVIC Systems Aktiengesellschaft (merger of Germany with foreign company, Article 43 EC) OJEC C289/13 [2003], opinion Advocate General Tizzano 7 July 2005 PR 106/05
12 January 2006	C-494/03 Senior Engineering Investments NV v. Staatssecr. van Financien (NL) (capital duty on informal capital, Article 43 EC, Directive 69/335) OJEC C21/23 [2004], opinion Advocate General Poiares Maduro, 14 July 2005
19 January2006	C-265/04 M. Bouanich v. Skatteverket (S) (repayment to non-residents of repurchased shares, taxation as capital gains or dividend, Articles 56, 58, 43, 48 EC), OJEC C228/22 [2004], opinion Advocate General Kokott, 14 July 2005
21 February 2006	C-152/03 Ritter-Coulais v. FA Germersheim (D) (compensation for loss from residence abroad), OJEC C158/8, opinion Advocate General Léger, 1 March 2005, PR 17/06
23 February 2006	C-253/03 CLT-UFA SA v. FA Köln-West (D) (discriminatory corporation tax rates for permanent establishments) OJEC C200/12, opinion Advocate General Léger 14 April 2005
23 February 2006	C-471/04 Keller Holding v. FA Offenbach/Main-Land (D) (tax deductibility of expenses for tax-free dividends from participations), OJEC C19/14

Appendix V Increasing opportunities for expansion strategies in the new wider Europe

The corporate tax planning and company law 'forum-shopping' practices, which can be implemented as a result of the ECJ's tax rulings on the freedom of establishment and the ECJ's company law rulings in the light of key differences between the national corporate tax laws and company laws of Member States, can be exemplified by a few practical cases. These cases (which are in no way exhaustive of the range of possibilities) show how new expansion strategies may allow internationally-oriented businesses to minimize corporate tax expenditure within the EC after its 2004 enlargement, and choose the most favourable company law irrespective of where the business activity is actually carried out within the EC.

CASE A: MINIMIZATION OF THE OVERALL APPLICABLE CORPORATE TAX RATE: SE FORM

An SE set up in the United Kingdom obtains £3 100 000 profit, which derives as to one-half from the UK market as to one-half from an export activity to all other Member States. The company is subject to the main corporation tax rate of 30%. It can foresee, thanks to a favourable market trend, that this level of profits will remain in the medium to long run and would like to minimize its overall corporate tax rate while keeping the part of its business activity in the United Kingdom. Through a comparison amongst the corporate tax regimes in all EC Member States which have currently implemented the ECS, it realizes that, for example, Latvia has a 15% corporate tax rate and that, just like the United Kingdom, taxes resident companies on their world-wide income and offers a tax credit for corporation tax paid in other countries. The SE plans a transfer of the registered office (together with the head office, under Article 8 of the SE Regulation) to Latvia with effect from the start of a new tax year. After making the transfer, it becomes subject to the 15% corporate tax rate on its world-wide income upon registration in Latvia. It subsequently opens a branch in the United Kingdom, from which it carries the part of its activity concerning the United Kingdom market and which continues to generate £1 550 000 profits. (Freedom of establishment under Articles 43 to 48 EC; Member States' liberty to allocate the powers of taxation between themselves, but under obligation to avoid juridical double taxation, ECJ *Van der Grinten* case; obligation on Member States not to discriminate against the SE as opposed to companies governed by national law, Preamble to the SE Regulation, recital (5).) On the profits deriving from the activity carried out through the United Kingdom branch, it is subject to the 30% main corporate tax rate and incurs a tax liability of £465 000: however, due to its new tax residence in Latvia, it can credit the tax paid by the branch in the United Kingdom against its corporate tax liability in Latvia, which is deemed to be about one-half (£232 500). Consequently, it does not incur corporation tax liability in Latvia. Accordingly, the SE avoids the tax liability that it would have definitively incurred had it kept its tax residence in the United Kingdom.

CASE B: MINIMIZATION OF THE OVERALL APPLICABLE CORPORATE TAX RATE

A French company, subject to a nominal corporate tax rate of 34.33%, would like to minimize its overall corporate tax rate. It realizes that, in Cyprus, a 10% corporate tax rate applies to resident companies, and that Cyprus, like France, considers a company as resident when it has its 'effective management' there. However, it also notes that, in Cyprus, 'effective management' is deemed to be located there if the board of directors of the company has a majority of Cyprus-resident directors and all meetings of the board are held in Cyprus.

The French company thus decides to 'migrate' to Cyprus for tax purposes, by appointing a majority of Cyprus-resident directors to its board and holding board meetings in Cyprus. This is sufficient to acquire residence in Cyprus for tax purposes and to be subject to a 10% corporate tax rate, on its world-wide profits. French tax authorities would be unable to impose 'exit taxes'. (Freedom of establishment: according to the ECJ, exit taxes are incompatible with the freedom of establishment, *Lasteyrie du Saillant*.) The French corporate tax rate would continue to apply to the part of the business which would continue to be carried out on French territory by means of a permanent establishment would be exempted in Cyprus.

CASE C: CHOICE OF MOST FAVOURABLE COMPANY TAX REGIME AND MOST ATTRACTIVE COMPANY LAW FORM WHILE CARRYING ON (MOST OF) BUSINESS ACTIVITY IN ANOTHER MEMBER STATE

German entrepreneurs wishing to operate mainly in the German market would like to take benefit from both a company law form more flexible than the GmbH (German private limited company) and a corporate tax rate lower than the German one irrespective of the level of profits. They realize that, from the company law perspective, despite the reduction of the minimum capital requirement of a GmbH to 10 000 Euros, both the United Kingdom and the Irish (Ltd) form remain more 'competitive' than the German form in terms of minimum capital and overall flexibility. They also note that, from the corporate tax perspective, the Irish nominal rate of 12.5% is more attractive than the German rate. The German entrepreneurs thus decide to incorporate a (Ltd) in Ireland, which is possible with only 2 Euros capital, and to exercise almost all of the activity of the company in Germany through a branch, which branch cannot be required, in Germany, to comply with German provisions on the minimum capital and cannot be subject to disclosure provisions other than those strictly deriving from the Eleventh Company Law Directive. (Freedom of establishment: ECJ judgments in *Centros* and *Inspire Art*.) The incorporation in Ireland qualifies the Ltd as resident in Ireland for corporate tax purposes, Ireland taxes the company on its world-wide income, by granting a credit for the tax paid in other countries, and the company formally does not transfer its place of central management and control to Germany, so that it remains resident in Ireland, under the terms of the Ireland-Germany DTC. When the branch in Germany generates high profits which are subject to the German rate, the German tax can be off-set in Ireland, thus resulting in a 0% effective corporate tax rate, as in this concrete situation the German tax is deemed to be higher than the tax on the activity carried out in Ireland from the head office (by definition, a higher amount of taxable profit in Germany than in Ireland, and with a higher rate). When the branch in Germany generates low profits which result in a German tax lower than the Irish tax, and the former is credited against the latter, the corporate tax rate remains 12.5%. The incorporation of the Ltd in Ireland thus allows the German entrepreneurs to benefit from both the Irish company tax and the Irish company law form while carrying on the business activity almost entirely in Germany.

CASE D: REDUCTION OF THE CORPORATE TAX BASE[1]

Location of Intangible Assets

Large cross-border enterprises which have their head office in a country and branches in several others can reduce their effective tax rate by allocating specific assets, which generate deductible elements in all jurisdictions such as depreciations, to branches located in a jurisdiction where they can benefit from the higher deductions from the taxable base. This can be exemplified by the Lithuanian corporate tax system, which has a particularly favourable depreciation rule as a location for intangible assets. In Lithuania, a special form of digressive depreciation (a declining balance method) can be used for intangible assets. The depreciation rate amounts to 66.67%: 66.67% can be written down in the first year; in year 2, ca 89% of the initial costs can be written down to lower the tax burden; in year 3, cumulative depreciation is 96%, which means the asset has almost been written down completely. In most other Member States, intangible assets can also be written down over a relatively short period, but only linear depreciation is allowed. This case is exemplified by Italy, where intangible assets can be written down for tax purposes over a three-year period with a linear depreciation method, so that, assuming a three-year useful life of the intangible asset, ca 33% is written down in a tax-efficient way in year 1 and ca 66% in year 2. In comparison with the Italian system, the Lithuanian system offers a crucial advantage, because almost 70% (against 33%) can be deducted in year 1, and ca 89% (against 66%) by year 2. As a result, the higher the overall profit of the business and the acquisition of new intangibles year by year, the higher the extent to which the creation by a company having tax residence in Italy of a branch in Lithuania, in which intangible assets can be 'parked', makes it possible to reduce the overall corporate tax base and therefore the effective tax rate: the amount of taxable profits by the Lithuanian branch is lower, due to new intangible assets being allocated amongst the assets of the branch, than the amount of taxable profits of a would-be Italian branch, and the tax resulting from the nominal rate of Italian corporate tax (33%), against which the tax paid by the Lithuanian branch can be credited, ends up applying to a lower amount of the world-wide corporate tax base.

Payment of Interest

A company based, for example, in Austria pays a 25% corporate income tax on a taxable profit which is calculated, amongst others, by deducting interest payments to lenders. The deductibility of interest payments by the company finds its counterpart in the fact that interest income earned by the recipient of the borrowed capital is treated as taxable income. The system of deductibility for the payer (taxation in the hands of the recipient) also applies in principle for interest payments between affiliated companies, provided the same conditions would have been agreed between unrelated companies. However, a group of companies may overcome this system by bringing in a company in Cyprus. If the Austrian company creates a subsidiary in Cyprus, and is subsequently provided with borrowed capital from this subsidiary, the interest payments to Cyprus reduce the taxable profits of the Austrian company, as the Interest-Royalties Directive does not permit withholding tax deduction in Austria. However, under Cyprus tax law, the interest payments are tax-free in the hands of the recipient company when, as in this case, this is a foreign-controlled company and interest arises from a foreign place of business. Moreover, if the Cypriot company pays out a dividend to its Austrian parent, this dividend remains tax-free in Austria, due to the choice by the national Austrian Law implementing the Parent-Subsidiary Directive of the exemption method rather than the indirect tax credit method. Through the Parent-Subsidiary Directive, withholding tax in Cyprus is also avoided. If a dividend is paid in Austria by the parent company to an Austrian shareholder, only a capital gains tax of 25% on distribution to natural persons applies; on the contrary, the overall tax burden, without the interposition of the Cypriot subsidiary, would be 43.75%, produced by the corporate tax of 25% at the company level and by the 25% capital gains tax at the partner level.

CASE E: DIFFERENCE BETWEEN CORPORATE TAX SYSTEMS USED AS A 'SAVINGS BANK'

Another company based in Austria and exercising a business activity with exports in all Eastern Europe markets, which has a favourable market trend and foresees that it is going to obtain high cash flows, would like to 'park' its liquid fund and save tax. It realizes that, under the Estonian corporate tax regime, undistributed profits are not taxed. Assuming an annual operating profit of 1.000 retained for 10 years at an internal interest rate for example of 6%, the Austrian company, in Austria, would have 18.600 left, whereas a company in Estonia, without distributing profits, would accumulate 29.800. After profits have been distributed and corporate tax paid in Estonia (24%), 22.648 would be available as a net dividend rather than 18.600. The Austrian company thus creates a 100%-owned subsidiary in Estonia and decides to exercise all its business activity through that subsidiary. (Freedom of establishment: according to the ECJ case law, the fact that a company set up in a Member State exercises all its business activity by means of a branch, agency or subsidiary in another Member State is entirely immaterial*: Segers, Centros, Inspire Art*.)

When the Estonian subsidiary pays out the dividends to the Austrian parent company, these dividends, as a result of the Parent Subsidiary Directive, are tax-free in Austria (recipient country). Because of the difference between the Austrian and Estonian corporate tax systems and the ECJ case law on the right of establishment, the Austrian company can thus use the Estonian subsidiary as a 'savings bank'.

NOTE

1. *Source*: Case D and Case E are drawn, with adaptations, from 'Tax concessions in the ten new Member States in the area of company taxation summary of the study of the BAK October 2005', by Otto Farny, Gertrand Lunzer, Martin Saringer, Norman Wagner and A.K. Wien.

Appendix VI Update

LATEST DEVELOPMENTS STRENGTHENING THE SCOPE FOR THE INTER-JURISDICTIONAL COMPETITION AND THE TOPICALITY OF THE 'SUPRANATIONAL SOLUTION'

Over the last few months, from June to October 2006, in the area of EC company law, in addition to the entry into force of the SCE on 18 August and of some national implementing acts, two Commission's proposals presented in the APCLCG (Chapter 3, par. 3.1.) have been adopted: the amendments to the Fourth and to the Seventh Directives on annual and consolidated accounts, introduced by Directive 2006/46/EC (Directive 2006/46/EC of 14 June 2006 in OJEC L 224/1 [2006]), and the simplification to the Second Directive on the formation of public limited companies and the maintenance and alterations of their capital, introduced by Directive 2006/68/EC (Directive 2006/68/EC of 25 September 2006 in OJEC L 264/32 [2006]). Directive 2006/46/EC increases the financial and non financial information to be disclosed by companies, in particular by listed companies which are required to include a corporate governance statement in annual reports, and establishes the collective responsibility of all board members for such information, but it also increases the companies' size below which Member States can partly exempt SMEs from both the requirements set by the Fourth Directive and its own disclosure requirements. Directive 2006/68/EC enables Member States to relax some procedural and substantive requirements previously set by the Second Directive, which latter, before these amendments, had consistently been regarded as part, together with the First Directive, of a 'first generation' of Directives characterized by a prescriptive nature and by few options for Member States (Chapter 3, 3.1. and Chapter 4, 4.1, 4.1.2.). Consequently, both Directive 2006/46/EC and Directive 2006/68/EC increase the scope for inter-jurisdictional competition, in the field of company law, in the regulation of both SMEs and public limited companies. SMEs, which represent the greatest part of EC businesses, are further encouraged to seek the jurisdiction with the comparatively lower disclosure obligations (as a result of the Directive 2006/46/EC). Public limited companies are also induced to structure in those jurisdictions where the implementation of Directive 2006/68/EC will lead to the minor requirements (as it was predictable: Chapter 4, 4.4.2.).

In the area of EC corporate tax law the 2005 Code of Conduct on transfer pricing proposed by the Commission (Chapter 1, par. 1.5, 1.5.1.) has been adopted by the Council in June 2006. Moreover, two important rulings have been issued in September 2006. In the first case, '*N*' (Case C-470/04, *N,* ruling issued on 7 September 2006), the ECJ ruled that Articles 43 EC precludes a Member State from establishing a system for taxing increases in value in the case of a taxpayer's transferring its residence outside that State, such as the system at issue. This involved taxation of a Dutch national on the latent increases in value of his shareholdings in Netherlands companies at the time of transfer of his residence to the United Kingdom, made the granting of deferment of the payment of the tax conditional on the provision of guarantee and did not take full account of reductions in value which may arise after the transfer of the residence and which were not taken into account by the host State (the United Kingdom). Interestingly, the plaintiff identified the obstacle to his freedom of establishment in the obligation he had to provide guarantee to obtain deferment of the payment of the tax, but the ECJ examined the system on the whole. Although the ECJ accepted, on the basis of *Marks & Spencer* (paragraphs 42 of N case, paragraph 45 of *Marks & Spencer*, Case C-446/03, *Marks & Spencer*, examined in Chapter 1, par. 1.4., 1.4.2.c), the Netherlands's justification whereby the provision at issue was designed to allocate the powers of taxation between Member States, the measure failed the 'proportionality test': the ECJ indicated that there were methods which were less restrictive of the freedom of establishment, and observed that the taxation of latent increases in value would have to take full account of reduction arising after the transfer of residence, unless such reduction has already been taken into account in the State of destination (which was not proven to be the case). (paragraphs 53–54 of N ruling).

It can be immediately noted that, either had Netherlands taken full account of any reduction in value arising after the residence transfer or had such reduction been taken into consideration in the United Kingdom for tax purposes, the situation of the Dutch national transferring its residence would not have been disadvantaged in comparison with the situation of a Dutch taxpayer remaining in the Netherlands. Consequently, this ECJ finding strengthens the conclusion, to be already drawn from *Marks & Spencer* (Chapter 1, par. 1.4.2.c and par. 1.5), that the situation of any (natural or legal) person exercising the freedom of establishment must never be disadvantaged, at intra-Community level, in comparison with that of any person remaining within a single Member State. As a result, it also indicates that a restrictive tax measure, even if acceptable as regards the restriction on the freedom of establishment on its own, risks failing the 'proportionality test' (and thus being incompatible with Articles 43 and 48 EC), whenever such a disadvantage arises (and the plaintiff evidences it before the ECJ) taking into consideration all EC jurisdictions involved. As a last and inevitable implication, it suggests that each individual Member State, before introducing any restrictive tax measure, must not ignore the overall situation in which the natural or legal persons moving from its jurisdiction (in the case of a Member State of departure, as in *N*) or coming into its jurisdiction (in the case of a Member State of destination, such as, for example, in the *St.-Gobain* case, Chapter 1, par. 1.4., 1.4.2.a) will find themselves, within the EC territory, due to the choices made also by other Member States. It thus confirms that only a co-ordination between Member States, such as that implied in the suggested supranational solution to the legal competition, can ultimately prevent a further erosion of national tax sovereignty by ECJ tax rulings.

The second case, *Cadbury Schweppers* (Case C-196/04, *Cadbury Schweppers*, ruling issued on 12 September 2006), concerned the application of a typical instrument which, within the EC and in the wider OECD context, is used to prevent tax avoidance: the controlled foreign companies (CFC) legislation, by which a State attributes to its residents, and taxes in their hands, the profits of a foreign company, controlled by these residents, which is resident in another State where the level of corporate tax is significantly lower. In the situation at issue, the United Kingdom applied its CFC provisions to a resident parent company having subsidiaries in Ireland, and basically argued that this measure could prevent transactions intended primarily to artificially transfer profits by the parent company to a low-tax State (Ireland) by means of a subsidiary established there (paragraph 48 of the *Cadbury Schweppers* ruling). Nevertheless, the ECJ ruled that Articles 43 and 48 EC preclude the application of CFC legislation, unless that application serves *only* to prevent wholly artificial arrangements intended to escape the national tax normally payable. In this regards, the ECJ also specified that such a tax measure must not be applied where, on the basis of objective factors which the interested company must be allowed to demonstrate, and which must be ascertainable by third parties with regard in particular to the extent to which the subsidiary physically exists in terms of premises, staff and equipment, it is proven that, despite tax motives, the subsidiary is actually established in the host State and carries on genuine economic activity. The ECJ highlighted that the freedom of establishment, exercised through a secondary establishment such as a subsidiary in another Member State, is intended to assist economic and social interpenetration within the EC through a genuine economic activity in the host State (paragraphs 52 to 54 of the *Cadbury Schweppers* ruling), and stated that a declared intention to obtain tax relief by means of this subsidiary (as in the case at issue) does not indicate a fully artificial arrangement. The above mentioned objective factors must be ascertained, and in this regard the ECJ clarified that an wholly artificial arrangement could exist in particular in the case of a letter box or front subsidiary (paragraph 63 to 68 of the *Cadbury Schweppers* ruling).

This ruling, while confirming that 'wholly artificial arrangements' need to be regarded as distortions in the functioning of the internal market (Chapter 1, par. 1.4, 1.4.2.b, par. 1.5. and par. 1.6.), leaves completely unaffected the scope for the type of forum-shopping at issue in the company law rulings *Segers*, *Centros* and *Inspire Arts* (Chapter 2, par. 2.3., and Chapter 4, par. 4.3., 4.3.2.), that is the creation by nationals of a Member State A of a company in Member State B and the carrying out of all activity of this company by means of a pseudo-foreign secondary establishment (branch or subsidiary) in Member State A, and thus maintains the scope for the abuses (distortions) lying behind this type of arrangement. This is because the ruling concerns not a further case of pseudo-foreign secondary establishment in which, de facto, the head office of a company is situated, but only the case of a foreign secondary establishment, such as a subsidiary. Moreover, the indication of the decisive factors (staff, premises) in assessing whether this subsidiary actually carries on genuine economic activity, and of a letter box or front subsidiary as a case of an wholly artificial arrangement, unintentionally ends up offering multinational groups advice on how to better switch their profits from one Member State to another. This is exactly what the ruling aims at avoiding, but, paradoxically, it risks being its ultimate effect for a simple reason: from a tax-planning viewpoint, no group would probably create a letter box or front subsidiary in a low-tax State, because this 'subsidiary', to the extent that it does not carry out any genuine economic activity in the host State and generates no profit there, cannot benefit from that location. By contrast, every group may wish to create a genuinely active subsidiary producing a certain taxable profit in that State: as the ruling is silent on which part of the group's economic activity need to be carried by this subsidiary in order for it to be considered as a 'genuine' establishment, multinational groups are ultimately free to devise the part of the activity to be carried out by the subsidiary, and to design the transactions between the subsidiary and the parent company, in such a way as to switch the profits to the low-tax State and the losses to the higher tax State. Thus, the effects of this ruling, in addition to making CFC legislation in practice inapplicable, may also potentially defeat the objectives pursued in Marks & Spencer (the prevention of artificial inter-jurisdictional losses transfers: Chapter 1, par. 1.4., 1.4.2.c) and amplify, rather then reduce, the scope for a tax competition on elements of normal tax regimes (such as tax rates) and the scale of the distortions caused by this competition.

Accordingly, all latest developments in the areas of both EC company law and EC company tax law increase the importance of a solution which, like the supranational solution to the legal competition suggested in this work, attempts *a priori* to minimize the (hidden) distortions in the functioning of the internal market in the two areas at issue and to help the achievement, together with this Treaty's goal, also of the 'Lisbon objective' (the minimization of distortions is particularly important in the current phase of continuing enlargement of the EC, with the 25 Member States becoming 27 Member States as of 1 January 2007 due to the entry of Bulgaria and Romania, and with further States possibly entering the EC in the next few years).

ECR UPDATE

The following ECJ rulings, which were not yet reported in the ECR at the time of submission of the work, have been reported during the early phase of the production process:

- *Keller Holding* ruling, in Chapter 1, par. 1.3, 1.3.1., Case C-471/04, *Keller Holding,* ECR [2006] I-2107;
- *CLT-UFA* ruling, in Chapter 1, par. 1.4, 1.4.2. a, Case C-253/03, *CLT-UFA,* ECR [2006] I-1831;
- *Marks & Spencer,* in Chapter 1, par. 1.4, 1.4.2. c, Case C-446/03, ECR [2005] I-10837;
- *SEVIC Systems,* in Chapter 2, par. 2.5, Case C-411/03, ECR [2005] I-10805.

Bibliography

Baelz, K. and T. Baldwin (2002), 'The end of the seat theory (*Sitztheorie*): the European Court of Justice decision in Üeberseering of 5 November 2002 and its impact on German and European Company law', *German Law Journal*, 12 (3), www.germanlawjournal.com/, 1 December.

Beveridge F. and C.A. Riley (1996), 'The tax goals of the EC', in Geraint G. Howells (ed.), *European Business Law*, Aldershot/Dartmouth, ch. 6, pp. 137–168.

Bolkestein, F. (2002), 'The future of European tax policy', *EC Tax Review*, 1 (11), 19–21.

Bolkestein, F. (2002), 'The new European Company: opportunity in diversity', address to a Conference, University of Leiden, 29 November.

Bouzoraa, D. (1997), 'The Parent-Subsidiary Directive: *Denkavit*'s Lessons', *European Taxation*, 1 (37), 14–18.

Burnside, A. (1991), 'The European company re-proposed', *Company Lawyer*, 11 (12), 216–220.

Cath, I.G.F. (1986), 'Freedom of establishment of companies: a new step towards completing the internal market', *Yearbook of European Law*, 247–261.

CCBE (Councils of the Bars and Law Societies of the European Union) response to the European Commission consultation on the cross-border transfer of the registered office of companies, 15 April 2004.

Charny, D. (1994), 'Competition among jurisdictions in formulating corporate law rules: an American perspective on the 'race to the bottom' in the European Communities', in S. Wheeler (ed.), *A Reader on the Law of the Business Enterprise*, Oxford Readings on Socio-Legal Studies, Oxford: Oxford University Press, pp. 365–391.

Commission Communication, 'Guidelines on company taxation' (SEC (90) 601 final).

Commission Communication, 'Towards tax co-ordination in the European Union: package to tackle harmful tax competition' (COM (97) 495 final).

Commission Communication, 'Towards an internal market without tax obstacles: a strategy for providing companies with a consolidated corporate tax base for their EU-wide activities' (COM (2001) 582 final).

Commission Communication, 'Modernising company law and enhancing

corporate governance in the European Union: a plan to move forward' (COM (2003) 284 final).
Commission Communication, 'An internal market without tax obstacles: achievements, ongoing initiatives and remaining challenges' (COM (2003) 726 final).
Commission Communication, 'On the work of the EU Joint Transfer Pricing Forum in the field of business taxation from October 2002 to December 2003 and on a proposal for a Code of Conduct for the effective implementation of the Arbitration Convention (94/436/EEC of 23 July 1990)' (COM (2004), 297 final).
Commission Communication, 'Working together for growth and jobs: a new start for the Lisbon strategy' (COM (2005) 24 final).
Commission Communication, 'The contribution of taxation and customs policies to the Lisbon strategy' (COM (2005) 532 final).
Commission Communication, 'Tackling the corporation tax obstacles of small and medium-sized enterprises in the internal market: outline of a possible Home State Taxation pilot scheme' (COM (2005) 702 final).
Commission Communication, 'Implementing the Community Lisbon Program: progress to date and next step towards a Common Consolidated Corporate Tax Base (CCCTB)' (COM (2006) 157 final).
Commission Conference, 'European Conference on company taxation: EU corporate tax reform: progress and new challenges', Rome, 5–6 December 2003, Presentations.
Commission, Final Report, *Etude de faisabilité d' un statut européen de la PME*, July 2005.
Commission Notice on the application of the state aid rules to measures relating to direct business taxation, OJEC C384/3 [1998].
Commission Press Release IP/04/270, 'Company Law: Commission consults on the cross-border transfer of companies' registered offices', 26 February 2004.
Commission Press Release IP/05/1403, 10 November 2005.
Commission Recommendation concerning the taxation of small and medium-sized enterprises, 90/394, 25 May 2004.
Commission Staff Working Paper, *Company Taxation in the Internal Market* (SEC (2001) 1681).
Commission Staff Working Paper, *Annex to the Communication to the Council, the European Parliament and the Economic and Social Committee Tackling the Corporate Tax Obstacles of Small and Medium-sized Enterprises in the Internal Market: Outline of a Possible Home State Taxation Pilot Scheme, Impact Assessment* (SEC (2005) 1785).
Committee of Independent Experts on Company Taxation (1992), *Ruding Report*.

Deininger, R. (2004), 'Case comment: impact of the ECJ *Inspire Art* decision', *The European Legal Forum*, 1 (4), 17–19.

Deloitte EU Tax Group (2004), *Study on Analysis of Potential Competition and Discrimination Issues relating to a Pilot Project for an EU Tax Consolidation Scheme for the European Company Statute (Societas Europaea)* (TAXUD/2003/DE/305), London, UK: Deloitte & Touche LLP, 18 August 2004.

Dine, J. (1989), 'The Community company law harmonisation program', *European Law Review*, 14, 322–332.

Dine, J. (1989), 'The harmonisation of company law in the European Community', *Yearbook of European Law*, (9), 93–120.

Dine, J. (1991–1994), *EC Company Law*, London, UK: Chancery Law Publishing, loose-leaf, ch. 1.

Drury, R. and A. Hicks (1999), 'The proposal for a European private company', *Journal of Business Law*, 429–451.

Drury, R. (2001), 'A European private company?', *International and Comparative Corporate Law Journal,* 2 (3), 231–250.

Du Plessis, J.J. and J. Dine (1997), 'The fate of the draft Fifth Directive on Company Law: accommodation instead of harmonisation', *Journal of Business Law*, 23–47.

Ebert, S. (2003), 'The European company in the level playing field of the Community', *European Business Law Review*, 2 (14), 183–192.

Edwards, V. (1999), *EC Company Law*, Oxford: Clarendon Press.

EUR-LAW (2005), *Investing in Europe: Modernisation of Company Law in Europe*, publication for the European Area of Freedom, Security and Justice, 2/2005.

European Industrial Relations Observatory (EIRO) of the European Foundation for the Improvement of Living and Working Conditions (2002), *The Involvement of Employees and Collective Bargaining in Company Restructuring*.

Faculty of Law, University of Bologna, papers for the International Congress 'Le imposte sui redditi e le riorganizzazioni societarie nell'esperienza europea: l'attuazione della Direttiva 434/90', 24–25 September 1999.

Faculty of Law, University of Bologna, papers for the International Congress 'Gruppi di societa' ed imposizione sui redditi: l'attuazione della Direttiva Cee 90/435', 29–30 September 2000.

Fitchew, G. (1992), 'The European dimension in company law?, *Company Lawyer*, 1 (13), comment.

Freedman, J. (1994), 'Small businesses and the corporate form: burden or privilege?', *Modern Law Review*, 4 (57), 555–584.

Frommel, S.N. (1988), 'EEC companies and migration: a setback for Europe?', *Intertax*, 409–414.

Gammie M. (2004), 'EU taxation and the *Societas Europaea*: harmless creature or Trojan horse?', *European Taxation*, 1 (44), 35–45.

Goldman, B. and A.L. Caen (1983), *Droit Commercial Europeen*, Paris, France: Dalloz, pp. 130–131.

Gonzalez Sanchez, E. and J.F. Fluxà (2006), 'Problems and options in calculating the tax base of companies in the European Union under Home State Taxation', *European Taxation*, 5 (46), 197–207.

Gutmann, D. and L. Hinnekens (2003), 'The *Lankhorst-Hohorst* case: the ECJ finds German thin capitalization rules incompatible with freedom of establishment', *EC Tax Review*, 2 (13), 90–97.

Hamaekers, H. (2003), 'Taxation trends in Europe', *Asia-Pacific Tax Bulletin*, 2, 42–49.

Helminen, M. (2004), 'The tax treatment of the running of an SE', *European Taxation*, 1 (44), 28–34.

Hicks, A. (1997), 'Legislating for the needs of small business', in Barry A.K. Rider and Mads Andenas (eds), *Developments in European Company Law*, vol. 2, London, The Hague, Boston: Kluwer Law International, pp. 35–96.

Hopt, K.J. (1998), 'Europaisches Gesellschaftrecht – Krise und Neue Anlaufe', *Zeitschrift fur Wirtschaftsrecht*, 19, 96–99.

Hopt K.J. (1999), 'Company law in the European Union: harmonisation and/or subsidiarity?', *International and Comparative Corporate Law Journal*, 1 (1), 42–61.

IBFD (1995), *Survey on the Implementation of the EC Corporate Tax Directives,* Amsterdam: IBFD Publications.

IBFD (2003), *Survey on the Societas Europaea*, Amsterdam: International Bureau of Fiscal Documentation.

Involvement and Participation Association (IPA) (1998), *Sharing the Challenge: Employee Consultation: a Guide to Good Practice*.

Johnson, M. (2004), 'Does Europe still need a Fourteenth Company Law Directive?', *Hertfordshire Law Journal,* 3 (2), 18–44.

Johnston, A. (2004), 'The European Takeover Directive: ruined by protectionism or respecting diversity?', *Company Lawyer*, 9 (25), 270–276.

Kieninger, E.M. (2005), 'The legal framework of regulatory competition based on corporate mobility: EU and US compared, Part II/II', *German Law Journal*, 4 (6), www.germanlawjournal.com/, 1 April.

Kok, C. (2001), 'EC update', *European Taxation*, 12 (41), 43.

Lannoo, K. and M. Levin (2002), *An EU Company Without an EU Tax? A Corporate Tax Action Plan for Advancing the Lisbon Process*, Brussels: CEPS Research Report, April.

Lisbon European Council, Presidency Conclusions, 23–24 March 2000.

Loussouarn, Y. (1990), 'Le droit d'etablissement des societés', *Revue trimestrelle de droit europeen*, 227–239.

Maisto, G. (2002), 'Shaping EU company tax policy: amending the tax Directives', *European Taxation*, 7–8 (42), 287–308.

Martin Jiménez, Alfonso J. (1999), *Towards Corporate Tax Harmonisation in the European Community: an Institutional and Procedural Analysis*, London: Kluwer Law International.

Merkt, H. (2001), '*Centros* and its consequences for Member State legislatures', *International and Comparative Corporate Law Journal*, 1 (3), 119–147.

Meussen, G. (2002), 'The EU-fight against harmful tax competition: future developments', *EC Tax Review*, 3, 157–159.

Mock, S. (2002), 'Harmonization, regulation and legislative competition in European corporate law', *German Law Journal*, 12 (3), www.germanlawjournal.com/, 1 December.

Morton, P. (2005), 'Report on the Joint CFE/CSE Seminar "Tax competition versus tax harmonization"', *European Taxation*, 1 (45), 25–26.

Nias, P. and N. Purcell (1999), 'Harmonization moves closer by stages', *International Tax Review*, July/August, p. 11.

OECD (1998), *Harmful Tax Competition: An Emerging Global Issue*, Paris: OECD.

Paris Chamber of Commerce, 'The European Private Company, Draft Regulation, Draft Regulation Comments', www.ccip.fr/English/ Studies,Reports,Proposals/Dossier.

Plasschaert, S.R.F. (2002), 'Further thoughts on the European Union Company Income Tax and its first cousins', *European Taxation*, 8 (42).

Plasschaert, S.R.F. (2002), 'Comprehensive approaches to EU company taxation: to which companies should they apply?', *European Taxation*, 1 (42), 336–45.

Rammeloo, S. (2002), 'Partnership law in the twenty-first century: "Europeization" versus "Law Competition"?', *Maastrict Journal of European and Comparative Law*, 1 (9), Editorial.

Rebberg, M. (2004), '*Inspire Art*: freedom of establishment for companies in Europe between "abuse" and national regulatory concerns', *The European Legal Forum*, 1 (4), 1–8.

Reindl, A. (1990), 'Companies in the European Community: are the conflict of law rules ready for 1992?', *Michigan Journal of International Law*, 1270–1293.

Roch, M.T.S. (2004), 'Tax residence of the SE', *European Taxation* 1 (44), 13–16.

Roussos, A. (2001), 'Realising the free movement of companies', *European Business Law Review*, 1 (12), 7–25.

Ruding, O. (2005), 'The past and the future of EU corporate tax', *EC Tax Review*, 1, Editorial.

Schon, W. (2000), 'Tax competition in Europe: the legal perspective', *EC Tax Review*, 2, 90–105.

Schon, W. (2002), 'Tax competition in Europe: general report' to the 2002 Lausanne Conference.

Schon, W. (2002), 'The European Commission's Report on Company Taxation: a magic formula for European taxation?', *European Taxation*, 8 (42), 278–286.

Schultz, A. and K. Eicker (2001), 'The European Company Statute: the German view', *Intertax*, 10 (29), 332–341.

Stein, E. (1971), *Harmonisation of European Company Laws: National Reform and Transnational Coordination*, Indianapolis: Bobbs-Merril Company Inc., ch. 2, pp. 24–57.

Szudoczky, R. (2006), 'EC update', *European Taxation*, 5 (46), 17–18.

Teichmann C. (2003), 'The European company: a challenge to academics, legislators and practitioners', *German Law Journal*, 4, 311–318, www.germanlawjournal.com/, 1 April.

Terra, B. and Wattel, P. (1997), *European Tax Law*, London: Kluwer Law International.

The Economist, 'Learning to live with uncertainty', 24–30 January 2004, p. 22.

The Economist, 'A taxing battle', 31 January–6 February 2004, p. 59.

The Law Societies, Joint Brussels Office, The Brussels Office Law Reform Update Series, *Company Law and Financial Services*, March 2006.

Thommes, O. (2004), 'EC law aspects of the transfer of seat of an SE', *European Taxation*, 1 (44), 22–27.

Timmermans, C. (1991), 'Methods and tools for integration: a report', in Richard M. Buxbaum, Gérard Herting, Alain Hirsch and Klaus J. Hopt (eds), *European Business Law, Legal and Economic Analysis on Integration and Harmonisation*, based on a conference held in 1988 in Lugano, Switzerland, Berlin: de Gruyter, pp. 129–148.

Tridimas, T. (1994), 'The case-law of the European Court of Justice on corporate entities', *Yearbook of European Law*, (13), 347–360.

Van Thiel, S. (2003), 'Removal of income tax barriers to market integration in the European Community: litigation by Community citizen instead of harmonization by the Community legislature?', in *EC Tax Review*, 4–19.

Vanistendael, F. (2000), 'Fiscal support measures and harmful tax competition', *EC Tax Review*, 3, 152–161.

Vanistendael, F. (2000), 'No European taxation without European representation', *EC Tax Review*, 3, 143.

Villiers, C. (1996), 'Harmonisation of company laws in Europe, with an introduction to some comparative issues', in Geraint G. Howells (ed.), *European Business Law*, Aldershot: Ashgate/Dartmouth, pp. 169–195.

Villiers, C. (1998), *European Company Law: Towards Democracy?*, Aldershot: Ashgate/Dartmouth, pp. 161–176.

Villiers, C. (2001), 'Reorganisation of European company structures in the twenty-first century', *International and Comparative Corporate Law Journal*, 2 (3), vii–x.

Wathelet, M. (2001), 'The influence of free movement of persons, services and capital on national direct taxation: trends in the case-law of the Court of Justice', *Yearbook of European Law*, (20), 1–33.

Wenz, M. (1993), *Die Societas Europaea (Se)*, Berlin and New York: Ducker & Humblot.

Wenz, M. (2004), 'The European company (*Societas Europaea*): legal concepts and tax issues', *European Taxation*, 1 (44), 4–8.

Werlauff, E. (2003), 'The SE company: a new common European company from 8 October 2004', *European Business Law Review*, 1 (14), 85–103.

Williams, David William (1998), *EC Tax Law*, London and New York: Longman, pp. 143–144.

Wooldridge, F. (1991), *Company Law in the United Kingdom and the European Community: Its Harmonisation and Unification*, Athlone, UK.

Wooldridge, F. (2003), 'Uberseering: freedom of establishment of companies affirmed', *European Business Law Review,* 3 (14), 227–235.

Wolff, G. (1993), 'The Commission's programme for company law harmonisation: the winding road to a uniform European company law?', in M. Andenas and S. Kenynon-Slade (eds), *EC Financial Market Regulation and Company Law*, London: Sweet & Maxwell, pp. 19–29.

Wouters, J. (1994), 'Fiscal barriers to companies' cross-border establishment in the case-law of the EC Court of Justice', *Yearbook of European Law*, (14), 73–107.

Xanthaki, H. (2001), '*Centros*: is this really the end for the theory of the siege reél?', *Company Lawyer*, 21, 2–8.

Further reading

Bisacre, J. (2001), 'The migration of companies within the European Union and the proposed Fourteenth Company Law Directive', *International and Comparative Law Journal,* 3 (2), 251–270.

Cerioni, L. (1999), 'The barriers to the international mobility of companies within the European Community: a re-reading of the case-law', *Journal of Business Law*, 59–79.

Cerioni, L. (2000), 'A possible turning point in the development of EC company law: the *Centros* case', *International and Comparative Corporate Law Journal*, 2 (2), 165–195.

Cerioni, L. (2003), 'The *Uberseering* ruling: the eve of a "revolution" for the possibilities of companies' migration throughout the European Community?', *Columbia Journal of European Law*, 1 (10), 117–137.

Cerioni, L. (2004), 'Intra-EC interest and royalties tax treatment', *European Taxation*, 1 (44), 47–53.

Cerioni, L. (2004), 'The amendments to the 1990 EC Tax Directives', *The European Legal Forum*, 02 (04), 139–148.

Cerioni, L. (2004), 'The approved version of the European Company Statute in comparison with the 1991 draft: some first remarks from the General Provisions and from the Directive on employees' involvement (Part I)', *Company Lawyer*, 25 (8), 228–242.

Cerioni, L. (2004), 'The approved version of the European Company Statute in comparison with the 1991 draft: some critical issues on the formation and the working of the SE and the key challenge (Part II)', *Company Lawyer*, 25 (9), 259–269.

Cerioni, L. (2005), 'Harmful tax competition revisited: why not a purely legal perspective under EC law?', *European Taxation*, 7 (45), 267–281.

Colombani, J.L. and M. Favero (2002), *Societas Europaea*, *La Societe Europeénne*, Paris, France: Jolis Editions.

Commission Communication on 'European contract law' (COM (2001) 398 final).

Commission Communication, 'A more coherent European contract law: an action plan' (COM (2003) 68 final.

Conci, P. (2004), 'The tax treatment of the creation of an SE', *European Taxation*, (1) 44, 15–21.

Dine, J. (2000), *The Governance of Corporate Groups*, Cambridge: Cambridge University Press.

Dine, J. (2001), 'Risks and systems: a new approach to corporate governance and to European employee consultation structures?', *International and Comparative Corporate Law Journal*, 3 (2), 299–313.

Dine, J., P. Hughes and R. Newey (1996–2006), *EC Company Law*, Bristol, UK: Jordans Publishing, looseleaf.

Dine, J. (2006), *The Governance of Corporate Groups*, Cambridge, New York: Cambridge University Press.

Edwards, V. (2003), 'The European company: essential tool or eviscerated dream?', *Common Market Law Review*, (40), 443–450.

IBFD (2006), *Survey on the Implementation of the Interest-Royalties Directive,* Amsterdam.

Wooldridge, F. (2001), 'Some new types of company and partnership in France and Germany', *International and Comparative Corporate Law Journal*, (2) 3, 211–229.

Index